The Scribes Manual for Law Review Editors

The Scribes Manual for Law Review Editors

Darby Dickerson
Brooke J. Bowman
EDITORS

Carolina Academic Press
Durham, North Carolina

LIBRARY OF CONGRESS CATALOGING-IN-PUBLICATION DATA

Names: Dickerson, Darby, 1963- editor. | Bowman, Brooke J., editor.
Title: The scribes manual for law review editors / edited by Darby Dickerson, Brooke J. Bowman.
Description: Durham, North Carolina : Carolina Academic Press, LLC, [2022] | Includes index.
Identifiers: LCCN 2022012719 (print) | LCCN 2022012720 (ebook) | ISBN 9781531022716 (paperback) | ISBN 9781531022723 (ebook)
Subjects: LCSH: Law reviews--United States. | Law--Study and teaching--United States.
Classification: LCC KF272 .S27 2022 (print) | LCC KF272 (ebook) | DDC 340.071/173--dc23/eng/20220526
LC record available at https://lccn.loc.gov/2022012719
LC ebook record available at https://lccn.loc.gov/2022012720

Carolina Academic Press
700 Kent Street
Durham, North Carolina 27701
(919) 489-7486
www.cap-press.com

Printed in the United States of America

Contents

Editor and Contributor Biographies

Kristen David Adams is the Wm. Reece Smith Jr. Distinguished Professor of Law and former Interim Dean and Associate Dean for Academic Affairs at Stetson University College of Law. She has authored or co-authored seven books and more than 20 law review articles. She teaches domestic and international commercial law, property law, and law and poetry. She also directs the Dispute Resolution Board at Stetson. Adams is an elected member of the American Law Institute, a member of the Council for the American Bar Association Business Law Section, a member of the American Bar Association Commission on Homelessness and Poverty, and an officer and fellow of the American College of Commercial Finance Lawyers.

Brooke J. Bowman is a Professor of Law at Stetson University College of Law, where she teaches Research and Writing, coordinates the Scholarly Writing Series, serves as Director of the Moot Court Board, and previously served as Interim Law Library Director. She serves as Managing Editor of *Perspectives: Teaching Legal Research and Writing* and served for ten years, including as Editor in Chief, on the editorial board of *Legal Writing: The Journal of the Legal Writing Institute*. She is a co-author of *ALWD Companion: A Citation Practice Book* (with accompanying Teacher's Manual), a practice book to accompany the 4th edition of the *ALWD Citation Manual*. She is also the editor of the *ALWD Online Companion* that accompanies the fifth and sixth editions of the *ALWD Guide to Legal Citations*.

Maureen B. Collins served as a Professor of Law at the University of Illinois Chicago and The John Marshall Law School for 17 years; she also served as the Director of Legal Writing at DePaul University College of Law for 14 years. She retired in May 2021. During her time at John Marshall and UIC, she served as the faculty advisor of the *Review of Intellectual Property Law*, which named its Excellence Award in her honor.

Mark Cooney is a Professor of Law and chairs the Research & Writing Department at Western Michigan University Cooley Law School, where he has advised the Law Review for ten years. He served as Editor in Chief of *The Scribes Journal of Legal Writing* from 2013–2022, and served as an Associate Editor for four years before that. Professor Cooney has published more than 40 articles on legal writing and other topics. His works have been quoted and cited by state and federal courts and have appeared in student-edited law reviews, peer-reviewed journals, and national periodicals. Cooney is a past chair of the State Bar of Michigan's Appellate Practice Section and has presented on legal writing topics in London, Chicago, Detroit, and elsewhere. He judges for the Center for Plain Language's annual ClearMark Awards and was a ClearMark Award co-recipient in 2018.

Darby Dickerson is the President and Dean of Southwestern Law School. Before joining Southwestern, she served as Dean at the University of Illinois Chicago School of Law, The John Marshall Law School, Texas Tech University School of Law, and Stetson University College of Law. She was President of the Association of American Law Schools during 2020, is a Past President and current Board Member of Scribes—The American Society of Legal Writers, an elected member of the American Law Institute, and a former Director of the Association of Legal Writing Directors. She has served as senior managing editor or managing editor of one student-edited law review and two peer-edited journals and as the faculty advisor for two law reviews. Her areas of teaching and scholarship include legal writing, drafting, editing, and citation; legal and higher education; torts; and pretrial practice. She was the author of the first four editions of the *ALWD Citation Manual*. Her awards and honors include the Burton Foundation Award for Outstanding Contributions to Legal Writing Education, ALWD's Darby Dickerson Award for Revolutionary Change in Legal Writing, the AALS Section of Legal Writing, Research, and Reasoning's lifetime achievement award, and the Scribes's Distinguished Service Award.

Brent Domann is a Reference Librarian and the Associate Director of Journals Programs at Michigan State University College of Law, where he also teaches courses on legal research and foundations of law. He manages the law school's digital repository and has helped transition the law school's journals to a digital publishing format.

Christine Anne George is the Assistant Director for Faculty & Scholarly Services and Editorial Coordinator at the Dr. Lillian & Dr. Rebecca Chutick Law Library at the Benjamin N. Cardozo School of Law. She manages the school's institutional repository and assists faculty and students with their online scholarly presence through social media and scholarly profiles. Her scholarship focuses on equity in citation, institutional repositories, and how to maximize scholarly impact. She previously held positions as the Archivist & Faculty Services Librarian at the Charles B. Sears Law Library at the University at Buffalo School of Law and a Tarlton Fellow at the Tarlton Law Library at the University of Texas School of Law.

Lindsey Gustafson is Associate Dean for Academic Affairs and the Arkansas Bar Foundation Professor of Law at the University of Arkansas at Little Rock William H. Bowen School of Law. She served as the founding Executive Editor of *The Journal of Appellate Practice and Process* and served on its editorial board until 2020. She was on the editorial board of *Legal Writing: The Journal of the Legal Writing Institute* for eight years, serving two years as Editor in Chief, and is a Co-Director of The Institute for Law Teaching and Learning. She has published articles on improving student scholarship and the impact of technology on student writing. She frequently presents at regional and national legal writing conferences on effective teaching methods. Gustafson also served as Executive Editor of the *Brigham Young University Law Review*.

Wes E. Henricksen is an Associate Professor of Law at Barry University. His scholarship focuses on how to stop or slow the spread of disinformation by politicians, the media, and corporations. Henricksen's recent publications have appeared in the *Cardozo Law Review*, *Utah Law Review*, and *Washington Law Review*. He is the author of *Making Law Review*, a guidebook for law students. Apart from his writing, he has also presented his research at numerous workshops, conferences, and law schools and appears regularly in the media. He teaches or has taught legal research and writing, securities regulation, and torts. He served as the Executive Notes & Comments Editor on the *Washington Law Review*.

Michael J. Higdon is a Professor of Law and Associate Dean for Faculty Development at the University of Tennessee College of Law. A former Editor in Chief of the *Nevada Law Journal* and a long-term faculty advisor to the *Tennessee*

Law Review, Higdon has authored law review articles that have appeared in journals such as the *Alabama Law Review*, *Duke Law Journal*, *Fordham Law Review*, *George Washington Law Review*, and *Iowa Law Review*. Higdon teaches in the areas of family law, wills and trusts, and legal writing.

Ashley R. Hilliard is an Assistant Professor at North Carolina Central University School of Law, where she teaches legal writing. While in law school, she served as Editor in Chief on the *North Carolina Central Law Review*. She received the Justice Robert Glass Award for Outstanding Service to the Law Review in 2016. After law school, she practiced criminal, family, and immigration law before entering academia full time.

Benjamin J. Keele is the Associate Director of the Ruth Lilly Law Library at Indiana University McKinney School of Law, where he also serves as a Lecturer in Law. He previously served as a reference librarian and adjunct professor of law at William & Mary Law School. While in law school, he was Editor in Chief of the *Indiana Journal of Global Legal Studies*. He is the faculty advisor for the *Indiana International and Comparative Law Review* and has published articles on improving law review operations.

Andrew W. Lang is the Head of Reference at the University of Pennsylvania Carey Law School's Biddle Law Library. Before moving to Philadelphia, he spent several years as a Reference Librarian at the Georgetown University Law Center in Washington, D.C., where he also coordinated the law library's journal liaison program. While a student, he served as Senior Managing Editor of the *Wisconsin Law Review* and as a Managing Editor on the *Wisconsin Journal of Law, Gender & Society*. He has written book reviews for *Law Library Journal* and *Library Quarterly*, regular columns for *Law Library Lights*, and co-authored a book chapter on sexual orientation, gender identities, and the law.

Teri A. McMurtry-Chubb is the Associate Dean for Research & Faculty Development and a Professor of Law at the University of Illinois Chicago School of Law. She is also an officer and director of Scribes—The American Society of Legal Writers. She has served as President of the Association of Legal Writing Directors, becoming the first person of color to head a national legal writing organization. McMurtry-Chubb has lectured nationally on structural discrimination in educational institutions and the workplace and is a leader in designing curricula to facilitate diversity, equity, and inclusion efforts. She is the author of numerous publications, including the books *Race Unequals: Overseer Contracts, White Masculinities, and the Formation of Managerial Identity in the Plantation Economy* and *Strategies and Techniques for Integrating Diversity, Equity, and Inclusion into the Core Law Curriculum*, and is a contributor to *Feminist Judgments: Rewritten Opinions of the United States Supreme Court*. In 2019, she received the 2018 Teresa Godwin Phelps Award for Scholarship in Legal Communication for her article, *The Rhetoric of Race, Redemption, and Will Contests: Inheritance as Reparations in John Grisham's* Sycamore Row, 48 U. Memphis L. Rev. 890 (2018). She also received the 2021 Thomas F. Blackwell Memorial Award for Outstanding Achievement in the Field of Legal Writing; she was the first person of color and first Black woman to achieve this honor.

Kristen E. Murray is a Professor of Law at Temple University Beasley School of Law, where she teaches appellate advocacy, education law, and legal research and writing. Murray previously taught at The George Washington University Law School, where she also served as the Associate Director of the Legal Research and Writing Program. She is a Lead Article Editor of *Legal Communication & Rhetoric: JALWD* and co-author of two books: *Scholarly Writing: Ideas, Examples, and Execution* and *The Legal Writing Companion: Problems, Solutions, and Samples*.

Clanitra Stewart Nejdl is the Head of Professional Development and Research Services Librarian at the Alyne Queener Massey Law Library at Vanderbilt Law School. She is also a Lecturer in Law at Vanderbilt Law, where she teaches first-year legal research and advanced legal research classes. Nejdl previously served as Reference and Instructional Services Librarian and Assistant Professor at the David C. Shapiro Memorial Law Library at Northern Illinois University College of Law. In that role, she served as a Perma.cc registrar and provided training to law review editors on using Perma.cc. Nejdl is an editorial board member of *AALL Spectrum*; her works appear in *The Second Draft*, *AALL Spectrum*, and *SC Lawyer* and the books *Integrating Doctrine and Diversity: Inclusion and Equity in the Law School Classroom* and *Introduction to Law Librarianship*. Nejdl received the 2021 Association of American Law Libraries' Emerging Leader Award and the 2017 AALL Minority Leadership Development Award.

Annalee Hickman Pierson is the Head of Reference and Faculty Services at the Howard W. Hunter Law Library at Brigham Young University. In that role, she oversees legal reference and faculty services, provides faculty research support, teaches in the first-year legal research and writing program, and produces scholarship that focuses on legal reference services, faculty services, legal research instruction, legal education, and law librarianship. Her scholarship has appeared in *Law Library Journal*, *Perspectives: Teaching Legal Research and Writing*, *AALL Spectrum*, *Student Lawyer*, *BYU Journal of Public Law*, and the book, *Introduction to Law Librarianship*. She currently serves as an editorial board member of *Legal Writing: The Journal of the Legal Writing Institute*. She has also served as an assistant editor for *Legal Information Review*, a peer reviewer for *Legal Communication & Rhetoric: JALWD*, and the faculty advisor for the *BYU Journal of Public Law*.

Polatip Subanajouy serves as the 2021–2022 Scribes Fellow and worked tirelessly with the co-editors on this *Manual*. He earned his J.D. in 2021 from the University of Illinois at Chicago, where he served as Executive Lead Articles Editor of the *UIC John Marshall Law Review*. He is a judicial law clerk in Cook County, Illinois.

Jessica Lynn Wherry is a Professor of Law, Legal Practice, at Georgetown Law, where she teaches legal research and writing courses to first-year and upper-level students. Before joining Georgetown's faculty, Wherry was Associate Professor of Legal Research and Writing, Associate Director of the Legal Research and Writing Program, and Co-Director of the Scholarly Writing Program at The George Washington University Law School. She is a Co-Managing Editor of *Legal Communication & Rhetoric: JALWD* and co-author of two books: *Scholarly Writing: Ideas, Examples, and Execution* and *The Legal Writing Companion: Problems, Solutions, and Samples*.

Pamela Wilkins is the Associate Dean for Academic Affairs and an Associate Professor of Law at Mercer University School of Law. During her time at the University of Detroit Mercy School of Law, she served as the law review faculty advisor for many years. She especially enjoys helping law reviews and faculties craft policies that ensure successful journals and happy, high-achieving students.

Austin Martin Williams is the Interim Director of the Law Library at Georgetown University Law Center. Before joining the Georgetown Law Library as the Deputy Director, he served as the Assistant Law Library Director at North Carolina Central University School of Law. While at NCCU, he also co-taught Law Practice Technology and served as an advisor for the *North Carolina Central University Science & Intellectual Property Law Review*. Before joining NCCU, he worked at Georgia State University College of Law. He is an active member of the American Association of Law Libraries and the Southeastern Chapter of the American Association of Law Libraries. He previously served as the Vice President of the Atlanta Law Libraries Association. He has published several articles, book chapters, and CALI lessons and presented at local, regional, and national conferences.

Carolyn V. Williams is an Assistant Professor of Law at the University of North Dakota School of Law, where she teaches legal writing, research, and advocacy courses. Before joining the North Dakota faculty, she was an Associate Professor of Legal Writing at the University of Arizona James E. Rogers College of Law. In law school, she was Editor in Chief of the *Arizona State Law Journal*. As a professor, she became the faculty advisor for the *Journal* and mentored subsequent EICs. She presented at the National Conference of Law Reviews many times on how to train staff members. She is an Article Editor of the *Journal of Appellate Practice and Process*, a faculty-edited law review, and the author of the seventh edition of the *ALWD Guide to Legal Citation*.

Introduction

We admit it. We're law review nerds. We were both editors on our respective reviews during law school, and we've gone on to serve as editors for several other academic journals.

We both loved the sense of community that came from being on law review—and especially on an editorial board. We thrived in a setting where we worked collaboratively with our peers; it was a less-isolating experience than preparing for classes and examinations. We were excited by being part of an enterprise with a common purpose: to help promote interesting ideas that might literally change the law and society. We appreciated working with other talented students and having the opportunity to interact with authors who were leaders in their fields. We dove into our own scholarly research and writing. And we even loved mastering a citation manual, so much so that one of us went on to write one, and both of us have focused our scholarly energies on improving legal citation and helping others to grasp the intricacies and mysteries of the cite-checking process.

But we also faced challenges as student-editors. We had to grapple with peers not meeting deadlines and submitting subpar work. We experienced the pain of "losing" edits that someone had spent significant time preparing—or discovering that new mistakes had crept into an article late in the process. We made grand plans for changes—only to learn that the law review didn't have the authority to implement those changes without faculty approval. We had to learn how to reach consensus when the board split on important matters. We endured some people not talking to others for a while—usually over something relatively petty. We worked long hours to balance our law review responsibilities, course work, and jobs. And for at least part of the time, we suffered from imposter syndrome: How did we get here? And when will people discover that we don't really know what we're doing?

But on balance, our law review experiences were the most significant of our law school careers. We walked away from our student-editor experiences with new and improved skills ranging from editing and communicating with authors to developing and sticking to a complex timeline and managing a staff. We've used these skills throughout our practice and academic careers—including our stints as senior academic administrators. We also gained confidence in our editing, writing, research, analytical, and leadership abilities. And the editor credential opened doors for professional positions that otherwise might not have materialized that early in our careers.

Our goal for this *Manual* is to help new editors understand their roles and responsibilities, learn how the review fits within their law school's program of legal education, anticipate challenges, plan for the year, and gain tips and ideas to improve the review. We hope faculty advisors and incoming editors will use this *Manual* during the annual transition process. We also hope editors will use the *Manual* as a resource when different challenges or questions arise during the year. The *Manual* can also assist law review members considering an editorial position and faculty members who teach seminars for student-editors.

To help readers navigate the *Manual*, each chapter starts with "Learning Objectives" to preview what editors will learn from studying the chapter. Each chapter ends with "Key Takeaways" that capture the top points the author hopes you will remember long after reviewing their chapter.

In addition to the chapters in this *Manual*, we encourage editors to review two symposia published specifically to train and help law review editors: *Stetson Law Review* Volume 30, Issue 2 (2000) (https://www.stetson.edu/law/lawreview/2000.php), and *Thomas M. Cooley Law Review* Volume 30, Issue 2 (2013) (available on HeinOnline). These issues include articles about selecting lead articles, cite-checking processes, working with peers, intraschool journal relations, and showcasing student scholarship.

We want to thank the chapter authors for sharing their expertise and insights that helped us turn our vision into reality. They have all worked on and with law reviews, whether as students, faculty advisors, senior law school administrators, law librarians, or all of those roles. So, when it comes to law reviews, they've been there and done that.

And we express our extreme gratitude to Polatip Subanajouy, the 2021–2022 Scribes Fellow and a recent law review editor, for his hard work on this *Manual*. We relied on his recent editorial experience to ensure that the *Manual* was sharing advice relevant and accessible to current editors. And his fresh perspective, attention to detail, and hard work made this *Manual* better than it otherwise would have been.

Before we end, we want to make a few final points about the *Manual*:

- We use the terms "law review" and "law journal" as synonyms. Regardless of your student-edited journal's name, this *Manual* is for you.
- We understand that different law reviews use different names for positions. In this *Manual*, "editor" refers to students selected for specific positions on the editorial board. "Member" and "staff member" typically refer to students on the law review who do not serve on the editorial board.
- Every law review is organized slightly differently and has slightly different policies and procedures. We understand that not all advice offered in this *Manual* can be translated to your journal, but we and the chapter authors have attempted to provide information about common practices. We encourage editors to direct specific questions about how your review or law school handles a particular issue to your faculty advisors.
- We and the chapter authors have made every effort to use gender-neutral and inclusive language throughout.
- As law review editors, you'll notice that the footnoting is light, and we've generally shunned speaking footnotes. This approach was intentional. We hope readers will engage with the main text without distraction, which we appreciate is not the approach most law reviews take regarding footnotes and citations.
- Following the advice of chapter author Christine George, in citations, we have listed all authors—instead of employing "et al."—so that each may receive credit for their work.

As Scribes President Susan Duncan mentions in the Preface, this *Manual* is just part of Scribes's commitment to law reviews. To supplement this *Manual*, we plan to hold regular webinars for editors and build an online repository for supplemental materials that will help editors with their work and connect them to each other.

Finally, we wish you the very best during your year as an editor. We hope this *Manual* can help you along the way and that you will have a successful year during which you produce great issues, learn a lot, and build relationships that will last a lifetime.

Darby Dickerson & Brooke J. Bowman
January 2022

Preface

To incoming law review editors: congratulations on your selection! We hope this *Manual for Law Review Editors* will help as you plan and navigate your year on the editorial board. For prospective editors and others, the *Manual* will provide you with an overview of how student-edited law reviews operate and the various considerations editors must balance. I am the current president of Scribes—The American Society of Legal Writers (scribes.org). Scribes is a nonprofit organization dedicated to excellent legal writing. The organization was founded in 1951 by the Chief Justice of the New Jersey Supreme Court. Its individual members include judges, attorneys, law professors, and others interested in improving legal writing, and its institutional members include law schools and courts.

For decades, Scribes has supported law reviews by presenting an annual award for the best student-written article in a law review. In addition, many Scribes members serve or have served as faculty advisors for law reviews.

Until 2017, the National Conference of Law Reviews held an annual training conference for incoming law review editors. Because the NCLR is no longer active, Scribes resolved to expand its outreach to law reviews and provide new services to law review members and editors. This *Manual*—which includes 19 chapters to help editors learn the intricacies of leading and managing an academic journal—is the cornerstone of these new services. Other services will include the following:

- regular webinars for law review editors and members;
- a biennial survey of law reviews that will help reviews and the legal academy better understand how law reviews operate; and
- an online portal that will serve as a national clearinghouse of information for student-edited law reviews.

We anticipate that the portal will include survey results, training videos and materials, and documents such as constitutions, policy manuals, style manuals, and competition packets that different law reviews have permitted us to share.

I want to thank Dean Darby Dickerson and Professor Brooke J. Bowman for editing this *Manual* and leading our other efforts to serve law reviews and law review editors. Dean Dickerson is a former Scribes president and continues to serve on the Scribes Board. Professor Bowman is a long-time Scribes member who also chairs the Law Review Award Committee. Both have extensive experience with law reviews, and both are long-time leaders in the academy. Scribes appreciates them donating their time and expertise to these important projects.

I would be remiss if I didn't invite each person reading this *Manual* to join and participate in Scribes. We have a special membership category for student-editors. Scribes members receive the *Scribes Journal of Legal Writing*, the *Scrivener* newsletter, weekly research and writing tips, and access to webinars about cutting-edge and interesting legal writing topics. Members are also invited to join committees, which provide opportunities to network with leading judges, practitioners, and law professors. Our committees help select winners for Scribes's annual Law Review, Best Brief-Writing, and Book awards and assist in other efforts to continue improving legal writing in the United States. I hope you will consider joining us!

Susan Hanley Duncan
Scribes President (2020–2022)
Dean, University of Mississippi School of Law

The Scribes Manual for Law Review Editors

1

Why Law Reviews Exist

Maureen B. Collins

LEARNING OBJECTIVES

After reviewing this Chapter, editors will be able to

- describe how legal journals are different from academic journals in many other disciplines;
- discuss the main contributions law reviews make to the profession, the academy, and society; and
- explain how the law reviews' gatekeeping function can impact the career trajectory of prospective and current law professors.

A. A Brief Introduction to Law Reviews in the United States

The law review has a long and storied history in U.S. legal education. The *University of Pennsylvania Law Review* was first published in 1852, and the *Harvard Law Review* in 1898. Since then, the law review has evolved into a prominent vehicle for shaping the law and developing new legal theories. Law review articles also advance individuals' academic careers. And unlike academic journals in other disciplines, law reviews provide opportunities for students to select and edit professional articles and publish their own scholarly pieces.

Law reviews address a variety of legal issues. Many are published quarterly, and for decades appeared in paperback format. Now, many are published online.[1]

1. For a detailed discussion of publishing, see Chapter 15 of this *Manual*.

Typically, a law review includes "lead articles" written by scholars, practitioners, and judges, and student articles, which some journals call "notes" or "comments." Historically, "comments" were shorter articles analyzing a single case, while "notes" were longer pieces addressing a particular topic. Some law reviews also publish shorter essays, speeches, and book reviews.

Today, more than 1,500 law reviews are published in the United States. Each accredited law school publishes at least one law review. When a law school has more than one publication, the other publications are frequently referred to as "law journals," although the terms "law review" and "law journal" are synonymous.

Academic journals exist in many disciplines, including medicine, science, and literature. But the law review is something of a unicorn. Most academic journals are governed by a board of experts and edited by noted professors who have a long history of writing articles. The law review, though, puts the power directly into students' hands. Although most reviews have one or more faculty advisors, for the most part, students select and edit the articles, create content, communicate with the authors, and manage the publication process and public relations. This "rare power"[2] creates opportunities and responsibilities that students in other disciplines do not have.

Law reviews have drawn criticisms. Law review articles are complex pieces of scholarship, and creating them requires extensive research, rigorous analysis, and a well-documented written explanation of the thesis. Although not universally true, many are regimented in style and format. Law review articles are longer than articles in many other disciplines, which often span fewer than ten pages. The length of law review articles is often due to long sections that trace the history of a legal concept or idea. The writing style and level of detail required to analyze a legal issue thoroughly may be considered dry and boring by those outside of the law—and perhaps to those who are less immersed in a particular legal subject. For many law reviews, author status matters. Journals often seek to publish articles written by professors from highly ranked law schools or considered leaders in their field.

Such criticisms, though, belie the valuable contributions these articles make. Law review articles create new knowledge, educate others about important legal topics, serve as the basis for legal reform, and more.

---

2. Eugene Volokh, Academic Legal Writing: Law Review Articles, Student Notes, Seminar Papers, and Getting on Law Review 177, 230 (4th ed. 2010).

A law review article can cover virtually any legal topic, from the law governing emerging technology to the criminalization of necrophilia to legal issues in Jane Austen's life and novels. And "flagship" or "general" law reviews may choose to publish any of them.

In the past few decades, many schools have established additional journals, many of which are known as "specialty" journals. Specialty journals, as the name implies, publish articles focused on a particular area, such as criminal law, environmental law, business, law, gender law, art law, or intellectual property, to name a few.

Initially, these specialty journals were considered second-tier in status and respect. But over time, specialty journals at some schools have become more highly regarded than the general review. Specialized journals have opened the door for scholars whose interests lie in less traditional areas or who may bring a different perspective than the authors offered invitations to publish in conservative law reviews.

If a journal's area of specialty is narrow, the number of articles received for consideration could be limited. In this situation, the editors may have to solicit articles—meaning they request particular authors to write specific articles for their journal—or publish less frequently. Some specialty journals publish just once a year.

More recently, blogs and online companions have become increasingly popular. These online resources tend to feature shorter articles, with more room for variation in format and subject matter. They reflect a trend away from the lengthy article filled with hundreds of citations and toward a more relaxed approach to communicating recent developments. At this point, though, a general movement away from the in-depth and complex analysis provided by the typical law review article does not appear imminent.

B. How Law Reviews Contribute to the Profession, Academy, and Society

To some, law reviews may seem like a relic. Certainly, many law review articles sit on the shelf, read only by a few scholars and loving members of the author's family. This view overlooks the vital purpose served by law reviews in three particular areas: shaping the law; hiring, promoting, and granting tenure to law faculty; and educating law students to engage in sophisticated legal thinking so they may assume leadership within the legal profession and academy.

1. Shaping the law

Dean Erwin Chemerinsky, a noted constitutional law scholar, reflected that "scholarship is, in essence, an act of faith that writing makes a difference."[3] While this thought may seem abstract, the impact of law review articles on the development and practice of law should not be underrated. Several important legal concepts, like the right of privacy and trademark dilution, were incubated in law review articles.[4] These articles, written by highly regarded academics, were responsible for changing how we think about and apply the law. And we learned about them because student law review editors selected the articles for publication.[5]

One reason that articles can have such an impact is the audience for which they are written. While most law reviews are widely available from several free, public sources, the targeted readers are fellow academics, jurists, and legislators who can shape the law. Law review articles cite other law review articles; the more citations, the more an idea can gain traction and prominence. Judges who read the articles might cite them to justify a particular interpretation or proposed modification of the law. And legislators might transform an idea into a bill that ultimately becomes a statute.

Law review articles may be particularly important in a new or controversial area of law. Our legal system, based on the principle of stare decisis, relies heavily on decisions made in the past. In essence, history guides the future.[6] By way of example, consider the question of liability for tainted blood products at the beginning of the AIDS epidemic. The extent of liability on blood banks for transfusions that infected the recipient was an untried area. At the time, receiving a tainted transfusion was tantamount to a death sentence. Yet no precedent existed for judges to follow. Instead, law review articles on the subject filled the gap by providing thoughtful, well-researched, and well-reasoned analysis of this complicated issue until a sufficient body of law developed.[7] The articles may have taken different positions and offered varying solutions, but they guided decision-making in the field.

---

3. Erwin Chemerinksy, *Why Write?*, 107 MICH. L. REV. 881, 893 (2009).

4. *See, e.g.*, ELIZABETH FAJANS & MARY R. FALK, SCHOLARLY WRITING FOR LAW STUDENTS: SEMINAR PAPERS, LAW REVIEW NOTES AND LAW REVIEW COMPETITION PAPERS 3 (5th ed. 2017).

5. *See id.* at 2.

6. *Id.* at 2.

7. *Id.* at 3–4.

Law review articles also offer a platform for advocacy and dissent. Law reviews provide a forum for exchanges among experts or emerging experts in the field. Law reviews can also promote new and diverse voices. While it can seem like the same authors from the same law schools publish on the same topic repeatedly, a third-year law student or junior professor with a novel idea or unusual perspective can wield influence. But for this to happen, editors must be willing to take a chance on the unusual or the untried. Nurturing these voices is an often-overlooked responsibility of the student-editors who determine the content and tone of their law review. It may mean publishing a non-traditional author from a lesser-known law school or promoting the ideas of a fellow student with something important to say. Although selecting a less well-known author may mean taking a chance, amplifying new voices can be one of the most rewarding experiences of serving as a law review editor.

2. Impacting the academy

Law reviews impact the academy in several ways. They fulfill an educational function for students. They can affect the prestige of their law school or university: a highly ranked law review adds polish to the institutional reputation. And they serve an important gatekeeping function in hiring, promoting, and granting tenure to law school faculty.

At most law schools, law review is an integral part of the curriculum. Often, student members and editors receive academic credit for their work. Some law schools require members or editors to complete an editing or scholarly writing course. Others grant credit for students writing their own scholarly pieces, editing others' work, and producing the journal. And, if academic credit is available for law review service, the school often charges students tuition, just as they would for other courses. In this way, the law review serves the same income-producing function as other courses. By granting credit, the institution recognizes the educational value of the work performed by the students.[8]

A highly regarded law review can also burnish the institutional reputation of a law school or university. Schools well established in the upper-echelon of legal education—Harvard, Yale, and company—have highly regarded law reviews that reflect their reputation for excellence. For those schools not atop the *U.S. News and World Report* rankings, the law review can be a vehicle for

8. For a discussion of school policies relating to academic credit for law review service, see Chapter 2 of this *Manual*.

upward mobility. Although the caliber of a school's law review is not technically a factor in the *U.S. News* rankings, 40% of that rank is determined by the combined opinion of faculty at other law schools (.25) and judges and practitioners (.15).[9] These are most law reviews' target audiences.

Law reviews are also subject to rankings. Each year, the Washington & Lee (W&L) University School of Law Library publishes a list of the top 400 ranked U.S. journals.[10] A law review is ranked using a quantitative analysis of the citations to articles in that review over five years. Specialty journals are ranked separately in several categories. Faculty members often use these rankings when deciding where to submit their articles and—when they receive multiple offers—which to accept. Law schools also use these rankings when evaluating whether to hire a prospective faculty member, promote a faculty member, and grant tenure to a faculty member. Consequently, editors should understand that the "rankings game" can impact where authors submit their work and where they will ultimately publish.[11]

Authors may also use an offer from a lower-ranked review as a steppingstone to convince higher-ranked reviews to consider and hopefully publish the piece. This process, known as "trading up," frustrates many editors who devote substantial time and effort vetting pieces, making offers, and communicating with authors, only to have them accept with a higher-ranked review. While pursuing rankings should not be the primary goal of a law review, editors should be mindful of the rankings and how they may impact the quality of the articles received and author conduct.

Law review editors might be surprised to learn that their decisions impact the selection, retention, promotion, and tenure of law school faculty. These days, most candidates seeking a full-time tenure-track position at a law school have already published multiple articles: likely one during law school and several during the years before they enter the teaching market. Even though law schools assign faculty members to read and evaluate the articles, they often use

---

9. For additional information on rankings for law schools, see Robert Morse et al., *Methodology: 2022 Best Law School Rankings*, U.S. News & World Rep. (Mar. 29, 2021), https://www.usnews.com/education/best-graduate-schools/articles/law-schools-methodology.

10. For more detail on the ranking process for law reviews, see *W&L Law Journal Rankings*, at http://go.wlu.edu/lawjournals [https://perma.cc/99HG-H9Y5].

11. Chapter 16 of this *Manual* incudes a discussion about journal rankings and the impact on author decisions and scholarly impact.

the candidate's placement of articles as a proxy for quality. Articles placed in flagship journals in T-14 schools are considered the coin of the realm.

Once on the tenure track, law schools expect professors to begin producing scholarship. Although schools understand that the quality of a professor's work and placements will develop over time, most expect professors to publish by at least the end of year two. New professors are under tremendous pressure to build a scholarly record to support their tenure dossier, which means they will be picky about where they submit their articles and where they choose to publish. Most will select the highest-ranking journal based on the W&L survey or the journal at the highest-ranking school using the *U.S. News* rankings. If their mentors are disappointed in the offers received, the professor often will withdraw the piece, rework it, and submit it during the next cycle.

To grant tenure—the most sought-after guarantee of academic job security—schools consider various factors. But among the most critical is a demonstration of scholarly accomplishment. Schools evaluate this metric through the quantity and quality of law review articles published by the faculty member. While promotion and tenure committees are now more willing to consider less traditional publications, including books, book chapters, blogs, and materials prepared for a practitioner audience, the law review article remains the gold standard.

As part of the tenure process, most schools require a candidate to have published at least three articles of significant length. While completing these articles, professors must also meet their teaching and service requirements. Internal committees of senior professors will carefully evaluate the candidate's scholarship. And almost all schools require that the candidate's scholarship be evaluated by multiple "external reviewers"—tenured full professors at peer or aspirational schools who are subject-matter experts in the areas in which the candidate writes. External reviewers will either prepare an in-depth critique of one article or a comprehensive review of the quality and complexity of the analysis of the candidate's body of scholarship. Again, the place of publication acts as a proxy for quality. Ultimately, the professor's academic career relies on the wisdom of student-editors accepting their articles for publication.

The significant influence of student-editors does not end with accepting a piece because the evaluation is based on the published piece, not the draft submitted. Frequently, if not universally, the finished product represents a collaboration between the author and the student-editor. Editorial suggestions might range from citation and grammar changes to direct challenges to arguments and analysis. Editors might also add references and sources, reorganize ideas, shift focus, refine the analysis, and rewrite passages for clarity and conciseness. These edits might improve—or weaken—an author's work, and thus their chances for promotion and tenure. Thus, editors should never forget the downstream and significant impacts of their work and choices.

The student-editor's impact may be particularly profound for a new professor whose primary publishing experience was as a law review editor. Professors who lack meaningful mentorship from their institutions may also rely more heavily on the work of a student-editor. Editors may not always be aware of those dynamics or the influence they may have. Put simply, student-editors have a remarkable impact on the shape and tenor of the law school faculty.

3. Training future leaders

Serving on a law review editorial board brings tremendous rewards, some more tangible than others. Most former editors will tell you that the experience was well worth the investment of time, effort, and intellect.

Being a board member requires a significant weekly time commitment, regardless of the specific position. Depending on an individual's specific board position, number of issues to be published, and general work habits, the work may be steady or come in waves—and some of the work is tedious and mind-numbing. On the other hand, serving on an editorial board allows you to develop relationships with experts and emerging experts, delve into new and often fascinating theories, hone your research and writing skills, build rapport with your peers—many of whom will become highly regarded professionals—and influence the development of the law.

Without question, the most quantifiable result of being a board member is the impact on job prospects. To be selected for law review opens many doors; to be an editor opens even more doors. For those seeking a judicial clerkship, serving as an editor is a credential many judges expect to see. Many large law firms begin their resume triage process by looking at particular schools. They then winnow the pool based on grades and law review service. To participate as a board member is to further distinguish yourself from other applicants.

The impact of board service is strong for a simple reason. Having served on a law review, and then on an editorial board, is an indicator of advanced writing and research abilities, the willingness to work hard to achieve goals, and a commitment to the law. Membership signals the ability to complete multiple tasks under time pressure and work in teams and the desire to work hard to achieve excellence. Having the credential on your resume is a bit like knowing a secret handshake. It creates a presumption that you are willing and able to join. Board experience magnifies that impact and further suggests that you are willing and able to assume a leadership position. This information may sound a bit elitist, and no doubt it is. But having identified yourself as a member of an elite group of law students is the result of natural talent, commitment, and a tremendous amount of hard work.[12]

Although it may be less quantifiable, the benefits of the experience and education of being a board member are no less important. Serving as a law review editor requires intellectual rigor, persistence, discipline, and creativity. The work involves juggling disparate tasks, time management, and strong people skills. These same attributes are crucial to the success of a first-year attorney. Experience in and mastery of them provide a leg up to new lawyers.

Being a law review board member introduces you to a select group of thinkers and actors in the legal community—both in practice and the academy. You may develop a bond with the author while working on an article. Your law review may decide to put on a symposium, and you will find yourself interacting with illustrious presenters. You may find yourself at a luncheon table surrounded by notable practitioners in the field. You may even meet your editorial board peers at a national conference and find yourself working at the same firm upon graduation. These opportunities are possible because you accepted the responsibility of being on the law review board.

From a more personal perspective, being on a law review board exposes you to ideas, concepts, and theories that you might not otherwise encounter. The smorgasbord of article topics submitted by authors is astounding. Some might not interest you, but others might pique a lifelong curiosity. Simply being exposed to this intellectual buffet is a benefit. As an editor, you will find yourself diving deep into a subject matter that might not relate to what you have experienced in law school or expect to experience in practice. Editorial service can prod you down the path of being a life-long learner. There are too few opportunities in life to do something like this. You can't help but grow from the experience.

---

12. For a discussion about member selection, including how journals evaluate student skills for law review, see Chapters 4 and 10 of this *Manual.*

C. Conclusion

This Chapter has addressed the benefits and a few downsides of life as a law review editor. Most would agree that the former considerably outweighs the latter. The job requires commitment and skill, grit, and grace. The demands on your time will be significant, but the sacrifices you make will pale in comparison to the experience you gain. Use this unique position of power to create a forum for new ideas and diverse voices. Work hard. Polish your skills. Build life-long relationships. Wield your influence for the good of the profession you have chosen.

KEY TAKEAWAYS

- In most academic disciplines, academic journals are peer-edited, meaning that the editorial board is composed of experts in the specific discipline.
- Because of their role in selecting articles for publication, student-editors wield enormous power in shaping the development of the law and impacting the academy.
- Although being an editor is time-consuming and can be difficult, the benefits and opportunities are worth the effort.

2

Law Review as an Academic Activity

Grades, Academic Credit, Accreditation Standards, and School Policies

Pamela Wilkins

LEARNING OBJECTIVES

After reviewing this Chapter, editors will be able to

- describe law school accreditation obligations that impact the law review;
- identify school policies that impact law review members and processes;
- differentiate editorial board responsibilities from faculty advisor responsibilities; and
- formulate solutions to common problems involving academic credit for law review service.

A. Introduction

Law reviews occupy a unique place among student organizations. On one hand, most law reviews are student-run: students select and edit articles, work with external authors, organize symposia, supervise classmates, and manage the organization's budget and logistics. Specifics vary by school, but law review editors generally enjoy considerable autonomy.

On the other hand, most law reviews are an academic endeavor: students often receive academic credit for their service, whether for writing their own scholarly article, performing staff work like cite-checking articles, or serving on the editorial board. As such, law reviews are subject to the law school's academic policies and procedures and accreditation standards, both of which limit the review's autonomy.

This Chapter has two principal goals. First, it addresses a common point of confusion among student-editors: which process, policies, and prerogatives do law review editors control, and which do the law school faculty and administration control? The faculty's and administration's authority stems in large part from the school's educational mission, accreditation standards, and policies. Second, the Chapter suggests how institutional stakeholders—editors, administrators, and faculty—can collaborate to avoid problems and build a strong student-led journal consistent with the law school's academic mission and accreditation obligations.

B. An Overview of Law School Accreditation and ABA Standards

An accreditor is an external, independent organization that certifies an institution meets certain predetermined minimum standards. Educational accreditation serves as an assurance of quality. Accreditation can be for the entire university, a particular school within a university, or a department. Accreditation standards vary by kind of institution and field of study. Although the United States Department of Education does not accredit institutions of higher education, it has recognized certain accrediting agencies as reliable authorities regarding the quality of education and training an institution provides.

The Council of the American Bar Association's (ABA) Section on Legal Education and Admissions to the Bar is the national accrediting agency for law schools. Its accreditation is powerful: most states require graduation from an ABA-accredited law school as a condition for admission to the bar.[1] Given this requirement, a law school's very existence generally depends on its accreditation status. In short, ABA accreditation is essential for most U.S. law schools.

---

1. Many states have exceptions to this requirement for lawyers who have been licensed in other jurisdictions for several years. For a summary of states' requirements, see *Chart 3: Domestic Legal Education* on the National Conference of Bar Examiners website, https://reports.ncbex.org/comp-guide/charts/chart-3/#1610142352111-e56b1dc2-06b5 [https://perma.cc/44KH-ASJA].

Each ABA-accredited law school is subject to regular review. In addition to filing an annual questionnaire that addresses topics such as enrollment, attrition, and type of courses offered, ABA-accredited schools undergo site visits every ten years. Before the site visit, schools answer an extensive questionnaire and provide a trove of documents and a self-assessment to the ABA. The ABA then appoints a volunteer team that typically includes a law dean, one or more professors with various experiences and expertise, a law librarian, a judge or practicing attorney, and a central university official (like a provost). The team serves as a factfinder by reviewing the written materials and visiting campus. The campus visit includes class observations; interviews with faculty, law administrators, student leaders, and university stakeholders; and group discussions with faculty, students, and often alumni and others from the community who work with the school. The process is time- and resource-intensive. The principal goal of the review process is to ensure a school's compliance with the ABA's accreditation standards, the *Standards and Rules of Procedure for Approval of Law Schools* (the ABA Standards or the Standards).[2]

The ABA Standards include seven chapters that address areas such as the law school administration, the program of legal education, the faculty, admissions and student services, the library, and facilities, equipment, and technology. The overarching goal is to ensure students receive a high-quality legal education that prepares them for the practice of law.

Chapter 3 is the source of most Standards that impact the law review. Titled "Program of Legal Education," Chapter 3 requires law schools to provide a rigorous education that prepares students to be "effective, ethical, and responsible" members of the legal profession.[3] This general requirement is given flesh through more granular requirements about the curriculum, credit hours, classroom minutes, academic advising, and other topics.

Chapter 3 sets a floor for law schools' programs of legal education. Schools may craft programs that serve their unique missions—which could be based on the rural or urban nature of the surrounding community, an institution's religious affiliation, an institution's status as an HBCU, etc.—but Chapter 3 applies to all schools. The Chapter 3 standards are both broad and narrow: broad, for example, by requiring that a school's program allows students to

---

2. *See* Am. Bar Ass'n Section on Legal Educ. & Admission to the Bar, 2021–2022 Standards and Rules of Procedure for Approval of Law Schools (2021), https://www.americanbar.org/groups/legal_education/resources/standards [https://perma.cc/6NP6-XV69].

3. *Id.* Standard 301(a).

attain competency in the "knowledge and understanding of substantive and procedural law";[4] narrow in their requirements that students receive at least six hours in experiential courses, take a professional responsibility class, and—most important here—have formalized and substantial writing experiences both in the first year and at the upper level.[5]

C. ABA Standards and School Policies Relevant to Law Reviews

1. Academic credit for law review generally

a. Relevant ABA Standards

If you receive academic credit for your work on law review, thank your school and Standard 305. Although schools are not required to award academic credit for law review service, Standard 305 allows it. Standard 305(a) provides that law schools "may grant credit... for courses that involve student participation in studies or activities in a format that does not involve attendance at regularly scheduled class sessions, including... law review."[6] Other provisions then limit the credit that schools can award.

Standard 305(b) guides schools in determining how many credits to award. Specifically, the credit "shall be commensurate with the time and effort required and the anticipated quality of the educational experience of the student."[7] Standard 310(b) provides a formula for determining the amount of work required to earn one credit hour. For courses that meet regularly during a fifteen-week term, one credit represents at least 42.5 hours of in-class instruction and associated out-of-class student work.[8] Thus, when schools grant academic credit for law review, students are expected to complete approximately 42.5 hours of law review work for each credit hour awarded.[9] Any law review credits

---

4. *Id.* Standard 302(a).
5. *See id.* Standard 303(a).
6. *Id.* Standard 305(a).
7. *Id.* Standard 305(b).
8. *See id.* Interpretation 310-1 (This calculation is based on 50-minute class sessions.).
9. *See id.* Standard 310(b)(2) ("A 'credit hour' is an amount of work that reasonably approximates... (2) at least an equivalent amount of work as required in subparagraph (1) of this definition for other academic activities as established by the institution.").

that meet the upper-level writing requirement also must satisfy Standard 303, which will be discussed later in this Chapter.

Just as Standard 305(b) concerns the amount of credit a school may award, Standard 305(c) addresses the evaluation of student work: "Each student's educational achievement in such a course [like law review] shall be evaluated *by a faculty member*."[10] Typically, the faculty advisor for the law review is charged with this duty. Although faculty advisors can and should consult with the editorial board, they cannot outsource the grading and assessment responsibilities to editors: the school—not the law review—awards academic credit.

Standard 311(c) also limits the number of credits a student can take at one time. Specifically, schools may not permit students to be enrolled in credits that exceed 20% of the total credits required for graduation.[11] For example, if a law school requires completion of 90 credits for graduation, then a student cannot be enrolled in more than 18 credits in any one semester. This limit includes credits for co-curricular activities like law review and moot court, and schools cannot waive this requirement.

Finally, Standard 311(b) states that students must take "at least 64" credit hours "in courses that require attendance in regularly scheduled classroom sessions or direct faculty instruction."[12] Interpretation 311-1(b) explains that these 64 credit hours do not include "[c]redit hours earned for participation in co-curricular activities such as law review, moot court, and trial competition."[13] For this reason, the school may limit the credits a student may earn for law review or other co-curricular activities or may provide self-audit checklists for students to ensure that they are meeting the 64-hour requirement. Some schools have also attempted to minimize the impact of Standard 311(b) on law review students by requiring them to take a seminar class as part of their service.

b. Relevant school policies

ABA Standard 308 requires that law schools "adopt, publish, and adhere to sound academic standards."[14] Because the ABA Standards only set a floor, most law schools have adopted specific policies designed to implement or augment the Standards. Schools also adopt policies to comply with universi-

10. *Id.* Standard 305(c) (emphasis added).
11. *Id.* Standard 311(c).
12. *Id.* Standard 311(b).
13. *Id.* Interpretation 311-1(b)(3).
14. *Id.* Standard 308(a).

ty-level accreditation rules, university expectations, and federal and state law. And some policies are created to ensure that the law school runs smoothly and that students are treated as equitably as possible.

For example, to comply with federal laws related to financial aid, the school may develop policies regarding the semester in which academic credit is earned. In the law review context, assume the school has a designated course for law review members writing their own scholarly papers. If a student registers for that course in the fall semester, federal regulations require that the student complete the vast bulk of the work for that project in the fall semester—the semester for which the school awarded the financial aid. The student cannot simply start the work in the fall and complete it over winter break or in the spring.

Federal financial aid regulations also require the school to report course drops, leaves of absences, and withdrawals as of the last day the student participated in the class. Thus, it is important that the law review implement weekly measures to track work and activity and contact the faculty advisor if students are not keeping up with their work or have stopped doing work or communicating with the law review about their situation.

Other policies that may impact the law review include religious and cultural holidays, academic integrity, incomplete grades, disability accommodations, non-discrimination, anti-harassment, FERPA and other student privacy policies, course registration, purchasing and contracting policies, and alcohol at student-led events. Senior editors should also become familiar with the academic calendar, including grade-submission deadlines.

Schools publish their academic policies in different places. Common examples include (1) in the Student Handbook, (2) in the law school or university course catalog, (3) on the Registrar's webpage, and (4) on a policy webpage. You must sometimes consult multiple sources to gather all relevant policies.

The relevance of some information will be immediately apparent; for example, if the school grants credit for law review, the course descriptions and specific credit hours should be in the Course Catalog. The relevance of other academic policies may be less apparent, but law review editors should familiarize themselves with the law school policies on the following issues:

- **Credit Hour Limits per Semester:** Many schools set a limit for permissible credit hours per term that is lower than the ABA requires. For example, if the ABA's upper limit is 18 credits in a term, a school may set a 16- or 17-credit limit. Some schools permit waivers of their internal limits, but law review members who receive academic credit should understand these limits.

- **Limitations on Pass/Fail Credits:** Most schools use a pass/fail grading system in awarding credits for law review service. However, many schools limit the total number of pass/fail credits students can take, and they may count law review and other co-curricular credits against that limit. The practical result may be that law review students have fewer options for electing pass/fail for other classes, such as externships. Such a policy also might dissuade students from participating in both law review and other co-curricular activities, such as moot court and other advocacy teams.
- **Limitations on Joint Service on Law Review and Other Activities:** Policies vary but may include limits on students' ability to participate in clinics, externships, or co-curricular competitions (moot court, dispute resolution, mock trial, etc.) during some semesters or to serve simultaneously on both the law review editorial board and the board of another co-curricular organization.

c. Best practices to prevent or mitigate common problems

An ounce of prevention is worth a pound of cure. Yes, it's a cliché, but it's a cliché because it's true. When editors understand problems that may arise, they can adopt a proactive approach to prevent problems.

The thorniest problems that typically arise concerning academic credit (excluding issues associated with the upper-level writing requirement, which is discussed below) are related to one another: first, role confusion, and second, nonfeasance.

Both editors and faculty advisors can suffer from role confusion. Editors might assume that the law review is entirely autonomous, that editorial board members are awarding academic credit and assigning grades, and that the only role of the faculty advisor is, well, advisory. Especially if they are new to legal education, faculty advisors may assume that advising the law review involves only the roles common to advising any student organization: wise counsel, patron, and cheerleader.

Moreover, role confusion provides fertile ground for the second major problem: nonfeasance, meaning the failure—whether by law review members, editors, or the faculty advisor—to fulfill their responsibilities. Those who do not understand their roles are not likely to perform them well.

Other common problems are more granular. Perhaps the registration process for law review creates risks of noncompliance with ABA or school standards regarding the number of credit hours per term. Perhaps information sessions about law review and advocacy competition teams are not clear about any limits on joint membership or participation.

Clarity, communication, and creating healthy systems prevent and mitigate issues of role confusion and nonfeasance. The same is true for the more granular problems. Specifics will vary by school, but editorial board members should take at least the following steps:

- **Read and keep copies of the current year's Chapter 3 of the ABA Standards, the school's Student Handbook, the law review bylaws, the Course Catalog entries related to law review, and any academic policies about law review service, the upper-level writing requirement, and awarding academic credit.** No substitute exists for knowing and understanding the policies that govern your institution and your organization. If you don't know where to find these policies or are not sure which policies might apply, the academic dean of your law school—often called the Associate Dean for Academic Affairs—is a good starting point. Because your faculty advisor works closely with the academic dean, it's a good practice to speak with your faculty advisor first and share that you would like to engage with the academic dean about specific matters. Another tip is to develop a timeline or checklist related to policy compliance for your term as editor.
- **Hold an initial meeting with the faculty advisor and the law school Registrar.** An organizational meeting should include the outgoing and incoming boards, the faculty advisor, and the Registrar. The meeting agenda should include the following: (1) roles, including that of the faculty advisor; (2) responsibilities of new members, returning members, and editors; (3) the faculty advisor's method of determining whether students have earned credit; (4) the method of registering students for law review; (5) any institution-specific issues and deadlines; and (6) preferred communication methods.

  The Registrar can help identify any prior problems with registration, grades, and academic credit and may propose a better process, which change might require further institutional approval. For example, if an institution does not automatically register students for law review, some students may forget to register, which creates a predictable and difficult set of problems (e.g., potentially excessive semester credits, failure to have enough credits for graduation, failure to qualify for financial aid, etc.). It is important to understand that registration systems work differently. For example, some schools do not permit direct registration for law review so non-members cannot register, while other schools' systems are constructed to require each individual student to register.

- **Meet regularly with the faculty advisor.** Regularly scheduled meetings throughout the term can help anticipate, avoid, and address problems. If the academic credits for law review are pass/fail, a faculty advisor's assessment responsibilities may be simple and rely heavily on reports by the editorial board: if students are doing the assigned work, credit shouldn't be an issue. That said, problems do arise, and no faculty advisor wants to learn of a problem at the end of the term, when it's too late for any constructive conversations or other steps to mitigate nonfeasance. You should also keep folders of each member's work, perhaps on TWEN, Canvas, or another course platform.

  Sometimes, when working with a faculty advisor, you need to "manage up." Advisors have other responsibilities or may be disorganized and advising student organizations can fall to the bottom of a to-do list. Suggesting a regular monthly or bi-weekly meeting allows the advisor to calendar the meeting and build it into their regular workflow.

  The problem of faculty nonfeasance can be complex, so know your boundaries ahead of time. If credits are not pass/fail and a faculty advisor asks you to assign grades for student work, you must say no. But you might want to discuss rubrics or checklists that you can complete to help the advisor determine grades. The same principle holds for pass/fail work. *Although faculty members may consider editorial board members' input, they may not outsource their grading responsibilities.* If an advisor pushes you or refuses to perform their role, consult the academic dean.

- **Include the faculty advisor (and possibly the Registrar and academic dean) in the orientation for new law review members.** Role confusion afflicts not only editorial boards but also new law review members. New members should understand how credit is awarded and should appreciate that the editorial board oversees the organization but the school awards academic credit and grades.

- **If necessary, amend the law review bylaws and discuss potential changes to course descriptions with the faculty advisor.** Recall that the ABA Standards require credit hours to reflect both time on task and the quality of the task. For example, arranging chairs may be time-consuming but not educationally valuable. Clear position descriptions not only reduce role confusion but also ensure that credit hours are commensurate with the kind and quality of the work. Of course, you do not have the power to change course descriptions—and bylaw changes may require faculty approval—but if such changes are appropriate, your faculty advisor can guide you through the school's processes.

Law review students tend to be ambitious and conscientious, so one can reasonably hope that editorial boards and faculty advisors will encounter few problems related to academic credit. However, hope is no substitute for good policy and best practices. This is nowhere truer than in the student-writing process.

2. Standard 303(a)(2): The upper-level writing requirement

For schools that allow students to fulfill the upper-level writing credit through the law review, Standard 303(a)(2) is a source of confusion about the division of power and responsibility between the editorial board and the faculty. However, a savvy editorial board can use the Standard to benefit the law review.

a. Overview of Standard 303(a)(2)

Standard 303 is the source of what many schools call the upper-level writing requirement. One mandated learning outcome for law schools includes competency in "legal analysis and reasoning, legal research, . . . and written and oral communication in the legal context."[15] Standard 303 is more specific, requiring "one writing experience in the first year and at least one additional writing experience after the first year, *both of which are faculty supervised.*"[16]

15. *Id.* Standard 302(b).
16. *Id.* Standard 303 (a)(2) (emphasis added).

Moreover, the experience must be rigorous. The ABA considers several factors in evaluating rigor, including "the number and nature of writing projects... the form and extent of individualized assessment of a student's written products, and the number of drafts that a student must produce for any writing experience."[17]

Law schools virtually always satisfy Standard 303's first-year writing requirement by offering one or two mandatory legal analysis and writing courses as part of the traditional first-year curriculum.

But there's more variation for the upper-level writing requirements. For example, schools may offer seminars—which allow students to write a traditional academic paper on a legal topic of interest—or advanced writing courses that focus on subjects like appellate advocacy or judicial opinion writing. Some schools allow students to write a significant paper as part of an independent study course supervised by a faculty member.

Seminars and practice-oriented advanced writing courses almost always meet the ABA's requirement that the academic experience be rigorous and include faculty supervision because a professor is assigned to teach the class as part of a regular course load. This course assignment includes responsibility for (1) creating and following a syllabus that generally includes intermediate assignments and formative assessments (outlines, rough drafts, etc.), and (2) submitting course grades by an institutional deadline. Students submit course evaluations that can be considered in the tenure and promotion process and in faculty annual reviews. Finally, when an ABA site team visits a school, it reviews syllabi to ensure rigor.

Many—but not all—schools allow students' law review articles, typically written by members during their first year of law review service, to fulfill the Standard 303 upper-level writing requirement. The number and kind of credits granted vary by school. One common law school policy is to grant two pass/fail credits for a thirty-page paper. Other schools may give three credits for a longer paper or may assign grades for the paper.

As the next section details, the practice of awarding academic credit and allowing a paper written as part of a law review service to fulfill the upper-level writing requirement presents a wonderful opportunity for law review members but poses potential landmines for both the law review and the school. Clarity about expectations will allow editors to realize opportunities and avoid or mitigate landmines.

---

17. *Id.* Interpretation 303-2.

b. Standard 303(a)(2) and academic credit for student papers: Opportunities and landmines

The opportunities are obvious. Law review members, who are often among the most academically accomplished students in their class, not only enjoy the opportunity to receive academic credit for writing about a subject of interest, but also have the chance to be published.

But landmines exist as well. First, when parties misunderstand one another's obligations, confusion or turf wars can arise. At most law schools, law review editorial boards jealously guard the journal's institutional autonomy. The student-writing requirement is typically imposed by the journal itself and is often supervised by an editor. The editorial board typically selects student works for publication. Within this context, a faculty member's heavy involvement in a student-writing project can sometimes feel to editors like meddling. The student-author may also be confused. What if the faculty member is dissatisfied with the student's work but the editors find it acceptable, or even good? If a student-author is meeting both with a faculty advisor[18] and an editor, who is the *real* boss?

Another challenge is faculty nonfeasance and outsourcing. Faculty members who have agreed to supervise student papers are all too often missing in action, underperforming, perpetually late, or apologetic but not apologetic enough to change. The result is confused and frustrated student-writers, work that isn't as strong as it could be, and editors who perceive little leverage over the underperforming faculty member.

Faculty nonfeasance usually results from a vacuum of accountability or equity structures at the law school. Regarding the accountability vacuum, teaching classes has a built-in accountability structure for professors. There's somewhere to be at certain times each week, with a general expectation of at least a semi-coherent lesson plan. Schools often impose an office-hour requirement and grading deadlines. Students complete course evaluations that administrators and other faculty members consider during annual reviews and

---

18. At many schools, each law review student has an individual faculty advisor (distinct from the law review advisor) during the note-writing process. Students may select these advisors based on subject-matter expertise or prior relationship, or the school may have a formal process for assigning advisors. At other law schools, the main faculty advisor for the law review plays a major role in advising on and assessing student notes and comments. Editors should learn and understand the structure at their institution. This section principally concerns situations in which students have individual faculty advisors for notes and comments, but the guidance can be adapted to other structures.

renewal, promotion, and tenure processes. For scholarship, faculty members must report on and show evidence of their scholarly progress at least once a year. Equally important, faculty members see teaching and scholarship as their core responsibilities.

Unlike teaching and scholarship, which have built-in accountability mechanisms, advising students completing their law review writing requirement often doesn't. There are often no expectations about whether faculty members have a duty to serve in that role or how to evaluate the faculty member's work. Furthermore, students have few effective means to pressure slack faculty members—other than to report the situation to the primary law review faculty advisor or a dean. Given the absence of accountability mechanisms, when coupled with faculty members' other obligations, it's easy for faculty members to procrastinate or otherwise let their advising responsibilities slide.

Regarding the equity vacuum, absent a provision in a union contract or school policy, most schools don't have formal mechanisms to require faculty members to serve as advisors or to limit their service. As a result, (1) the "popular" professors—who are often a personality type that struggles with saying no—serve disproportionately; (2) woman and POC faculty serve disproportionately, especially when schools have few women or POC faculty; and (3) some faculty members do not serve at all or serve infrequently.

The equity and accountability vacuums hurt the law review, affected professors, and the institution itself. The law school suffers for many reasons, including that its compliance with Standard 303(a)(2) and Interpretation 303-2 may reasonably be called into question. Is the writing experience truly rigorous when faculty members aren't holding up their end of the bargain? Moreover, the primary law review faculty advisor may be the technically designated professor, and colleagues' nonfeasance puts the advisor in a thorny situation both practically and ethically.

Ideally, you won't face these dilemmas as an editor. But if you do, understanding editors' roles versus faculty advisors' roles will help. Faculty members *must* advise and *must* determine whether academic credit is appropriate. Those are institutional responsibilities and conditions of accreditation. However, depending on your law school's policies, the law review likely retains autonomy regarding several issues, including (1) whether the student-author has satisfied the standards for the law review itself, and (2) which student pieces should be published.

Moreover, don't underestimate your own power as an editor. You now know your institution's obligations to the ABA and have a sense of the institutional interests at stake. You also know that the Dean and the Associate Dean for Academic Affairs prioritize institutional compliance with accreditation standards; thus, chances are the law review's faculty advisor shares similar concerns. Accordingly, consider the following steps:

- **Learn your institution's policies regarding faculty responsibilities concerning the upper-level writing requirement generally and law review student works specifically.** In addition to checking for written policies, contact the law review's faculty advisor. Some relevant questions include the following:
    - Who on the faculty is responsible for advising students during the student-writing process: the law review's main faculty advisor, a group of assigned faculty members, faculty members selected by students, someone else?
    - What are faculty members' responsibilities regarding the school's upper-level writing requirement?
    - Are they required to hold conferences, review outlines, or comment upon a certain number of drafts?
    - Do faculty members have limits on how many student-authors they can supervise per semester or academic year?
    - Do faculty members receive institutional credit for serving as advisors for student articles?
    - Is the work recognized by law school or university administration in the annual review process?
    - Is the *absence* of such advising by faculty members—those who say no again and again—recognized in the annual review process?
    - If a law review member has an issue with an individual faculty advisor, how should that member proceed?
    - What if the faculty advisor and editors give the member conflicting advice?
    - Is there a process you can develop to coordinate comments before sharing them with the student-author?

These questions will help you and the student-authors and will help determine whether the school has policies that ensure compliance with ABA Standard 303.

- **If there are policies on the books but that are not enforced, meet first with the law review's faculty advisor and potentially the Associate Dean for Academic Affairs.**
- **If the school lacks formal policies, speak with the law review faculty advisor and the Associate Dean for Academic Affairs about developing such policies.** If faculty advising of student-authors is a free-for-all, then speak with the faculty advisor and the academic dean about developing common expectations for advising. In a perfect world, advising would be considered part of each faculty member's formal workload.
- **Hold an orientation meeting with advisors, student-authors, the law review faculty advisor, and (ideally) the Associate Dean of Academic Affairs to set common expectations.** Even if the school's policies are nonexistent or sub-optimal, most people want to do the right thing. Although you have no formal power over faculty members—and many may skip the meeting—explaining the law review's interests and expectations will help create a set of shared expectations. You're more likely to get what you want if you ask for it directly.
- **Take institutional steps to make strong faculty advising visible within the law review and at the institution.** How? Your imagination is the only limit! Many law reviews give awards for a faculty member of the year, but all too often, that's another popularity contest or a way to recognize a faculty member who worked hard. Ideas might include
    - recognizing the faculty advisor when a student's work is selected for publication;
    - asking student-authors to thank their advisors in their paper and with a formal letter that faculty members can use for their renewal, promotion, or tenure file;
    - allowing student-authors to nominate an Advisor of the Year;
    - emailing the Dean and Associate Dean for Academic Affairs about faculty members whose work has been especially conscientious or otherwise notable; and
    - when you are permitted, nominating high-performing faculty members for university awards.

- **Encourage law review members to write outside of Constitutional Law and Criminal Procedure.** There are *lots* of interesting topics in law, and that Estates & Trusts professor may be a great advisor—and may help a student draft a paper that will serve their future professional interests in a way that writing about the Fourth Amendment may not.

Finally, remember that the law review editorial board and the law school share common interests. Both want the law review to succeed. Both want students to succeed. Both want students to write excellent papers and earn academic credit. Engaging in best practices and remembering common interests will minimize frustrations and conflicts and result in both better work and happier stakeholders.

KEY TAKEAWAYS

- ABA Standards require faculty members to assess student work and award academic credit.
- Faculty members' responsibilities for determining academic credit cannot be delegated to student editors, although faculty members may seek input from editors.
- Read the relevant accreditation standards and policies as your editorial term begins.
- Regular communication between editors and faculty advisors prevents problems.
- In addition to the law review's faculty advisor, the Associate Dean for Academic Affairs and the Registrar are good sources of information and support.

3

The Business of Law Reviews

Darby Dickerson

LEARNING OBJECTIVES

After reviewing this Chapter, editors will be able to

- identify the journal's legal status and relationship to the host law school;
- compile a comprehensive list of business-related questions to address during the editor transition process;
- assemble key business-related documents, policies, and procedures to review carefully;
- discuss a wide variety of business-related matters with the journal's faculty advisor and law school administrators;
- differentiate business matters over which the law review likely has authority from those where it lacks authority to act independently; and
- plan how to handle the journal's business matters professionally and effectively.

A. Introduction

A law review is an academic journal and a business. It's a business because the members produce and distribute a product. This Chapter will address many business concepts that journal editors must understand to operate the journal effectively during their term. More specifically, these concepts include

- the journal's legal status and relationship to the law school;
- governing documents;

- budgets and finances;
- contracting authority;
- fundraising;
- on- and off-campus events;
- working with law school staff;
- physical space; and
- websites and webpages.

The final section of this Chapter addresses several miscellaneous, but nonetheless important, business matters. Other chapters cover additional business topics like publishing or printing the journal,[1] ensuring compliance with copyright law,[2] and supervising other journal members.[3]

B. Legal Status and Relationship to the Law School

Virtually all student-edited law reviews in the United States are attached to a law school. But journals have different legal statuses and relationships to their schools. A law journal may operate as a recognized student organization, a functional department within the law school, an academic program, or a separately incorporated legal entity. Even within a single law school, journals may have different relationships to their schools. For example, The Harvard Law Review is formally independent of Harvard Law School.[4] It is published by the Harvard Law Review Association, a separate 501(c)(3) nonprofit organization.[5] Yet, the Harvard Business Law Review is a student organization of Harvard Law School.

---

1. See Chapter 15 of this *Manual*, which addresses journal production and dissemination.

2. See Chapter 17 of this *Manual*, which discusses a variety of copyright issues relevant to law reviews.

3. See Chapters 9 and 12 of this *Manual*, which provide advice about different aspects of peer supervision.

4. *About*, HARV. L. REV., https://harvardlawreview.org/about [https://perma.cc/E2XM-6GKU] (last visited Jan. 8, 2022).

5. *See* Harv. L. Rev. Ass'n, *Form 990 for Period Ending June 2020*, PROPUBLICA: NONPROFIT EXPLORER, https://projects.propublica.org/nonprofits/display_990/42104292/05_2021_prefixes_01-04%2F042104292_202006_990_2021051818121895 (last visited Jan. 8, 2022).

Early questions that the incoming Editor in Chief should ask are, "What is the journal's legal status?" and "How is the journal organized within or in relation to the law school?" The answers to these threshold questions will determine how the journal responds to myriad business matters. The incoming EIC should pose these questions to the outgoing EIC, the journal's faculty advisor, or the school's academic dean. That being said, using self-help, it's often possible to discern the journal's status from the "About" or "Background" section of the journal's webpage. In addition, if the EIC suspects that the journal is published by a separately incorporated entity, the EIC can search the relevant secretary of state's website or sites like ProPublica, which post tax returns and 990 forms for many nonprofit organizations.

1. Journals that are part of the law school

Most journals are part of their law school and do not have a separate legal identity. Being part of a law school means that journals likely do not have their own banking account, cannot execute contracts in the journal's name, and must abide by relevant school policies and procedures. In short, the journal likely lacks the authority to act independently on most business matters. But lacking authority is not necessarily "bad"; instead, it may mean that the school has arranged the journal's business affairs to allow editors to focus on editing and related academic pursuits.

But the status inquiry doesn't end if the EIC discovers that the journal is not a separately incorporated entity. Instead, the EIC should determine how the journal is viewed within the school.

If the journal is a recognized student organization—akin to the Black Law Students Association or the Environmental Law Society—then the journal likely has some reporting relationship to the Student Affairs Office (or a similar office that works with student organizations). That relationship, in turn, could mean that the Student Affairs Office sets the journal's budget, assists with reimbursements, approves all events, and might require that designated editors submit certain regular reports or attend certain meetings and training sessions.

If the journal is viewed solely as an academic program—like the Moot Court Board or a concentration program—the EIC likely reports only to the designated faculty advisor, who will serve as the liaison to other administrators, help develop the budget, and assist with other operational matters in addition to submitting grades and providing guidance and advice about article selection, editing, and member interactions.[6] Status as an academic program might give the journal more freedom over the events it holds and how it manages its other affairs.

If the journal operates like a functional department within the law school—akin to the business office or IT department—it's likely that a full-time staff member has been assigned to work with the journal. That staff member, and not the EIC, will be considered the department head. This structural arrangement may mean that the journal has a bit more business authority than the other arrangements, but every school is different, and context matters.

2. Journals published by separately incorporated entities

Editors on journals that are published by a separately incorporated entity may have more business-related responsibilities than editors on journals that are subsumed within the law school. Status as a separate organization carries additional duties, such as ensuring that annual corporate filings and tax returns are accurate and submitted timely and that adequate insurance is purchased and the entity notifies the insurance broker of any potential claims (e.g., threats or service of a lawsuit, slip-and-fall, etc.). And if the entity owns or leases a separate building, then the responsibilities increase exponentially.

Separate status likely means that the journal can contract in the name of the separate entity, develop and administer its own budget, register its own trademarks, and develop its own policies on various business-related matters. But separate status does not mean that the law review can act in a way that conflicts with the policies or procedures of its affiliated law school or university. Because the journal name typically includes the name of the affiliated law school or university—and especially if the law school awards academic credit for law review service—a memorandum of understanding or similar agreement likely exists between the law school or university and the entity that publishes the journal. That agreement probably includes provisions requiring that the journal abide by important law school policies, such as its nondiscrimination and conflict-of-interest policies. The incoming EIC should ask about this type of agreement, review it carefully, and then discuss it with the senior staff member of the separate entity and likely the dean of the affiliated law school to ensure that everyone understands each parties' rights and responsibilities.

---

6. For information regarding how editors interact with the journal's faculty advisor regarding grades and academic credit, see Chapter 2 of this *Manual*.

Separately incorporated journals are found at different types of schools. A few examples include the Columbia Business Law Review (specialty journal at a private law school), Mississippi Law Journal (general journal at a public law school), and Western State Law Review (general journal at a private law school).

But before becoming concerned that you've taken on more responsibility than you had anticipated, speak with the outgoing EIC because the affiliated law school likely has developed a structure and assigned staff to help ensure the journal remains in compliance with relevant laws and regulations. Even if the school has not provided structure and resources, the nonprofit that publishes the journal may have experienced staff or an advisory board, and the outgoing EIC hopefully has a checklist or timeline for all business-related steps required by law or regulation.

One key, though, is to ensure that the current EIC can locate the original Internal Revenue Service Determination Letter evidencing the Section 501(c)(3) tax-exempt status and any amendments.

3. Nonprofit status

Most, but not all, law schools are nonprofit organizations under Internal Revenue Code § 501(c)(3). And most separate entities that publish student-edited law journals also appear to be 501(c)(3) nonprofit organizations.

The benefits of 501(c)(3) status include exemption from federal income tax and possibly state income, sales, and employment taxes, exemption from federal unemployment tax, and reduced postal rates. Donors to 501(c)(3) organizations are allowed to claim a tax deduction for the contributions.

To be tax-exempt under Section 501(c)(3), the organization must not serve a private interest, and its net earnings must be used solely to advance the organization's charitable cause. Education is a qualifying charitable purpose. Section 501(c)(3) organizations cannot act to influence legislation in a substantial way, participate in campaign activities, or endorse political candidates. They typically cannot engage in lobbying. To maintain the status, the 501(c)(3) organization must remain true to its original charitable mission (for example, an educational institution must continue to provide education and not shift its mission to providing shelter to unhoused persons). While some unrelated business income is allowed, the organization may not receive substantial income from unrelated business operations.

While this Chapter only scratches the surface of this topic, editors should recognize types of activities that might jeopardize Section 501(c)(3) status. As noted above, danger zones include lobbying, participating in political campaigns or endorsing political candidates, veering away from the organization's founding mission, operating for an individual's private gain, and engaging in material, unrelated business activities (e.g., selling large quantities of merchandise). An organization can also lose tax-exempt status by failing to file federal and state tax returns for three consecutive years and failing to register with the relevant state authority.

C. Governing Documents

Regardless of the journal's legal status and relationship to its host school, the journal likely has governing documents that new editors should review, abide by, and if appropriate, consider updating. These documents might be titled "constitution," "bylaws," or "articles of incorporation," and a journal might have more than one of these documents.

The constitution identifies the organization's name, purpose, mission function, membership (e.g., eligibility, number), organizational structure (e.g., executive board, officers, committees, advisors), selection and removal processes, and required meetings. The constitution may also include provisions about how to amend the constitution and dissolve the organization.[7]

An organization's bylaws are its operating manual. They provide accountability, transparency, and consistency. Schools often expect that a journal's bylaws address the planned timing and frequency of publication; the proposed format (online or print); the timing and selection process for new members and editors; and duties associated with each editorial position. Bylaws might include nondiscrimination or diversity statements, information about the Americans Disabilities Act, and anti-plagiarism policies; alternatively, these matters might be included in a separate staff or editor handbook or manual.[8] If

---

7. Bert Markgraf, *How to Write a Constitution for a Nonprofit Organization*, AZ CENT., https://yourbusiness.azcentral.com/write-constitution-nonprofit-organization-15590.html [https://perma.cc/4KQL-FUX4] (last visited Jan. 8, 2022); Student Orgs. & Activities Div. of Student Affairs, *Student Organization Constitution Writing Guide*, NW. U., https://www.northwestern.edu/studentorgs/org-officers/annual-requirements/writing-a-constitution/assets/soa-student-constitution-template-033117.pdf [https://perma.cc/63ZZ-68RN] (last updated Spring 2017).

8. *E.g.*, *Bylaws*, HOUS. BUS. & TAX L.J., https://uh.campuslabs.com/engage/organization/hbtlj/documents/view/570907 [https://perma.cc/VK23-B9XJ] (last amended Apr. 18,

the organization does not have a constitution, matters traditionally addressed in the constitution might be incorporated into the bylaws.

For journals published by entities separate from the affiliated school, the articles of incorporation document the corporation's creation and organization.

These documents and any internal handbooks, manuals, and policies should be kept in a relatively secure, centralized location that editors over the years can access. A network drive on the law school's system can be a good choice. A cloud-based system in an individual editor's name, on the other hand, is not an appropriate location.

In addition to the governing documents, journals often create handbooks, manuals, policies, and internal guides to help ensure consistency from one volume or editorial board to the next and memorialize helpful practices. Besides studying the documents to understand how to run the law review, editors should, on some regular basis, review these documents and consider whether they should be amended. As a rule of thumb, a review every three or four years is reasonable. It's wise to involve the faculty advisor in any review, as that individual may be able to help identify law review policies and documents that conflict with current law school policies or changes in state and federal law.

Changes to governing documents must be made according to the terms set forth in the document and often require approval by the law school administration or faculty, or in the case of a separate entity, the board of directors (as opposed to the editorial board). Navigating these processes can take time, so start any desired amendment process over the summer or as early in the academic year as possible.

Following any amendment, do not delete or discard the former document; instead, establish an archive in case you need to retrieve the historical document for any reason.

D. Budgets and Finance

As a business, the journal will have a budget that reflects the revenue the journal is expected to earn and the expenses the journal is expected to incur. It's

---

2017); *Bylaws*, St. Mary's L.J., https://commons.stmarytx.edu/thestmaryslawjournal/StMLJ_Bylaws.pdf [https://perma.cc/2N65-LQ52] (last amended Feb. 22, 2021); *Establishing a New Law Journal or Review*, U.C. Irvine Sch. L., https://www.law.uci.edu/campus-life/student-organizations/resources/new%20law%20journal.html [https://perma.cc/8D8L-JEBW] (last visited Jan. 8, 2022).

important for the EIC and Business Manager, if any, to understand the budget and how to manage it during their term. The journal will also likely need to make purchases, reimburse members for certain expenses, and deposit checks or receive other revenue.

Questions for the new editors to ask during the transition process include the following:

- How is the journal funded? Does the school provide operational funds (which generally means money from tuition dollars) to run the journal?
- How does the budget-development process work? When does it start and conclude? Who is involved? What input will current editors have in the process?
- How can current editors access the budget and determine how much money remains? What happens if the journal needs to purchase an item that's not included in the current budget? Can the journal overspend in one line item and offset that by underspending in another line item? What happens if the journal exceeds the allocated budget?
- If the journal earns revenue on subscriptions, royalties, or from other sources, where does the revenue go, and how is it used? For example, does the journal get to keep the funds, or do the funds go to the law school generally? The answers will often depend on how the journal is structured and funded. If the journal receives a check or other funds, how should it proceed (e.g., take the check to the law school's business office)?
- Does the journal have its own banking and checking accounts? If so, who has access? Do signature cards need to be changed when editors change? Does the journal or school have a policy regarding banking and checking accounts or check-signing? Are any law school or entity staff listed on the account? Who reviews the bank statements, and on what basis? Must the bank statements be provided to anyone else, such as a law school official, auditor, or tax preparer? How should an editor proceed if they suspect embezzlement, misuse, fraud, or another problem, whether involving another journal member or not?
- Does the journal have a credit card? If so, in whose name is the card? Do new cards need to be issued to new editors and canceled

for outgoing editors? Must an individual complete designated training before becoming eligible as a cardholder? Does the faculty advisor or another staff member have a school credit card that can be used for journal purchases? What is the limit on each credit card? Who pays the balance, and when? Does the law school or university have specific policies relating to credit cards? What happens if an editor or the journal misuses the credit card?

- How can the journal procure supplies it may need—such as new citation manuals, paper for copiers and printers, pens, etc.—or make other payments (e.g., conference registration, down payments for events, etc.)? Must the journal use designated vendors? Does the school have a procurement policy? If so, how can editors access it (for public schools, it's usually on a website)? Is there a tax-exempt certificate the journal must use when making purchases? If so, how can the journal obtain the current-year certificate?
- Can a journal member buy an item or make a payment and receive reimbursement? If so, how does that process work? Does the journal need a FOAPAL or similar set of accounting numbers to code purchases and requests for reimbursements? Are requests for reimbursement submitted online or via a specific hard-copy template? What are the deadlines by which requests for reimbursement must be submitted?
- Does the school have special rules regarding travel? For example, has the school or state imposed maximums on meals and hotel costs? Is advance permission required for travel? If so, who approves travel for journal members, and how much notice is required? Does the school have corporate accounts (and thus special rates) with certain hotels and carriers?
- Do other departments' budgets cover items that might benefit the law review? For example, can the law review request that the law library purchase certain materials on the library's budget? Or can IT purchase new computers for the journal, with the IT budget?

If you are fortunate enough to have a law school staff person assigned to work with the journal, that staff member may know the answers to many of these questions and handle many of the business functions. If your journal does not have an assigned staff member, your faculty advisor may—but likely will not—know the answers to these and related questions. If your journal has a reporting relationship with the Student Affairs Office, that office can walk you through the answers and processes and may provide some staff support for more complex transactions. But if you need assistance, the best place to look is your law school's business, accounting, finance, or administrative support office (names will vary across schools).

The most important caveat is not to spend any member's personal funds before understanding how the budget, purchasing, and reimbursement works. Otherwise, that member may have unintentionally made a gift to the journal.

E. Contracting Authority

A related issue is whether any editor can sign a contract on behalf of the journal. If the journal is part of the law school, the answer is likely "no," other than perhaps signing a standard copyright agreement that the law school or university has approved. Most law schools and universities have policies or procedures about who can sign a contract and the review process that must be completed before anyone at the school can sign an agreement.[9] Most typically, a designated employee—often the dean or a chief operating or financial officer—must sign all contracts after review by the General Counsel or a procurement or purchasing officer. So, editors and members should never sign any agreement without first understand schooling policies and procedures.

For journals published by separate entities, it may be that certain editors are delegated to bind the host entity on certain matters, but the wisest course is to ask questions before negotiating or signing any contract.

For journals situated within larger universities, it's important to understand that the contract process may take weeks or even months to complete, so plan wisely and balance patience with professional prodding. Also consider how to involve your faculty advisor if you feel like the process has stagnated or your matter has dropped to the bottom of someone's pile of work.

---

9. *E.g.*, *Contract Approval and Signature Authority Policy*, CATH. U. AM., https://policies.catholic.edu/finance/finance/Contracts/index.html [https://perma.cc/93ZK-LLZM] (last revised Oct. 4, 2011); Off. of Gen. Counsel, *Signature Authority*, U. S. CAL., https://generalcounsel.usc.edu/signature-authority [https://perma.cc/PP75-8MN6] (last visited Jan. 8, 2022).

On a related point, new editors should ask for access to ongoing agreements that impact journal operations. Examples might include a publisher or printing contract, a contract with a freelance designer, proofreader, or web designer, or a contract to hold next year's banquet at a certain venue. New editors should review and abide by all contracts, calendar all important milestones, deadlines, and renewal dates, and ensure they pass access and important information to the new board at the end of their term.

F. Fundraising

Many journals seek to increase their revenues through fundraising, whether by approaching alumni for donations, hosting a fundraiser, or selling merchandise. Sometimes, the supplement is needed merely to publish the journal. Other times, journals hope to host events for members, establish scholarships for editors, or buy items like cords or gifts for graduating members.

The cardinal rule is to speak with your faculty advisor and the head of the law school's development, fundraising, or institutional advancement office before planning any fundraising activities. If the journal reports to the Student Affairs Office, include that office's primary contact in any discussions. As noted earlier, some activities might jeopardize the journal's tax-exempt status, while other activities might impact the school's relationship with donors or prospective donors. For example, the law school will likely be reluctant to permit the journal to solicit all former journal members because the school might be working on a major gift proposal for one or more alumni. It would be a shame for all involved if a donor gave $100 to support the journal when capable of giving much more, maybe even to support the journal or its members.

Students often underestimate the time and effort required to raise even modest sums. Any fundraising will require the support of law school staff members. For example, they will need to acknowledge the gift, record the gift, and send a gift receipt for tax purposes—at a minimum. Advancement offices tend to protect staff time and have their eye on "ROI"—return on investment. If your event will take significant staff time to raise a few hundred or thousand dollars, expect your request to be denied.

A better approach is to take a long view and offer to have several editors to help the advancement office with their projects. For example, that office frequently needs students to pose for photographs, write testimonials, draft thank-you notes to annual-fund donors, and maybe even to join visits with donors or prospective donors who served on the journal. By assisting in these ways, you will educate the advancement office about the journal and its importance to the law school and will be top-of-mind as they speak with donors about potential student scholarships and other projects.

One other topic is to understand whether any endowments or restricted accounts exist to support the journal or its editors. An endowment is a fund given by a donor, usually for a specific purpose; the principal may never be touched, but part of the interest may be used annually. A restricted account is a fund for a particular purpose, all of which may be used for that purpose. Endowments and restricted funds may be used to pay editors stipends or scholarships, purchase technology for the journal, or sponsor certain journal events, like an annual gala. Once you understand whether these accounts exist, ensure they are being used. Sometimes, funds are established, but over time, someone forgets about them, and they go unused for some period (although most schools have tracking processes to ensure this situation does not occur).

G. Events

Many journals sponsor a variety of events during the year, ranging from open houses for prospective members, meals during new member orientation, awards ceremonies and year-end banquets, "book parties" to celebrate the publication of a specific issue, symposia, conferences, alumni gatherings, and career panels for members.

As explained elsewhere in this Chapter, it's important for the journal to coordinate with key law school staff before planning and announcing any events. Among the various issues that the journal and school must consider and discuss are whether

- a budget exists for the event;
- the event is appropriate for the journal to host and consistent with school policies (e.g., alcohol rules, fundraising, etc.);
- on-campus or off-campus space for the event can be reserved or procured;

- law school staff or the faculty advisor must be present during the event;
- the event conflicts with other school events or the academic calendar; and
- appropriate risk-management processes have been built into the event (e.g., transportation, severe weather, alcohol, security, insurance, etc.).

Pop-up events under the journal's sponsorship are likely not feasible, and planning for major events may take at least six months (contract approval, venue reservations, invitations, etc.). Therefore, the incoming board should discuss what events it plans to host during the coming year, and before leaving for the summer, should meet with the faculty advisor, Student Affairs Office, and other key administrative contacts to discuss the proposed events and how to move forward in an organized manner consistent with school policies and protocols.

If you want the dean or other administrators or faculty to attend your event, give them notice as soon as feasible, because calendars fill up quickly. And understand that many deans have event request forms they ask groups to complete so they can understand the event and be prepared to participate effectively. The dean's executive assistant typically can provide that form and give preliminary information about the dean's availability to attend an event on a given date.

It's not wise to circumvent these policies and protocols because individual members may be opening themselves to personal liability should anyone be injured or killed, or property is damaged. Even if no one is hurt and no property is harmed, individuals could be subject to individual or organizational discipline or other sanctions under the school's honor, professionalism, or disciplinary codes. Members could also tarnish their reputations and thus damage future career prospects and destroy relationships with the faculty advisor and other journal members.

H. Working with Law School Staff

Depending on your journal's situation, you may have one or multiple full-time law school staff assigned to work with your journal or multiple journals or student organizations, you may have a part-time staff member assigned to work with your journal, or you may have no staff members assigned to work with your journal.

If your journal has an assigned staff member, the EIC should understand

- **To whom the staff member reports.** The staff members typically will report to another employee, such as a director or dean, not to student-editors or even the journal faculty advisor. That supervisor will handle HR matters such as approving vacation and other time off, approving any timesheets, and handling annual performance reviews. The EIC should build a relationship with the supervisor so that the journal is aware when the staff member will be off work, and the EIC should ask whether the supervisor will want input for the staff member's annual review. The EIC should also understand their role vis-à-vis the staff member; for example, can they assign work to the staff member and if so, is the type of work limited? The EIC should also understand how to properly submit a concern about a staff member through the proper chain-of-command and with appropriate attention to privacy and related concerns.
- **The status of each staff member assigned to work with the journal.** In most cases, the staff member is likely to be a non-exempt employee, and in some circumstances, the staff member may be a member of a union or subject to the terms of a collective bargaining agreement. Non-exempt employees work set hours each week (such as 8:00 a.m. to 5:00 p.m., Monday through Friday); any adjustment to that schedule typically must be approved in advance by the staff member's supervisor. Non-exempt employees typically get a set lunch break and possibly other set breaks during the day. If they work more than a pre-established number of hours per week, they are entitled to overtime. At most schools, overtime must be both budgeted and approved in advance by the supervisor. Many times, staff want to do the best possible job for the journal, and they will stay late or check emails and perform work on weekends and holidays on a "volunteer basis." But the law does not permit such volunteering, and the journal should understand that the school will be subject to federal wage-and-hour liability if the staff member does not accurately record all hours worked. For these reasons, it's important for the EIC to know the hours the staff members are allowed to work and when breaks should

occur—and to respect those parameters and ensure that other members also respect them. If the journal has a special need—for example, an evening event where they need the staff member's help or extra work needs to be performed to meet a deadline, the EIC should speak with the staff member's supervisor and potentially the school's HR director to ensure that laws, policies, and collective bargaining agreements are honored. These restrictions also mean that editors must plan their work and projects and stick to planned timelines because not doing so may mean paying overtime (assuming a budget and supervisor approval) or completing the work without staff assistance.

Editors should appreciate that long-term staff members know more about producing the law review than new or even outgoing editors, and they should respect the staff members' experience and knowledge and treat them as valuable team members. Seek their input. Ask questions. Never adopt an "I'm going to be a lawyer, but you're an administrative assistant" attitude.

To help build a positive working relationship, get to know the staff member. How does the person prefer to communicate? Email? Teams messaging? In person? Does the staff member have any other preferences the editorial board can honor? What does the staff member enjoy about the position, and what are the main challenges? Don't gossip about prior boards but do seek input about how you can help improve the operation.

If the journal doesn't have an assigned staff member, you're likely going to work with a wide array of staff across campus: in the business office, student affairs, security, housekeeping/maintenance/facilities, print shop, IT, advancement/fundraising, Registrar, and more. Again, take time to learn people's names and functions. Treat them kindly and professionally. Ask questions instead of barking commands. Be understanding if they refer you to another department or need time to fulfill your request. Most law schools are understaffed, and most staff are overworked. But most also love working with students and want to help you as best they can given school policies and workload constraints. Consult the journal's faculty advisor if you hit obstacles or can't navigate the administrative bureaucracy. If the faculty advisor is not available or unhelpful, consult the HR director for employee-related matters and the law school's academic dean for other guidance.

During your term, consider how the journal can express gratitude to the staff—not just your main staff contacts, but different departments that supported your work. Examples might include thank-you notes (with the staff member's supervisor copied), small birthday or holiday gifts (many schools restrict employees' ability to accept gifts other than de minimum gifts), and recognition in the journal or during a year-end banquet.

I. Physical Space

Questions related to journal space include (1) whether the journal has or needs physical space, (2) how the physical space is maintained, (3) how to care for equipment in the physical space, (4) who can access the space and how to keep those in the space safe, and (5) what the journal can do in its designated physical space. This section addresses these topics and concludes with a few thoughts about other spaces on campus that the journal might use.

1. Journal space in general

While many journals may have their own space—whether on or off campus—others may share space or have no designated physical space. As the number of journals and other activities or departments within a law school proliferate, physical space can become a precious resource. On the other hand, as tools like Zoom, Canvas, and Box have developed, it's become easier—and often more convenient—for editors and members to publish the review from separate, remote locations.

If your journal has substantial physical space on the law school campus that you are not using for journal work, you might consider being a good citizen and discussing with your faculty advisor whether you should relinquish the space. Of course, once you give up space, there's little chance of getting it back, so be sure to consider future boards when you make these decisions. If you return space or agree to share space with another journal or student organization, consider whether you will ask the school for any consideration in return. For example, in a shared space situation, maybe lockers or room dividers would be desirable. But be reasonable with your requests because if your journal is located on property owned by the law school or university, the journal is akin to a non-rent-paying tenant, at best, which means you typically don't have much leverage.

On that note, your school may, at some point, decide to move the law review's physical space. If this situation occurs, hopefully the law review will be given sufficient time to plan for the move. Schools most typically make these decisions at the end of the academic year or early in the summer, to be ready for the next academic year. Incoming EICs should speak with the outgoing EIC and faculty advisor about whether the school is considering space shifts. If so, ask to be part of the discussions about the new space so you can help ensure that the new space is located in an appropriate area, is adequately furnished, lit, and organized, is accessible during reasonable hours, and will otherwise work well for journal members.

Also work with the school to develop a plan that will allow the journal to move at a more convenient time and not in the midst of the write-on competition or just a few days before new member orientation. Ask about moving logistics, including who will box and unbox the journal's materials, who will move and reconnect computers and other electronic equipment, how to update items (like letterhead) that might have a physical room number printed on it, and when signage will be installed for the new office.

If your journal shares space, evaluate how sharing impacts your operation so you can develop effective protocols. For example, if three journals share an office with one large conference table, no journal should be able to monopolize the table for days or weeks by laying out articles or cite-and-source materials. If the office has shelf space, label which shelves belong to which organization.

If your journal lacks space but has decided that it needs physical space to run the organization effectively, speak first with your faculty advisor. The faculty advisor will then likely need to speak with the administrator who assigns space on campus. That administrator should have a good idea of what, if any, space might be both open and appropriate for a journal. If no offices are available, another person to speak with is the law library director. As libraries shift from physical to electronic resources and eliminate computer labs, they often have unused or underused spaces they might be willing to designate for journal use, especially if that means attracting more students into the library.[10]

2. Maintaining the journal's physical space

If your journal has physical space, it's important to understand who maintains that space. For example, the law school or university might have a housekeeping or maintenance staff that cleans all law school spaces, including

---

10. For more information about working with librarians to obtain space in the library for journal use, see Chapter 6 in this *Manual*.

journal space. Or the school might outsource cleaning and maintenance to vendors. If the journal is separately incorporated and housed off-campus, its members might be responsible for upkeep or contracting with a company to clean and maintain the space.

With regard to housekeeping functions, editors should ask when the cleaning occurs. Does it occur early in the morning, late at night, or at variable times during regular business hours? You need to understand this information because if you plan an editorial board meeting in your space at 3:00 p.m., but the cleaning crew comes between 2:00 p.m. and 4:00 p.m., you don't want to be competing with a vacuum cleaner. If members can access journal space 24/7, you will want to alert both the members and the cleaning crew so that no one is startled, especially if cleaning occurs late at night or before school opens in the morning.

It's also important to learn what cleaning entails. Does the cleaning crew empty trash daily, vacuum weekly, and dust and clean surfaces each Friday night? Editors should think about how the type and frequency of cleaning might impact operations. For example, if you keep stacks of documents on the floor, is it clear what is trash and what is not trash? If you have a high-traffic area, is weekly vacuuming sufficient, or do you need daily or twice-weekly vacuuming? If the staff cleans surfaces, how do they interact with papers that might be stacked or strewn on a desk or table-top?

To discover these answers, ask your faculty advisor to connect you with the administrator who supervises the housekeeping function. You might want to ask that person and the lead worker to tour your offices so you can share information about the operation and develop ways that housekeeping staff can do their job effectively while not negatively impacting journal operations. You might also want to discuss related topics, such as adding recycling bins.

Editors should be considerate and notify housekeeping if any extraordinary cleaning needs arise (e.g., someone spilled a pot of coffee on the carpet). Editors should also remind members to clean up after themselves (e.g., wash coffee mugs, clean out the fridge regularly, throw away food and drinks, etc.) so that housekeepers can perform their designated jobs. And editors should stress that journal members treat all law school staff and outside vendors with respect. Without housekeeping services, journal members would have to assume that responsibility and would have less time to focus on writing and editing. Developing a system to thank those who serve the journal will go a long way toward maintaining positive relationships and helping the law review obtain fast service when needed.

At some schools, housekeeping and maintenance are separate functions. Maintenance work includes painting, replacing light bulbs, responding to leaks, resolving plumbing issues, addressing electrical problems, and moving heavy furniture. Schools often have a "ticket system" that units must use to request work. Ask whether your school has such a system and ensure that multiple members are trained to use it. Other schools have a reporting system where a unit calls a certain person or office to request help. In this case, the EIC will want to designate editors who can request maintenance service on the journal's behalf.

Editors should understand what they can do to the physical space without permission. For example, many schools do not allow students to repaint space or order new furniture without special permission and following school processes. Some schools will have protocols about hanging pictures or using tape on walls. Others may prohibit organizations from covering glass windows. On a related note, all schools must comport with fire codes and not block or impede means of egress. When in doubt about what you can do to the journal's physical space, ask your faculty advisor to arrange a meeting with the appropriate school administrator.

Finally, the incoming EIC should ask the outgoing EIC about any space-related issues that might need to be addressed over the summer. Examples might include replacing some very old chairs or improving the lighting. Once that list is compiled, the incoming EIC or their designee should meet with the journal's faculty advisor and the administrator who oversees maintenance to discuss what steps might be taken to address the issues. Some issues might have to wait until the school has an opportunity and the ability to budget for the project. Other matters might be placed on a summer schedule easily handled before the new school year begins.

3. Equipment in the journal's physical space

The journal office might include computers, monitors, printers, copiers, telephones, a fax machine, refrigerator, microwave, and more. It's important to understand who is responsible for maintaining these items and how the journal can obtain service if something malfunctions or breaks.

Your law school or university's IT department is likely the first point of contact for most of these items. It's worth meeting with the head of IT to understand when computers and related equipment are replaced or reimaged, how data is archived, and when the school forces updates to school computers. You also need to understand how to request service and who to call when issues arise.

Members also need to understand how the telephone system works. Basic questions include where to find the manual for the phone, what the number or extension is, whether the number can be forwarded to a personal phone, whether messages can be set to appear as text in an email, how to change the voicemail message, how to check voicemail, how to place a call on hold, how to transfer a call, and how to set up a conference call.

Related phone considerations include ensuring that the journal has a professional voicemail message, establishing a system to check voicemail regularly, understanding whether members can make international calls without a special code, determining whether the law review is billed for phone calls, and training members how to answer calls professionally. On this last point, consider posting a short script near each phone. For example, "XX Law Journal. This is [insert first name] speaking. How may I help you?"

Regarding printers and equipment like fax machines, determine who owns or leases the equipment, the costs and billing arrangements, any limits associated with the equipment (e.g., whether a different pricing structure kicks in after 10,000 copies in any given year), any codes or passwords needed to use the systems, and contact information if emergency maintenance is needed. If not already established, editors should also develop policies about appropriate member use of the equipment. For example, may members use the printer for non-journal projects?

For equipment like refrigerators and microwaves, it's prudent to establish a protocol for students to use it (e.g., labeling food, establishing a cleaning schedule). Also understand who to call for service (someone at the school or a vendor). Finally, understand whether the journal has the authority to acquire and install new equipment. For those questions, start with your faculty advisor.

4. Access and safety

Two basic access questions are whether the journal office is accessible to individuals with physical disabilities and who has permission to enter the journal office.

a. Accessibility

Although law schools and universities are bound by federal and state laws that require physical spaces to be accessible to those with disabilities, that does not mean that all spaces within your school are accessible. Through safe-harbor provisions in building codes and other regulations, organizations have been permitted to retain some non-accessible features that were acceptable at a certain point in time.

New EICs should evaluate the journal's space from a physical accessibility standpoint. Must individuals use one or more steps to enter the office or any internal space? Is elevator access reliable? Is there an accessible restroom within a reasonable distance of the office? Also notice whether members seem to have trouble with any access issues, like opening doors, turning on lights, and sitting at tables. Encourage member feedback—preferably on an anonymous basis—about the space and accessibility issues. Many individuals have "invisible" disabilities and needs you may not anticipate. And students with disabilities often hope that the journal and law school will improve access without forcing them to go through a time-consuming accommodations process.[11] That being said, editors should be familiar with the school's accessibility policies and understand how to help a member seek needed accommodations, if requested.

b. Permitted access

Editors should consider who can access the journal office. And if the journal space has multiple offices, who can access each one. Questions that the editorial board should answer—potentially in connection with the law school—include the following:

- During what hours may members access the office?
- Will editors, or certain editors, have more expansive access than general members?
- Do law review editors have access to the office beyond the times the law school is open to other students?

---

11. Belynda Cianci, *Accessibility in the Workplace: How to Make Your Office More Inclusive*, Robin, https://robinpowered.com/blog/accessibility-inclusion-in-the-workplace [https://perma.cc/M4GS-V7FR] (last visited Jan. 8, 2022); *Disability Accommodations and Resources: Making Offices Accessible*, U.C. Santa Cruz, https://ada.ucsc.edu/facilities-access/office%20accessibility.html [https://perma.cc/7P3J-BP34] (last modified Mar. 9, 2018).

- How do members access the office? Is the door simply left open or unlocked? Are keys distributed? Is there a pin pad? Is access via a student ID or fob?
- May members use the office when not engaged in journal work?
- When are guests allowed in the office?
- Is there a limit on the number of guests that a member may bring into the office at one time?
- Are access policies written and available to members?
- What is the consequence for members who violate access policies?
- Which law school employees have access to the office?
- Do any vendors (e.g., outsourced cleaning crews) have access to the office?

The answers to these questions likely will generate additional questions, such as the following:

- If the door is generally kept open, how does a member proceed if the door is locked? Under what circumstances may a member decide to lock the office?
- If access is via a pin pad, how frequently is the code changed, and how are those changes communicated to members?
- If access is via a key, how are keys distributed, how will the law review prevent keys from being duplicated, and how will the law review proceed if keys are lost or not returned?

Answering as many of these questions upfront—and sharing the answers with all members—will help avoid issues and conflicts during the year. And as with most administrative matters, be sure to include the journal's faculty advisor and other relevant law school administrators in your discussions about office access.

c. Safety and security

Editors must be sensitive to office security issues. In terms of the physical office, editors should connect with the faculty advisor and campus security or police staff to understand any unique safety issues related to the journal space. For example, if members have 24/7 access to the space, you might develop a system to alert security about who is in the office and when they leave. You might ask whether safety walks are available for members working late at night. You might work with administrators to ensure that the lighting around the office is appropriate. You might review the campus's annual security report (which should be readily available on the school's website) to learn about safety issues and challenges you had not considered before you assumed your editorship. You might learn about whether security cameras are present and are well-maintained. You might confirm that you can hear emergency announcements over the PA system when in the journal office. And you might consider requesting that panic buttons be installed in certain locations within the office.

But as with other matters, safety equipment comes with a price tag, and in public and larger private universities, procurement rules and systems take time and planning. So, you may need to work with the law school to develop a longer-term plan to enhance office safety.

Develop a plan to educate members about safety issues. For example, emphasize the importance of not propping doors open, of following all safety protocols, and not engaging in high-risk activities in the office. The office is for working, not playing Nerf basketball or holding late-night poker games (with or without alcohol).

In addition, you should know some basics about applicable school insurance policies and how to report accidents, injuries, and emergencies. Your faculty advisor, the outgoing EIC, and the school's chief business or administrative officer should be able to help you learn about these matters. Two important pieces of advice are to always call 911 in case of emergency (then call campus security or campus police) and post in various places around the office—including near each phone and entrance—a notice that includes (a) a reminder to call 911 in case of emergency, (b) the phone number for campus security or police, and (c) the street address, building name, and room number of the office to help guide first responders to your exact location.

5. Appropriate use of journal space

As noted above, the journal office is a workspace and must be used as such. Using the office for other purposes can open the school or sponsoring entity to liability, which may or may not be covered by adequate insurance.

If you plan to hold an event, such as an open house or holiday party, in your physical space, confer first with your faculty advisor. It's also usually advisable to confer with the Student Affairs Office, which may be able to help you develop a sound plan that mitigates risks.

Having alcohol in the office is not recommended and likely violates both school policy and federal law. The Federal Drug-Free Workplace Act of 1988 and the Drug-Free Schools and Communities Act and its amendments of 1989 require all federal grant recipients to certify a drug-free environment. Most universities receive federal grants and are thus subject to this law. Most schools also ban drugs on campus for the same reason—even if you are in a state where marijuana is legal or decriminalized.

And as noted earlier, any use of the space must comport with school policies, building and fire codes, and other laws and ordinances. For that reason, students likely are not permitted to sleep overnight in the office at all or on a regular basis.

6. Other space on campus

Even if your journal has dedicated office space, members likely will need to use other spaces on campus. For example, you may need to reserve a conference room for editorial board meetings, reserve library study rooms for 1:1 editor-student author meetings, or use library spaces for cite-checking.

It's important to understand how to reserve or request to use these spaces. Even if the conference room you like to use is right across the hall from the journal, it's likely controlled via a master reservation or calendaring system. If the outgoing editors don't explain how to reserve rooms on campus, contact your faculty advisor. If the faculty advisor isn't sure how to proceed, check the list of law school administrators and look for titles like "Director of Calendar and Events" or "Associate Dean for Administrative Services." If you can't easily find the correct person, the Registrar can be a helpful resource.

Try to reserve rooms that you anticipate you will need as early as possible, which often means 30–60 days before a new semester begins. But all schools differ. And if you reserve space and don't need it, be sure to cancel your reservation. If you forget to reserve a room and another group with a reservation appears, be graceful and exit. Depending on the complexity of the room-reservation system, one or two editors may need to seek training on and access to that system.

Regarding library space, contact the law library director to learn whether the library already has space reserved for journal use. Many libraries reserve shelves and carrels for journal members. For additional information on this topic, consult Chapter 6 in this *Manual*, titled "Working with Law Librarians."

J. Websites and Webpages

Journals may (1) maintain a separate website, (2) maintain a webpage within the law school's website, or (3) have a webpage within the law school's website that is maintained by law school staff. The website or webpage is an important business resource. Journals may use it to receive submissions, educate potential authors and members about the journal, publish current or past issues, and share news.

The first step is determining what arrangement exists. If the journal maintains its own website, outgoing editors must transfer passwords, style guides, and other relevant information during the transition process.

Regardless of the arrangement, the EIC should assign one or more editors to update the website so that it doesn't fall out of date and thus leave a negative impression on those who might visit. Individuals assigned to update the website may need training about how to perform this task properly. For standalone webpages, that might include knowledge about the content-management system or even basic coding. Or it might involve working with an outside consultant. For webpages, it will mean liaising with the appropriate law school staff member and understanding the updating process.

A crucial issue for standalone websites is ensuring that they meet accessibility standards. For example, images should include alt-text, written transcripts should be provided for videos and podcasts, and PDFs and other documents should themselves be accessible.[12] Otherwise, the journal or school may be subject to liability if a lawsuit or Office of Civil Rights complaint is filed.[13]

---

12. *Web Content Accessibility Guidelines (WCAG) Overview*, Web Accessibility Initiative, https://www.w3.org/WAI/standards-guidelines/wcag/ [https://perma.cc/25CK-NHMZ] (last updated Dec. 6, 2021) (Shawn L. Henry ed.); *Accessibility Basics*, USA Ability, https://www.usability.gov/ what-and-why/accessibility.html [https://perma.cc/Z4CT-H9BB] (last visited Jan. 8, 2022).

13. *Web Accessibility Lawsuits: What's the Current Landscape*, Essential Accessibility, https://www.essentialaccessibility.com/blog/web-accessibility-lawsuits [https://perma.cc/J7Y6-675L] (last updated Apr. 20, 2021); *Overview of Website Accessibility Laws*, Siteimprove, https://siteimprove.com/en-us/accessibility/accessibility-laws [https://perma.cc/G5UP-B6EN] (last visited Jan. 8, 2022).

Other issues to consider when reviewing and updating websites and webpages include ensuring that the journal or designated school official

- follows copyright and other IP laws;[14]
- uses law school and university logos appropriately and with permission;[15]
- secures the website from hackers;[16]
- makes regular backups;
- protects member privacy by confirming with the Registrar that members have not opted out of providing directory information and not publishing photos or information that might put individuals in danger (e.g., if a member is a domestic violence survivor);[17] and
- uses inclusive language.[18]

K. Miscellaneous Matters

Given the differences in how journals and law schools are structured, it's not possible to predict all business matters that an editor might face. While the major ones are addressed above or in separate chapters, below are a few more

---

14. *Websites: Five Ways to Stay out of Trouble*, STAN. LIBR., https://fairuse.stanford.edu/overview/website-permissions/websites [https://perma.cc/478G-ZDK4] (last visited Jan. 8, 2022).

15. *E.g.*, Office of Auxiliary Enters., *Trademark Licensing*, HOW. U., https://auxiliary.howard.edu/services/trademark-licensing [https://perma.cc/78AU-MBMC] (last visited Jan. 8, 2022); *Brand Guidelines*, U. CAL., https://brand.universityofcalifornia.edu/terms-of-use.html [https://perma.cc/24GU-3ZXC] (last visited Jan. 8, 2022).

16. Lucy Carney, *How to Secure a Website*, WEBSITE BUILDER EXPERT (last updated Dec. 5, 2021), 2021), https://www.websitebuilderexpert.com/building-websites/how-to-secure-a-website [https://perma.cc/7XSF-YLJ9].

17. *Protecting Student Privacy, Directory Information*, U.S. DEP'T EDUC., https://studentprivacy.ed.gov/content/directory-information [https://perma.cc/ABF7-JY4K] (last visited Jan. 8, 2022); *see, e.g.*, *FERPA*, STETSON U., https://www.stetson.edu/administration/registrar/ferpa/index.php [https://perma.cc/5QFP-7LTP] (last visited Jan. 8, 2022) ("Request to Withhold Directory Information").

18. *Inclusive Language Guide*, OR. HEALTH & SCI. U. (Feb. 2021), https://www.ohsu.edu/sites/default/files/2021-03/OHSU%20Inclusive%20Language%20Guide_031521.pdf [https://perma.cc/LQ8W-SAQR].

questions that incoming editors need answered to help run a smooth and effective operation:

- **Running meetings:** Running board and other meetings is a part of journal life. If you've not run a meeting before, take time to conduct research or complete a mini-course via LinkedIn learning or another source, and consult the faculty advisor or your mentors. Familiarize yourself with Robert's Rules of Order,[19] but realize that you need not run every meeting so formally or strictly. Prepare an agenda, ensure that someone is assigned to take and produce written minutes, stay on point and watch the time, treat everyone with civilly and respect—and insist that all other participants do the same, accept constructive feedback gracefully, and re-evaluate your process and strategy when a meeting doesn't go exactly as you planned.
- **Files:** This Chapter has mentioned various documents and files: constitution, bylaws, handbooks, manuals, etc. The journal also likely has electronic and possibly physical files for each article accepted, each issue, etc. If past editors have not already devised a logical, well-organized electronic filing system, it's worth your time to assign that task to an appropriate editor. Spend time discussing categories of folders (e.g., Governing Documents, then a subfolder for Bylaws, then files for different final versions of the Bylaws, and potentially a subfolder for the draft of Bylaws revisions), file naming conventions (e.g., a descriptive name then date then editor initials), and similar issues. Time devoted to this task will save time during the year as you need to locate specific documents. If the journal has paper files, ensure they are well-organized. Find the journal's or school's document retention policy and take time during your year to purge files that should not be retained per the policy. And if the journal has significant physical files even after complying with the document retention policy, consult with appropriate law school staff about the possibility of digitizing files.
- **Receiving physical mail:** How and where is physical mail delivered? If the journal must pick up mail from a mailroom, where is it, and

---

19. Robert's Rules of Order, https://robertsrules.com (last visited Jan. 8, 2022).

what are the hours? Must the journal designate specific people to pick up the mail, or may any journal member ask to gather the journal's mail if an appropriate student ID is produced?

- **Sending physical mail:** How can the journal send mail via the U.S. Post Office, FedEx, UPS, or another delivery service? Is there a set drop-off spot or box on campus? What is the latest pick-up time? Where are packaging materials located? Does the journal have its own postage meter? If so, how do you use it, and how is it refilled? Does the journal or school have a special permit to send mail at a reduced rate? If so, who has that number, and what is the process to use it? Does the journal have accounts with FedEx, UPS, or other services, and if so, who has the account number? How can the journal send physical materials to another department (e.g., "interoffice mail")?
- **Working with other journals:** If your school has multiple journals, find your counterpart in the other journal and work through these business matters together. The law school staff will also appreciate holding a single meeting with all journals instead of multiple meetings with each journal.

Finally, you don't know what you don't know. So unexpected business matters may pop up. When they do, stay calm, consult your assigned staff member or faculty advisor, and develop an action plan consistent with school and journal policies.

L. Conclusion

By the end of the year, many editors will have gained valuable and transferable business skills in addition to honing their writing, editing, time management, and interpersonal skills. Near the end of your term, take time to reflect on these skills and related accomplishments and add them to your resume. For example, you might be able to incorporate statements like "prepared agendas for and presided over 15 editorial board meetings"; "developed and successfully managed a budget of $50,000"; "worked with the law school administration to evaluate the accessibility and safety of the law journal's physical space"; and "worked effectively with the law school administration to raise three significant scholarships for the law review." These types of skills and accomplishments will serve you well in life and your career and may be even more attractive to some employers than touting your editing skills.

KEY TAKEAWAYS

- Editors must understand the status of the review and the review's relationship to the affiliated law school; in addition, the editors must understand their role in maintaining the journal's or school's 501(c)(3) nonprofit status.
- The business aspects of running a law review are as significant as the publishing responsibilities and can provide editors with the opportunity to develop key business skills that employers will value.
- Editors often lack the authority to handle business matters like executing contracts or making purchases without the sign-off of law school staff; accordingly, editors must understand the limits of their authority and the school procedures relevant to the review's operations.
- The incoming EIC and Business Manager (or similar position) should, as part of the editor transition process, learn as much as possible about the law review's business operations, gather and review all key documents and policies, and meet before leaving for the summer with the faculty advisor and key law school employees about important business matters.
- Always be courteous and respectful to school staff who assist the law review—and find ways to thank them for their efforts.
- Plan ahead and be patient, as certain business processes may take many months to complete.

4

Diverse, Equitable, and Inclusive Practices for the Law Review and Legal Scholarship

Teri A. McMurtry-Chubb

LEARNING OBJECTIVES

After reading this Chapter, law review editors will be able to

- develop equitable recruitment and retention practices for law review members;
- assess scholarship that engages critiques of the law;
- identify citation inequities; and
- incorporate critical citation practices into manuscript review.

A. Introduction

On March 17, 1982, the day honoring Ireland's most famous and celebrated patron saint, the thirtieth volume and seventeenth issue of the University of Michigan Law School's student newspaper *The Res Gestae* "hit the stands."[1] St. Patrick received only a passing mention, but the headline "Review Nixes Affirmative Action" conjured a different shade of green best reserved for feelings of envy.[2] The author of the piece detailed a discussion by the Law Review and faculty members about the lack of racial and ethnic diversity on the Law

1. Barry Rudofsky, *Review Nixes Affirmative Action*, RES GESTAE, Mar. 17, 1982 http://repository.law.umich.edu/res_gestae/439 [https://perma.cc/G83M-RB3R].

2. *Id.* at 1.

Review. When the piece was published, only two Black law students had joined the Law Review, and their membership had concluded 17 years prior.[3]

The debate split along racial lines, though not cleanly or for similar reasons. A year earlier, the Harvard Law Review had adopted an "affirmative action plan" that "allow[ed] [minoritized] students seeking to join the Review to submit a personal statement for consideration."[4] In the statement, "[Law] Review staff [were asked] to consider that [the minoritized students] were members of an 'historically underrepresented racial or ethnic group' or that they have overcome 'economic, societal or educational obstacles.'"[5] Yet the requirement of competitive grades remained for the students who opted to submit a statement.[6] The Michigan Law Review editorial board tabled the discussion about implementing such a policy, citing a "[lack] of support [by] the majority of the staff."[7] Far from dead, the issue resurrected the following year.[8]

The Editor in Chief of the law review during the affirmative action discussion, a White man, reasoned that if law review were a marker of high achievement among law students, then an affirmative action policy would undermine it and "be of dubious value."[9] A Black law student recognized that affirmative action plans like the one implemented by the Harvard Law Review could stigmatize students but ultimately concluded that "if it can be demonstrated that more [Black students] on Law Review will increase opportunities for employment and increase the numbers of [Black faculty members], then it will outweigh any stigma attached to it."[10]

The President of La Raza took a slightly different view, arguing that minoritized students take longer to become socialized into law school and should be given an additional opportunity in their second year to apply.[11] Echoing this sentiment, Professor Sallyanne Payton, the first Black person to graduate from Stanford Law School, a former member of the Stanford Law Review, and a faculty member at the University of Michigan Law School, asserted that

---

3. *Id.*
4. *Id.*
5. *Id.*
6. *Id.*
7. *Id.*
8. *Id.* at 1–2.
9. *Id.* at 2.
10. *Id.*
11. *Id.*

> [law] is the study of the culture of the white ruling class. If the students didn't grow up with them then without that level of exposure [through a "first-class private school or a highly integrated public school"] then it is hard to understand the thinking patterns of judges and faculty members.[12]

However, Professor Payton ultimately concluded that any recruitment policies that the Law School adopted should be the same for all students.[13]

Although these debates about more equitable law review recruitment practices occurred over thirty years ago, they endure in the present day. If our starting premise is Professor Payton's contention that "law is the study of the culture of the white ruling class," then what is its impact on the law review as a training ground for law students in the scholarly discourse of the profession and as a forum for legal scholars to discuss the theory and practice of the law? Accordingly, the purpose of this Chapter is to explore diversity, equity, and inclusion on the law review. Because law students have varied experiences with assessing the quality of scholarly work that engages issues of race, class, gender, and sexuality, the balance of the Chapter will equip members with the tools to reject author education and school ranking as proxies for excellence and scholarship quality. The Chapter also will provide guidance for writing student articles that enter critical discourse. It concludes by examining critical citation practices that widen the field of acceptable legal discourse.

B. Equitable Recruitment and Retention Practices for Law Review Members

Recruitment into and matriculation through law review are typically cast in terms of post-graduation opportunities—namely, clerkships, prestigious (and lucrative) jobs in law practice, and academic and judicial appointments. The focus on post-law school opportunities obscures law as a discipline and legal education as a socialization process into the discourse communities of legal practice and legal scholarship.[14] The rigorous nature of required legal research

---

12. *Id.*

13. *Id.*

14. Teri A. McMurtry-Chubb, *Toward a Disciplinary Pedagogy for Legal Education*, 1 Savannah L. Rev. 69, 87 (2014).

and writing curricula are effective in preparing students to write legal memoranda, trial and appellate briefs, client demand letters, and a host of other writing genres commonly utilized in litigation. Like seminar courses, independent study electives, and other upper-division courses, the law review provides students with the opportunity to engage in scholarly research and writing. Law reviews are also the fora for legal disciplinary scholars to examine, debate, and explore the law and the most pressing legal issues confronting the United States and the world. As such, membership in the law review also requires law students to evaluate legal scholarship based on the appropriate standards for the discipline—law—and the existing conversations and critiques of scholars who have written in the subject area and on the same or a similar topic.

Because the law review serves as a training ground for producing legal scholarship and a referee for publication, the means commonly used to assess student readiness for law review—first-year grades and write-on competitions—are deficient.[15] They fail to select the students most qualified to produce and evaluate scholarly work and disproportionately exclude racially minoritized students from participation.

The skill set commonly associated with law review members' success includes "research skills, technical editing [and proofreading] abilities, leadership traits, maturity, dependability, communication skills, interest in scholarly publishing, originality of perspectives stemming from background, [and the] ability to work with others."[16] Critical reading and focus are also skills necessary to understand sources gathered from research and the context in which the author's inquiries emerge. Grades on law school exams and the ability to write on a topic under time constraints in a closed research universe are poor measures for whether students possess or can learn these skills.

Transparency in the recruitment process—and tailoring it to best meet the challenges that law review students will encounter—has the best promise of facilitating racial diversity efforts. Although much has been made of whether students of color have a unique "voice"[17] that would somehow justify their

---

15. *See, e.g.*, Paul Willison, Comment, *Rethinking the Writing Competition: Developing Diversity Policies on Law Journals After FASORP I and II*, 71 Case W. Res. L. Rev. 351, 390–92 (2020); Sharon E. Rush, *Beyond Admissions: Racial Equity in Law Schools*, 48 Fla. L. Rev. 373, 388–90 (1996).

16. Mark A. Godsey, *Educational Inequalities, the Myth of Meritocracy, and the Silencing on Minority Voices: The Need for Diversity of America's Law Reviews*, 12 Harv. Blackletter L.J. 59, 77 (1995).

17. *See, e.g.*, *id.* at 68–72.

inclusion and necessitate "non-traditional" recruitment methods, this line of reasoning is flawed. First and foremost, students of color are valuable as law students and law review members. The minimal redress for law schools' systemic exclusion of racially minoritized students is their entrance into law school and their full inclusion into all that it has to offer. The belief that students of color are valuable only if they justify their existence at the law school by bringing new ideas or insights about racial inequities trades on the worst racial ideologies. Namely, by valuing them only for their perceived racial identities, law schools and law reviews reinforce the notion that students of color alone are inadequate and do not deserve to be there.

While it is true that people of color share experiences with racial oppression and occupy cultures that differ from those of White students, racial and ethnic diversity are poor proxies for perceived critical ideas about the law. The study of racial inequity in the law and society is a study—people of color have shared knowledge about racial inequality from their own experiences, but their personal experiences do not make them experts in the histories, traditions, laws, and policies that bring about racial inequity. The law review should welcome students of color and allow them to write about whatever subject they choose. They should have no more pressure than any White student to write about issues of social justice or racial oppression. Rather, if the goal of the law review is to have a group of students who desire to write about race, class, gender, and sexuality, then recruitment processes should be tailored to attract the students most qualified (or at least most interested) to write in these areas and assess the quality of writing in the review as well.

The recruitment process should match the skill set needed for the law school to produce a top-notch law review. The editorial board and a representative group of faculty by race, gender, subject matter expertise (including librarians), rank (faculty with the titles of assistant, associate, and professor), and status (contract faculty and non-tenure-track faculty) should work together to attract, select, and retain the most qualified students. The committee that chooses the faculty should include the Editor in Chief, Managing Editor, Lead Articles Editor, Online Editor (if applicable), and a representative staff member in consultation with the faculty advisor for the law review and possibly the Associate Dean for Research at the law school. Law reviews are student-run, but this does not mean solely student-run. In areas of legal scholarship, second- and third-year law students are still novices as compared to faculty members who have published numerous articles and books and are accustomed to working with law review editors as authors. Faculty guidance is indispensable—not only in the area of scholarship but also in choosing which students can write competently in a variety of subject and topic areas and later serve as peer mentors. Additionally, students of color who might not otherwise be encouraged to apply may do so because of the presence of diverse faculty members they respect and trust.

Holistic recruitment practices that are most equitable for everyone have the greatest chance at attracting racially and ethnically diverse law review members. To that end, the law review should invite all rising second- and third-year (and the part-time equivalent) students to apply for the law review, with most slots reserved for rising second-year students to create institutional memory and stability of service.

The materials in the application package should include a resume and cover letter that highlight the applicant's experience with editing and proofreading, online and print publications, leadership, team building, and any undergraduate or graduate work related to research and writing ability. Applicants should also provide a sample of the last scholarly paper they have written (whether in law school or another discipline) with information about the course, assignment for which the paper was written, writing process (Were multiple drafts required? Did the student receive editing assistance?), and the final grade received. Finally, any letters of recommendation should include the applicant's legal research and writing professor, as well as any professors who may have supervised the applicant's scholarly writing before or during law school.

With respect to legal research and writing professors, these are the law professors who have the most contact hours with the first-year students and are uniquely situated to comment on a student's research, analytic, writing, and citing abilities. If the law review decides to solicit letters of recommendation from legal research and writing professors, keep in mind that these professors have a disproportionately heavy workload due to the number of assignments, grading, and student contact hours their jobs require. A letter from the law review Editor in Chief to the Dean recognizing their work as service to the law school will help ensure this aspect of a legal research and writing professor's work is included in any employment evaluation.

After the joint editor-faculty committee reviews the applications, it will decide which applicants should proceed. This initial review is necessary to weed out applicants who lack scholarly research and writing experience. The next stage of the recruitment process should include a series of tasks aligned with the skills needed to perform as a law review member. These skills include scholarly research, editing and proofreading, source attribution, and technical citation practice. Examples of possible tasks and the rationale for each include the following:

> **Scholarly Research:** Research skills to produce scholarly work require applicants to demonstrate that they understand how to locate and organize research in a particular subject area and topic. For this task, applicants would be asked to research an area of interest highlighted in their application materials and produce a table or chart that lists the sources by type. Each source should be annotated to explain its significance to the research question.

A partial response and scoring rubric for this exercise might take the following form:

SCHOLARLY RESEARCH ASSIGNMENT

Sample Research Question: Can a work of fiction that depicts violence be used as evidence against the writer in a criminal trial?

Source 1: *State v. Hanson*, 731 P.2d 1140 (Wash. App. 1987).

Source Type	Case
Annotation	While on trial for first-degree assault, Gerald Hanson testified on direct examination that he had never committed a crime of any kind. He also stated that despite serving in the Vietnam War, he had never killed anyone. After several sidebars with counsel concerning the line of questioning, the judge allowed the prosecutor to question Mr. Hanson about fiction that he had authored. The fiction that was the subject of the questioning involved violence by a Vietnam War veteran and a widower wronged by his new wife, which caused him to become violent toward her. The prosecutor's subsequent questioning revealed that Mr. Hanson was a widower, he had remarried, and his second wife planned to divorce him at the time the crime for which he was charged was committed; the crime was not committed against his second wife, but against a grocery store clerk. The jury subsequently convicted Mr. Hanson, and he filed an appeal.

continued

continued

Source Type	Case
Annotation	The appellate court found that the trial court ruling admitting his fictional writings was more prejudicial than probative when Mr. Hanson's character was at issue in the trial and the prosecutor articulated no motive about his alleged commission of the crime. Fictional writings are not probative, because a writer's tendency toward violence cannot be inferred from the nature of their writings. Consequently, a court's admission of such writings can result in unfair prejudice to the defendant because the jury might use the writings to arrive at the faulty conclusion that the defendant committed the crime charged. This outcome is especially likely when a prosecutor articulates no motive for a seemingly random violent act.
Significance	Key in the court's holding was that the prosecutor failed to offer a motive for the crime alleged, and that the violence in Mr. Hanson's writings (domestic violence and violence by a war veteran) was not similar to the crime alleged (a random shooting of a grocery store clerk). If the prosecutor had offered a motive for the crime, and both the crime alleged and the motive were congruent with Mr. Hanson's fictional work, it is possible that the court would have reached a different conclusion.

Source 2: Jason E. Powell, Note, *R.A.P. Rule Against Perps (Who Write Rhymes)*, 41 RUTGERS L.J. 479 (2009).

Source Type	Law Review Article
Annotation	In this student note, the author explores the constitutional and evidentiary implications when a court admits a criminal defendant's rap lyrics as evidence in a criminal trial. Powell places hip-hop culture in an oppositional frame to the legal system and criminal law as a whole. As an artistic expression, hip-hop critiques law enforcement's encroachment in minoritized communities and, by implication, the courts that evaluate it as an art form.

Source Type	Law Review Article
Annotation	The animus generated between the culture and courts causes the former to render it unprotected and outside of artistic expression, just as it renders its practitioners unprotected from disproportionate police interventions and criminal convictions. Powell further illustrates this animus through a smattering of federal appellate court decisions that demonstrate how evidentiary standards are bent to allow the lyrics to stand as evidence of criminality and the courts to deny them First, Fifth, and Fourteenth Amendment protections. Powell's solution to this legal conundrum is for courts not to allow rap lyrics as evidence of anything, unless the lyrics refer to the crime at issue in a manner only those who could have committed it would know.
Significance	This article provides context for why the courts categorize certain forms of artistic expression as outside of the protections of the First Amendment. The history, context, and culture of the expression (hip-hop vs. crime fiction) determine whether the court will treat it as art or evidence of guilt, intent, or motive.

GRADING RUBRIC FOR SCHOLARLY RESEARCH ASSIGNMENT

		(A)	(B)	(C)	(D)	(F)
Source	Source selected is relevant and necessary to resolve the research question					
Source Type	The types of sources selected are sufficiently varied and appropriate for the resolution of the research question					

(A) Excellent **(B)** Good **(C)** Average **(D)** Below Average **(F)** Poor

continued

continued

		(A)	(B)	(C)	(D)	(F)
Annotation	The annotation demonstrates that the applicant understands the structure, purpose, and function of the source (e.g., for cases: facts, reasoning, and holding; for scholarly work: thesis, argument, and evidence) and its relationship to the issues implicated by the research question					
Significance	The applicant connects the main arguments or holding from the source to the resolution of the research question					

(A) Excellent **(B)** Good **(C)** Average **(D)** Below Average **(F)** Poor

Editing and Proofreading: Editing is the process of sharpening the thinking and reasoning in a piece of writing. Proofreading is the process of correcting grammatical, structural, and usage errors. Applicants would be asked to edit and proofread a draft seminar paper or article. The committee would assess the quality of the edits according to how well they improved the thoughts the author desired to convey. The applicant's proofreading ability would be evaluated based on how their suggested corrections improved the readability and clarity of the author's language.

Source Attribution: A large part of a law review editor's job is to chase down citations in accepted manuscripts. In a task associated with this skill, an applicant would be provided with a few pages from a draft article or seminar paper and asked to locate a number of the sources cited. Next, the applicant would explain whether the source as cited accurately represented the author's argument or statement and why. This task would give potential law review members a peek at how citations are used in scholarly work.

Technical Citation Practice: Students end their first year with a range of competency in citation practice. Lack of knowledge or technical expertise should not be penalized. Rather, students should be given the opportunity to demonstrate their ability to learn the broad concepts behind citation rules. Thus, assessing students' technical citation ability and supplementing it with instruction should be the goal. Taking each student through a series of citation tutorials that measure their current skill level in context will help them to understand that citation skills can be attained by practice and immersion.

The final step in the selection process should determine the range of skill levels that students possess (measured by the previous tasks and others identified in each candidate's application materials) in addition to the myriad subject areas that students are competent to write in and evaluate. This assessment will help the law review link its members with the goals of the publication to represent the entire student body of the law school in race and ethnic make-up, subject-matter interest, and writing proficiency. Moreover, a law review that represents its student body stands well-equipped to understand and accept a range of manuscripts that represent the legal academy and address pressing issues in the law.

Beyond selecting new members, law review editors should not be elected but should be selected through an application process designed to attract students with the skill sets needed for each position and to lead effectively. Examples of selection criteria would include an applicant's ability to mentor new law review members; the quality of an applicant's editorial and proofreading based on author evaluation; and the quality of an applicant's own article as compared to their peers at the law school and nationally based on a sampling of student notes and comments published in the same year. Ultimately, structuring the law review recruitment and retention process in a manner that removes the proxies for an applicant's ability is an important first step toward achieving diversity, equity, and inclusion.

C. Assessing Scholarship That Engages Critiques of the Law

Students enter law school having completed a variety of undergraduate majors and advanced study that may not have implicated the law. Because first-year classes do not usually include discussions of critical legal scholarship, it is unlikely that students who join law review in their second year will be sufficiently knowledgeable in it to assess the quality of manuscripts that adopt this approach. The following descriptions are meant to familiarize law review editors with some of the major critical legal subject areas and movements within legal education and scholarship. Often, without understanding this work, law review editors rely on implicit biases and proxies for legitimacy, quality, and excellence that cause them to reject critical legal scholarship. Developing knowledge about the basic tenets and broad inquiries in these areas will position editors to evaluate fairly the scholarly work that engages these theories.

1. Critical legal studies

The first scholars who gathered for the Conference on Critical Legal Studies (CLS) in 1977 would, through subsequent meetings, collaborations, and publications, develop a field bent on elucidating the contradictions between legal objectivism (the law as the embodiment of moral and ethical truths that are objective, knowable, and normative) and legal formalism (the law as "neutral," apolitical, and determinative of legal outcomes).[18] CLS can be distilled to its inquiries about the role of the market in reproducing hierarchy and protecting inequality, primarily as those inquiries relate to class-based social relationships.[19] CLS scholars uncover the existing hierarchies in jurisprudence and lawmaking and seek strategies to resolve them.[20] *The Politics of Law: A Progressive Critique*, anecdotally referred to as the "CLS manifesto," explains that CLS

> is an attempt to develop progressive, critical analysis of current trends, decisions, and legal reasoning and the operation and social role of the law in contemporary American society. We do not, as some progressive approaches have in the past, dismiss the law as a sham or a subterfuge; our criticism takes seriously the law's doctrines, principles, methods, and promises. Critical analysis exposes the law's proclamations of inevitability, reason, and logic as false necessity and false legitimacy, and opens up the possibility of alternatives. This provides both a deeper understanding of law and society and an essential tool

---

18. Mark Kelman, A Guide to Critical Legal Studies (1987); Roberto Mangabeira Unger, *The Critical Legal Studies Movement*, 96 Harv. L. Rev. 563, 564–67 (1983).

19. Unger, *supra* note 18, at 567–73.

20. *See, e.g.*, The Politics of Law: A Progressive Critique xxxii (David Kairys ed., 3d ed. 1982).

> for engaging in the immediate, ongoing contest over values and priorities in the law.[21]

Additional works that provide an overview of the key themes CLS engages include the following:

- Alan Hunt, *The Theory of Critical Legal Studies*, 6 OXFORD J. LEGAL STUD. 1 (1986).
- Allan C. Hutchinson & Patrick J. Monahan, *Law, Politics, and the Critical Legal Scholars: The Unfolding Drama of American Legal Thought*, 36 STAN. L. REV. 199 (1984).
- Duncan Kennedy, *Legal Education and the Reproduction of Hierarchy*, 32 J. LEGAL EDUC. 591 (1982).
- Mark V. Tushnet, *Critical Legal Studies: A Political History*, 100 YALE L.J. 1515 (1991).
- G. Edward White, *The Inevitability of Critical Legal Studies*, 36 STAN. L. REV. 649 (1984).

2. Feminist jurisprudence/feminist legal theory

Feminist jurisprudence centers women in its examination of the law, legal systems, and judicial decision-making. It operates from the premise that the law centers men and heterosexuality, which has enshrined inequities based on patriarchy and heteronormativity.[22] Feminist legal theory can be viewed as a response to CLS and its failure to grapple with patriarchy in its examination of class, social relationships, and legal indeterminacy.[23] As feminist scholar Robin West articulated in *Jurisprudence and Gender*, "[B]y virtue of their shared embrace of the separation thesis, all of our modern legal theory—by which I mean 'liberal legalism' and 'critical legal theory' collectively—is essentially and

---

21. *Id.*

22. *See, e.g.*, Ann C. Scales, *Towards a Feminist Jurisprudence*, 56 IND. L.J. 375, 375 (1981) (arguing that her article "demonstrates the necessity of making a feminist evaluation of our jurisprudence and of taking a jurisprudential view of feminism"); *see also* Patricia A. Cain, *Feminist Jurisprudence: Grounding the Theories*, 4 BERKELEY WOMEN'S L.J. 191, 191–93 (1988–1990); Robin West, *Jurisprudence and Gender*, 55 U. CHI. L. REV. 1, 2–3 (1988).

23. *See e.g.*, Patricia A. Cain, *Feminist Legal Scholarship*, 77 IOWA L. REV. 19, 20 (1991); West, *supra* note 22, at 2; Ann C. Scales, *The Emergence of Feminist Jurisprudence: An Essay*, 95 YALE L.J. 1373, 1376–77 (1986).

irretrievably masculine."[24] Recently, feminist jurisprudence has been employed to analyze the common law in Anita Bernstein's *The Common Law Inside the Female Body*[25] and rewrite key Supreme Court opinions in the Feminist Judgments Project.[26]

Additional works in feminist jurisprudence/feminist legal theory include the following:

- Patricia A. Cain, *Feminist Jurisprudence: Grounding the Theories*, 4 Berkeley Women's L.J. 191 (1988–90).
- Bridget J. Crawford, Kathryn Stanchi, Linda L. Berger, Gabrielle Appleby, Susan F. Appleton, Ross Astoria, Sharon Cowan, Rosalind Dixon, J. Troy Lavers, Andrea L. McArdle, Elisabeth McDonald, Teri A. McMurtry-Chubb, Vanessa E. Munro & Pamela A. Wilkins, *Teaching with Feminist Judgments: A Global Conversation*, 38 Minn. J. L. & Ineq. 1 (2019).
- Lisa R. Pruitt, *A Survey of Feminist Jurisprudence*, 16 U. Ark. Little Rock L. Rev. 183 (1994).
- Ann C. Scales, *The Emergence of Feminist Jurisprudence: An Essay*, 95 Yale L.J. 1373 (1986).
- Kathryn M. Stanchi & Jan M. Levine, *Gender and Legal Writing: Law Schools' Dirty Little Secrets*, 16 Berkeley Women's L.J. 3 (2001).

3. Critical race theory

Critical Race Theory (CRT) is the progeny of CLS and the People of Color Legal Scholarship Conferences (POC LSC), which historically have served as fora for Black law professors to discuss their scholarship in a supportive environment.[27] In 1989, the first critical race theory conference, The Wisconsin Conference on Critical Race Theory, was held in Madison,

---

24. West, *supra* note 22, at 2.

25. Anita Bernstein, The Common Law Inside the Female Body (2018).

26. Feminist Judgments: Rewritten Opinions of the United States Supreme Court (Bridget J. Crawford et al. eds., 2016).

27. Linda S. Greene, *From Tokenism to Emancipatory Politics: The Conferences and Meetings of Law Professors of Color*, 5 Mich. J. Race & L. 161, 162–65 (1999) [hereinafter Greene, *Tokenism*]; *see also* Linda S. Greene, *Critical Race Theory: Origins, Permutations, and Current Queries*, 2021 Wis. L. Rev. 259 [hereinafter Greene, *Critical Race Theory*].

Wisconsin.[28] Its purpose was to evolve an analytical framework adequate to center the experiences of people of color in interpretations of the law and legal systems.[29] This work continued at subsequent POC LSC throughout the 1990s, and by the late 90s had expanded to include Asian, Latinx, and LGBTQIA+ law professors of color.[30]

In their book *Critical Race Theory: An Introduction*, CRT scholars Richard Delgado and Jean Stefancic explain that "critical race theory questions the very foundations of the liberal order, including equality theory, legal reasoning, Enlightenment rationalism, and neutral principles of constitutional law."[31] CRT (including the LatCrit, AsianCrit, QueerCrit, and ClassCrit movements) explores these broad themes:

- "[Racism] is ordinary, not aberrational—'normal science,' the usual way society does business, the common, everyday experience of people of color in [the United States].... [R]acism is difficult to address or cure because it is not acknowledged. Color-blind or 'formal' conceptions of equality, expressed as rules that insist only on treatment that is the same across the board, can thus remedy only the most blatant forms of discrimination...."[[32]]
- "[Our] system of white-over-color ascendency serves important purposes, both psychic and material, for the dominant group.... Because racism advances the interests of both white elites (materially) and working-class Caucasians (psychically), large segments of society have little or no incentive to eradicate it."[[33]]
- "[T]he 'social construction' thesis [of CRT] holds that race and races are products of social thought and relations. Not objective, inherent, or fixed, they correspond to no biological or genetic reality; rather, races are categories that society invents, manipulates,

---

28. Greene, *Critical Race Theory*, *supra* note 27, at 262; Greene, *Tokenism*, *supra* note 27, at 172–73.

29. Greene, *Critical Race Theory*, *supra* note 27, at 262–63; Greene, *Tokenism*, *supra* note 27, at 173.

30. Greene, *Critical Race Theory*, *supra* note 27, at 263–64.

31. Richard Delgado & Jean Stefancic, Critical Race Theory: An Introduction 2–3 (3d ed. 2017).

32. *Id.* at 8.

33. *Id.* at 8–9.

or retires when convenient.... That society... endows [physical attributes] with pseudo-permanent characteristics is of great interest to critical race theory."[34]

- "[Dominant] society racializes different minority groups at different times, in response to shifting needs such as the labor market.... Closely related to differential racialization—the idea that each race has its own origins and ever-evolving history—is the notion of intersectionality and antiessentialism. No person has a single, easily stated, unitary identity.... Everyone has potentially conflicting, overlapping identities, loyalties, and allegiances."[35]
- "A final element concerns the notion of a unique voice of color. Coexisting in somewhat uneasy tension with antiessentialism, the voice-of-color thesis holds that because of their different histories and experiences with oppression, black, American Indian, and Latino writers and thinkers may be able to communicate to their white counterparts matters that the [White people] are unlikely to know."[36]

Additional works in CRT include the following:

- Robert S. Chang & Neil Gotanda, *The Race Question in LatCrit Theory and Asian American Jurisprudence*, 7 NEV. L.J. 1012 (2007).
- *ClassCrits Mission Statement*, 43 SW. L. REV. 651 (2014).
- Darren Lenard Hutchinson, *Ignoring the Sexualization of Race: Heteronormativity, Critical Race Theory and Anti-Racist Politics*, 47 BUFF. L. REV. 1 (1999).
- Margaret E. Montoya & Francisco Valdes, *"Latinas/os" and Latina/o Legal Studies: A Critical and Self-Critical Review of LatCrit Theory and Legal Models of Knowledge Production*, 4 FIU L. REV. 187 (2008).
- Francisco Valdes, *Theorizing "OutCrit" Theories: Coalitional Method and Comparative Jurisprudential Experience—RaceCrits, QueerCrits and LatCrits*, 53 U. MIAMI L. REV. 1265 (1999).

---

34. *Id.*
35. *Id.* at 9–10.
36. *Id.* at 10–11.

- Adrien K. Wing, *Is There a Future for Critical Race Theory?*, 66 J. Legal Educ. 44 (2016).

4. Critical race feminism

The origins of critical race feminism (CRF) can be traced to the work of sociologist Patricia Hill Collins and her ground-breaking book *Black Feminist Thought: Knowledge, Consciousness, and the Politics of Empowerment*, which theorizes the phenomena of multiple interlocking oppressions (e.g., race, class, and gender) using the intellectual traditions of Black women. In her words, Black feminist thought "reflects diverse theoretical traditions such as Afrocentric philosophy, feminist theory, Marxist social thought, the sociology of knowledge, critical theory, and postmodernism."[37] It is significant because Black women's experiences and interactions guide its theoretical frames. They are neither abstract nor grounded in White feminist theory or Western cultural imperatives.[38] CRF builds on this tradition, in response to the silences in feminist jurisprudence and CRT, to center the experiences of women of color. As Richard Delgado wrote in his foreword to CRT and CRF scholar Adrien K. Wing's *Critical Race Feminism: A Reader*,

> Wing's encyclopedic yet tightly organized collection of cutting-edge essays on critical race feminism not only lays bare the workings of patriarchy and racism in subordinating women of color, but it shows why conventional approaches fail. Feminism is white-themed, while civil rights discourse is largely geared toward the problems of men of color. The world of the woman of color is unique; it is not a combination the two worlds of black men and white women, A plus B equals C.[39]

Additional works in CRF include the following:

- Sahar F. Aziz, *Coercing Assimilation: The Case of Muslim Women of Color*, 24 Transnat'l L. & Contemporary Probs. 341 (2015), and 18 J. Gender Race & Just. 389 (2015–16).

---

37. Patricia Hill Collins, Black Feminist Thought: Knowledge, Consciousness, and the Politics of Empowerment loc. 126 (Kindle 2d ed. 2000); *see also* Patricia Hill Collins & Sirma Bilge, Intersectionality (2016).

38. Collins, *supra* note 37, at loc. 126–51.

39. Critical Race Feminism: A Reader xiv (Adrian K. Wing ed., 2d ed. 2003).

- Sumi K. Cho, *Converging Stereotypes in Racialized Sexual Harassment: Where the Model Minority Meets Suzie Wong*, 1 J. Gender Race & Just. 177 (1997).
- Berta Esperanza Hernandez-Truyol, *The Gender Bend: Culture, Sex, and Sexuality—A LatCritical Human Rights Map of Latina/o Border Crossings*, 83 Ind. L.J. 1283 (2008).
- Teri A. McMurtry-Chubb, *Writing at the Master's Table: Reflections on Theft, Criminality, and Otherness in the Legal Writing Profession*, 2 Drexel L. Rev. 41 (2009).
- Joanna Woolman & Sarah Deer, *Protecting Native Mothers and Their Children: A Feminist Lawyering Approach*, 40 Wm. Mitchell L. Rev. 943 (2014).

D. Critical Citation Practices

Citation practice involves more than ensuring that the format is technically correct according to a disciplinary citation manual. On the contrary, citation is part of the process of building a canon of thought in a discipline—the act of setting the boundaries for who can have conversations in the discipline and how they are permitted to have them. Who is cited reflects which knowledge producers in the discipline are respected and seen as integral to continuing existing conversations. In this sense, citation practices go hand-in-hand with knowledge production—particularly epistemology (how we know what we know). Among the discourse community of legal scholarship, we "know" because who (the scholar; the law school where they are employed; the law school they attended) and what (the rank of the publication in which their work is cited; how the work is constructed/arranged) tells us how we should know.[40]

Legal education does not critique its scholarly norms but encourages conformity and adoption of them. For students in any discipline,

> to internalize the norms, conventions, and standards of [the legal profession] is to adopt the worldview associated with that profession.

---

40. Michael J. Higdon, *Beyond the Metatheoretical: Implicit Bias in Law Review Article Selection*, 51 Wake Forest L. Rev. 339, 342–51 (2016); Rachel J. Anderson, *From Imperial Scholar to Imperial Student: Minimizing Bias in Article Evaluation by Law Reviews*, 20 Hastings Women's L.J. 197, 212, 215 (2009).

> Scholars who master a professional style are themselves to some extent mastered by that style. Enculturated into a particular epistemic and institutional order, we learn to uphold and enforce professional codes that designate certain conventions as appropriate, objective, and ethical.[41]

This process is evident in how law students are first enculturated into the scholarly legal discourse community through the publication of what is now *The Bluebook*.[42]

Writing to the men of the Yale Law Journal as its Editor in Chief in 1920, Karl Llewellyn authored the booklet, "The Writing of a Case Note," as their guide for style and citation.[43] He casts the basic parts of the genre as consisting of a heading (keywords that comprise a mini index for the Note), the digest (a statement of the facts and holding for the case being analyzed), and the write-up.[44] In his words,

> The write-up in general covers one and only one point.... The write-up contains three main things, in as brief a compass as possible:
>
> > (1) **The state of the law:....** The aim of the statement of the law is two-fold: to prepare the reader to see the effect of the law of this new case; and to prepare him, by following the line of reasoning suggested in the arrangement of material, to agree with the writer's view of the case. A case-note is so brief that its argument *must* be presented more by *arrangement* of the thoughts than by *words* of explanation. In this training lies one of the greatest values to the writer. Any new point of view, or novel analysis, or helpful interpretation of the authorities, must, to get across, appear (or be prepared) in this portion of the write-up. It will then be driven home by (2) the statement of the bearing of the principal case upon the state of the law; this fits the principal case into the frame prepared; and finally, by (3) the writer's opinion of the principal case which should in most cases merely

---

41. Audrey Thompson, *Gentlemanly Orthodoxy: Critical Race Feminism, Whiteness Theory, and the* APA Manual, 54 Educ. Theory 27, 27 (2004).

42. The Bluebook: A Uniform System of Citation (Columbia L. Rev. Ass'n et al. eds., 21st ed. 2020).

43. Karl Nickerson Llewelyn, The Writing of a Case Note (1920), https://openyls.law.yale.edu/bitstream/handle/20.500.13051/17645/FacColl_L77_pamphlets_no1_1_200_dpi.pdf?sequence=2&isAllowed=y [https://perma.cc/6XM6-X255].

44. *Id.* at 7.

> make articulate the impression the reader already has been made to gather. (2) and (3) are combined: "But the instant case very soundly follows. . . ." (1), (2) and (3) need not appear in this order. But they are all present, express or implied, in every case-note.[45]

Central to the write-up is the analysis, which "[traces] the development of the particular point of law under discussion, bringing forth all sides of the question."[46] Llewellyn advised his law journal colleagues to "[s]how the position taken by the principal case and conclude with your idea of the decision and possibly, a prediction as to whether or not it will be followed. Never state this dogmatically, but as a suggestion, thus: It would seem...etc. It is submitted...etc."[47] As to the matter of citations, he instructed, "[always] cite authorities at the end of the sentence, *never in the middle*. Do not make your analysis merely a summary of the holdings. Use quotations only when absolutely necessary."[48]

In the volume following that for which Llewellyn served as Editor in Chief, William Murray Field, the Case and Comment Editor, offered a series of "rules" for citations within the analysis.[49] He indicated how to cite cases on point with the premises advanced in the analysis; those that contain dicta; and those that "squint[ ] toward [the author's] point," as well as directions for typeface conventions and instructions for citing to articles in the *Yale Law Journal* and legal treatises.[50] The significance of this section of the guide is that Field links the substance of the work to its presentation. The primacy of case law and precedent is taken as a given, as is its place at the center of appropriate legal analysis. Moreover, the range of available citation forms focuses on *how* the referenced case authority can be used—to directly support a proposition, to vaguely suggest or encourage a proposition, or to cosign an observation about a case that a jurist espoused in the opinion—and the *types* of authority that may be used (cases, *Yale Law Journal* articles, and legal treatises). As Llewellyn

---

45. *Id.* at 5–6 (emphasis in original).
46. *Id.* at 7.
47. *Id.*
48. *Id.* (emphasis in original).
49. *Id.* at 7–8.
50. *Id.*

emphatically stated in his booklet, "The ultimate authorities are and remain the cases and statutes."[51]

This socialization process through the lens of citation and knowledge production excludes non-conforming scholars. Because most students on a law review will be required to write a Note, the means of communicating its contents and the sources relevant to its production become the default manner of thinking about legal scholarship. Although Llewellyn authored his booklet more than 100 years ago, the basic structure and function of the Note remain the same. As late as 1986, the Note has been summarized in much the same terms as Llewellyn used,[52] and in 2017, mastery of legal citation was touted as proof that the author is "'on the team'—that you made it through law school and you actually learned something from it."[53]

The role of citations in shaping legal scholarship is problematic because citation standards reflect Western (White) cultural and masculine norms of construction and dissemination.[54] Essentially, citation practices center Western (White) ways of knowing and indicia of "quality" in gauging the value of scholarship in a discipline. In doing so, citation practice narrows the scope of acceptable legal scholarship by privileging arrangement and argumentation styles that center Western norms. By restricting the sources of knowledge that are citable or making sources outside of their purview challenging to cite, they limit how scholars of critical legal studies, feminist jurisprudence, critical race theory, and critical race feminism (to name a few) are able to enter existing conversations, start new conversations, or present knowledge in ways that reflect different cultural imperatives. For the unsuspecting law review editor, this norm means that the default selection of "quality" manuscripts pursuant to existing standards in the discipline will work implicitly to exclude non-conforming voices.[55] The voices that are silenced overwhelmingly belong

---

51. *Id.* at 4.

52. Richard Delgado, *How to Write a Law Review Article*, 20 U.S.F. L. Rev. 445, 447 (1986).

53. Sean Burke, *How to Write a Law Review Article*, 99 J. Pat. & Trademark Off. Soc'y 113, 126 (2017).

54. *See generally* Elizabeth Berenguer, Lucy Jewel & Teri A. McMurtry-Chubb, *Gut Renovations: Using Critical and Comparative Rhetoric to Remodel How the Law Addresses Privilege and Power*, 23 Harv. Latinx L. Rev. 206 (2020); Teri A. McMurtry-Chubb, *Still Writing at the Master's Table: Decolonizing Rhetoric in Legal Writing for a "Woke" Legal Academy*, 21 Scholar 255 (2019).

55. Anderson, *supra* note 40, at 204–08.

to scholars who write about issues of particular importance to minoritized communities.[56]

Patricia Williams's germinal work, *The Alchemy of Race and Rights*, is illustrative in this regard. Williams writes,

> Legal writing presumes a methodology that is highly stylized, precedential, and based on deductive reasoning. Most scholarship in law is rather like "old math": static, stable, formal—rationalism walled against chaos. My writing is an intentional departure from that. I use a model of inductive empiricism, borrowed from—and parodying—systems of analysis, in order to enliven thought about complex social problems. I want to look at legal issues within a framework inscribed not just within the four corners of a document—be it contract or the Constitution—but by the disciplines of psychology, sociology, history, criticism, and philosophy. The advantage of this approach is that it highlights factors that otherwise go unremarked.[57]

In each part of her book, Williams presents a series of reflections as diary entries that serve to report her life as she experiences it, in so far as her life highlights legal subjects and challenges legal principles, all given meaning through inductive empiricism—reasoning by experience. The journey through which Williams leads the reader privileges the chaotic nature of continuing life experiences; they are—in and of themselves—sources of authority and subjects of analysis. In building her narrative in this way, Williams reveals law as the same; sources of authority that are fluid, episodic, relational, and ever-changing. Her experiences are briefly punctuated by legal cases, statutes, law review articles, and other interdisciplinary scholarly works, which serve only as supplements to her experiential knowledge; they are both forward-looking and backward-looking points of departure, telling simultaneous and parallel stories.

What critical citation practice means in this context is that law review editors should evaluate manuscripts for their adherence to the standards of the subject area and topic written about, not according to standards that privilege one method of arrangement and organization or stilted notions about which sources are "acceptable." This practice is particularly important for scholarship that challenges existing legal systems and reimagines the law as a conduit through which justice flows.

---

56. *Id.* at 210–12.

57. Patricia Williams, The Alchemy of Race and Rights 7 (1991).

Scholars of color whose work critiques legal systems and practices that replicate inequity are often excluded from the lauded canonical works. The exclusion manifests as a failure of scholars who are writing in the same or similar subject and topic areas to cite their work. Citation metrics can be a factor in hiring, tenure, and promotion decisions and in establishing the credibility of a scholar. Thus, for those decision-makers who regard low citation metrics as an indication of poor-quality scholarship, excluding these scholars from discourse could be detrimental to their careers.[58]

Richard Delgado, in his article *Imperialist Scholar*, gives some insight into why critical scholars may not be cited.[59] He points to false perceptions about objectivity in writing about race, namely that White authors are "neutral" and authors of color are not, and to ego and the need for majority authors to maintain control of the discourse to mediate the rate of change.[60] Similarly, feminist legal scholar Pat Cain argues that the legal academy, where the balance of power is disproportionately male, has met feminist jurisprudence with "silent dismissal to polite questions revealing a significant lack of understanding."[61] Delgado identified typical strategies to marginalize critical scholars, which in the present day we describe as mansplaining, whitesplaining, tone policing, gaslighting, co-opting, and trivializing.[62] These tools have also been employed to ostracize law professors who teach legal writing as scholars and knowledge producers in the academy, which effectively excises their scholarly contributions from the canon of legal scholarship as a whole.[63]

Law review editors should be cognizant of citation inequities. In addition to reviewing citations for technical correctness and accuracy for the proposition cited, editors must also ask the question of who is being cited. Excluding minoritized voices from legal discourse not only denies their scholarly con-

---

58. For more information about citation metrics, see Chapter 16 of this *Manual*.

59. Richard Delgado, *The Imperial Scholar: Reflections on a Review of Civil Rights Literature*, 132 U. Pa. L. Rev. 561 (1984).

60. *Id.* at 573–78.

61. Patricia A. Cain, *Feminist Legal Scholarship*, 77 Iowa L. Rev. 19, 29 (1991).

62. Richard Delgado, *The Imperial Scholar Revisited: How to Marginalize Outsider Writing, Ten Years Later*, 140 U. Pa. L. Rev. 1349, 1358–68 (1992).

63. *See also* Higdon, *supra* note 40, at 351–52. *See generally* Teri A. McMurtry-Chubb, *Writing at the Master's Table: Reflections of Theft, Criminality, and Otherness in the Legal Writing Profession*, 2 Drexel L. Rev. 41 (2009); Kathryn M. Stanchi, *Who Next, the Janitors? A Socio-Feminist Critique of the Status Hierarchy of Law Professors*, 73 UMKC L. Rev. 467 (2005); Toni M. Fine, *Legal Writer's Writing: Scholarship and the Demarginalization of Legal Writing Instructors*, 5 Legal Writing 225, 227 (1999).

tributions to a particular subject area and topic but also weakens the overall arguments that the author who excludes them seeks to advance. Movements like @blacknbluebook—a Twitter account maintained by law professors who seek to "[d]ecolonize the legal academy one cite at a time"—that highlight the scholarly contributions of legal research and writing professors, clinicians, law librarians, and all legal scholars outside of the top 14 schools (as ranked by *U.S. News and World Report*) are resources for editors to ascertain the full scope of contributors to scholarly knowledge. As the law review is both a forum for the exchange of scholarly ideas and a gatekeeper of the profession, it can do no less in its quest for diversity, equity, and inclusion.

KEY TAKEAWAYS

- Law reviews should develop and implement recruitment practices that attract and retain members based on their skills, abilities, and potential to strengthen the scholarly quality of the law review.
- Law reviews should create an environment of scholarly inquiry and curiosity among members that encourages the respectful engagement of scholarship that critiques the law and legal systems.
- Editors should recognize how the relationship between the substance of legal scholarship and common citation practices marginalizes minoritized scholars and scholarship.
- Editors should respect non-conforming modes of writing style and arrangement.

5

Understanding Philosophical Movements Law Review Editors May Encounter

Kristen David Adams

LEARNING OBJECTIVES

After reviewing this Chapter, editors will be able to

- recognize that not all journal articles are written the same way; while some are entirely pragmatic in tone, others take a more theoretical approach and might reflect one or more of the schools of thought presented in this Chapter;
- differentiate key philosophies from one another; and
- appraise a prospective article based on how well it reflects a philosophy it purports to represent.

A. Introduction

This Chapter provides a series of thumbnail sketches on the following movements in legal philosophy that you may encounter as a law review editor:

- formalism;
- natural law;
- positivism;
- legal realism;
- law and economics;
- critical legal studies;

- feminist jurisprudence;
- queer theory;
- empirical scholarship;
- interdisciplinary legal study; and
- mainstream legal scholarship.

The Chapter also includes guidance on evaluating a prospective article and a reading list of jurisprudential sources. This Chapter is, of course, not a substitute for a course in jurisprudence, and if you find yourself intrigued by these materials, please consider taking such a course.

Please note that the boundaries between the bodies of legal philosophy presented here are porous rather than distinct. A scholar might identify with more than one philosophy, and significant overlap can exist within the schools of thought. One example is the emergence of law and economics from legal realism. Thus, law and economics may be seen as representing and incorporating many traditions of legal realism. A second example can be found in the commonalities that may exist between critical legal studies and law and economics. Although the former is commonly seen as a left-leaning philosophy and the latter a right-leaning philosophy, they both see the law as in some ways a political construct that is connected with, rather than independent from, other disciplines.

B. Formalism

Formalism, sometimes referred to as "classicism," is often associated with Harvard Law School and the legacy of Christopher Columbus Langdell, who served as its dean from 1870 to 1895. Much of contemporary legal education has its foundation in Langdell's "case method," through which law students learn the law by studying appellate opinions. Before the case method, new lawyers learned through apprenticeships rather than formal education.

For formalists such as Langdell, law was a science, and this science could be reduced to a few key rules and principles. These rules and principles were then carefully applied by judges in rendering their opinions. A key tenet of formalism is that judges discern and apply the law, but do not create law. Langdell was also an amateur botanist, and it is sometimes said that he applied the same art of classification to both botany and law. Along with Langdell, his Harvard colleagues Joseph Beale and Samuel Williston are also associated with the formalism of this time.

Although many schools of thought presented in this Chapter were formed in response to formalism, it would be inaccurate to assume that formalism is no longer used in any way. In addition to its influence on legal education, formalism still influences the work of the American Law Institute, and especially its Restatements. These works reflect a desire to distill the key principles and rules of a body of law so that it can be correctly applied. Formalism is still also a subject of discussion in contemporary law reviews.[1]

C. Natural Law

Natural law may be the oldest of the legal philosophies. It dates back to the ancient Greeks and has been associated with Plato, Cicero, Aristotle, Thomas Aquinas, William Blackstone, John Finnis, and Lon Fuller, among others. For Cicero, law was divine in origin and could be discovered by humans exercising their highest and best powers of reasoning. The Catholic Church's Code of Canon Law is another example of natural law rooted in divine principles. Natural law is not, however, merely an ancient theory, and despite its emphasis on morality, it is not always associated with religious thought. In the early 1940s, Harvard Law professor Lon Fuller developed a secular natural-law theory, in significant part in response to the rise of legal positivism, described below, which dominated that time period.

One who follows natural law is sometimes called a "natural lawyer." For the natural lawyer, the validity of law is inextricably tied to its moral correctness. Indeed, thirteenth-century Italian philosopher St. Thomas Aquinas is credited as having defined natural law as "right reason."[2] Thus, for the natural lawyer, the law cannot be morally wrong, because if any putative law is morally wrong, it does not qualify as law and would thus not have the force of law. The natural law consists of a body of moral standards that are capable of justifying and guiding political authority, and that can, in turn, create binding legal rules. Morality, then, is both the source of the law and the purpose of the law.

---

1. *See, e.g.*, Paul Troop, *Why Legal Formalism Is Not a Stupid Thing*, 31 Ratio Juris 428 (2018); Brian Leiter, *Legal Formalism and Legal Realism: What Is the Issue?*, 16 Legal Theory 111 (2010).

2. Analytic Jurisprudence Anthology 4 (Anthony D'Amato ed., 1996).

Legal realism, discussed below, is in part a response to—and critique of—natural law.

D. Positivism

Positivism is often described in opposition to natural-law theory. For the natural lawyer, the *content* of the law helps to determine whether it qualifies as law, because only that which is morally correct can have the force of law. For the positivist, the *process* by which the law was developed—such as through legislation or judicial precedents—determines whether it qualifies as law. Thus, for the positivist, an unjust law can still qualify as law, and only factual sources such as legislative history showing how and by what authority the law was created are needed to determine what the law is. The content of the law is a question of fact rather than a question of morality.

Positivism is sometimes called "the command theory of law," reflecting the understanding that law is "a command issued by a sovereign and backed by a sanction."[3] This famous phrase can be traced to English philosopher Thomas Hobbes's *Leviathan*, written in 1651.[4] Even so, positivism did not emerge as a distinct field of legal philosophy until much later with the work of English philosophers Jeremy Bentham and John Austin in the late 1700s and early 1800s. Positivist legal scholars use the phrase "rule of recognition" to describe a rule that is used to determine whether a given law is valid.[5] In addition to the scholars already mentioned, English philosopher H.L.A. Hart and Austrian philosopher Hans Kelsen are among the more famous positivist legal scholars.

One critique of legal positivism is that it is morally untenable. Lon Fuller, who called for something of a revival of natural-law theory in the 1940s, did so in response to what he saw as the danger of legal positivism. If the law need not have any moral dimension to qualify as law, then any legal order with coercive power would be considered valid, even if it came from a system of

---

3. Bailey Kuklin & Jeffrey W. Stempel, Foundations of the Law: An Interdisciplinary and Jurisprudential Primer 143 (1994).

4. Thomas Hobbes, Leviathan or the Matter, Forme & Power of a Commonwealth, Ecclesiasticall and Civil 193 (A.R. Waller ed., Cambridge U. Press 1904).

5. Frederick Schauer & Walter Sinnott-Armstrong, The Philosophy of Law: Classic and Contemporary Readings with Commentary 31 (1996).

tyranny rather than a system of democracy.[6] To accommodate despotism was, to Fuller, unacceptable. This critique may be overstated, as positivists would admit that the law is often the vehicle chosen to enforce or effectuate societal norms that are seen as desirable.

E. Legal Realism

The origins of legal realism have been traced to a statement made in 1924 by American philosopher John Dewey: "The actual life of the law has not been logic: it has been experience."[7] These words that launched the philosophical movement that became legal realism were originally spoken by United States Supreme Court Associate Justice Oliver Wendell Holmes, whom Dewey credited. These words also reflect that logic, rules, and principles do not accurately describe how the law operates—or how judges decide cases. Realists are interested in the sociology of law and the factual patterns to be found in judges' decisions.

Legal realism dominated the field of legal scholarship in the 1920s and 1930s. Yale Law professor Karl Llewellyn,[8] the principal architect of the Uniform Commercial Code, has been credited as the first to describe the emerging body of jurisprudence as "legal realism."[9] Legal realism was, at least in part, a response to concerns that neither natural law nor positivism provided a realistic view of how legal systems actually work, hence the name "realism." Some of the most famous realists, in addition to those mentioned above, were American lawyer Felix Cohen and Jerome Frank, who served on the United States Court of Appeals for the Second Circuit.

Legal realism rejects the idea that the law can be mechanically and objectively applied to the facts of a given case. As Karl Llewellyn stated, "[T]here is less possibility of accurate prediction of what courts will do than the traditional

---

6. Lon L. Fuller, *Positivism and Fidelity to Law—A Reply to Professor Hart*, 71 Harv. L. Rev. 630, 638–39 (1958).

7. John Dewey, *Logical Method and Law*, 10 Cornell L. Rev. 17, 21 (1924) (quoting Justice Oliver Wendell Holmes).

8. For a discussion of Professor Llewellyn's influence on student-edited law reviews through his work as Editor in Chief of the Yale Law Journal, see Chapter 4 of this *Manual*.

9. The Canon of American Legal Thought 133 (David Kennedy & William W. Fisher III eds., 2006).

rules would lead us to suppose."[10] Instead, law can be best understood by applying the social sciences and studying the law as actually applied, rather than the law as it exists in theory. The distinction between "law in books" and "law in action" arises from this attempt to distinguish between the "real reasons" for a judge's decision and the reasons as articulated in the judge's opinion.[11]

Realism has been referred to as the prediction theory of law.[12] For the realist, the way to make the law more certain—and thus more predictable—is to learn more about how the law actually operates and how judges actually reach their decisions. Thus, in realism, the law consists not of the rules themselves, but the behavior of officials (such as individual judges) as predicted by applying legal principles and understanding the social interests and public-policy conceptions of individual judges.

One hallmark of legal realism is its view that law is indeterminate; yet legal realism has been described in ways that reflect these same qualities of being "ambiguous, unsettled, and undefined."[13] Legal realism is sometimes critiqued—even caricatured—as "the jurisprudence of legal incertitude and arbitrariness."[14] A famous—and inaccurate—criticism from the early days of legal realism was that realists claimed the law was a result of nothing more than "what the judge had for breakfast."[15] This criticism suggests that realism is not so much a philosophy of law as a body of observation of how the law has developed. Although this critique is not without foundation, it does discount the extent to which realist scholars concern themselves with legal doctrine, procedure, and concepts, in addition to observation.

F. Law and Economics

As the name suggests, law and economics draws from the field of economics and uses methods drawn from science. This work is often associated with conservative economists from the University of Chicago. Modern law and economics began in the early 1960s with works by British economist Ronald

10. *Id.* at 153.
11. Laura Kalman, Legal Realism at Yale, 1927–1960, at 7, 9 (1986).
12. Analytic Jurisprudence Anthology, *supra* note 2, at 183.
13. Neil Duxbury, Patterns in American Jurisprudence 65 (1995).
14. *Id.* at 66.
15. Kuklin & Stempel, *supra* note 3, at 155.

Coase and Guido Calabresi, who is both a Yale Law professor and a judge on the United States Court of Appeals for the Second Circuit.

Law and economics emerged as a coherent school of thought in the early 1970s. But its roots are much older, dating back at least to the 1890s when United States Supreme Court Associate Justice Oliver Wendell Holmes stated, "For the rational study of law the black-letter man may be the man of the present, but the man of the future is the man of statistics and the master of economics."[16] Much of the "old" law and economics of the late 1800s and early 1900s was centered on macroeconomic concepts and national economic issues such as antitrust law, while the newer law and economics focuses on microeconomics and concepts of efficiency.

The major claim of law and economics is that the law can be both improved and better understood by applying economic principles in a way that has been termed "the application of rational choice theory to law."[17] Thus, the law and economics scholar might seek to demonstrate how economic forces shape the law or how the law creates economic incentives, or to evaluate some aspect of law based on its efficiency or inefficiency. In doing so, the scholar might apply a cost-benefit analysis to evaluate the anticipated effect of some change in the law.

Law and economics has been credited with bringing some aspects of the scientific method—including theorizing and testing—into the field of legal scholarship and the study of law. Law and economics is also characterized by a particular kind of research method—empirical research. Empirical scholarship is discussed as a separate heading later in this Chapter.

Yale Law professor Owen Fiss has criticized *both* law and economics and critical legal studies (discussed later in this Chapter) as being dangerous because both are "united in their rejection of law as public ideal."[18] He contends both schools of thought could "mean the death of the law, as we have known it throughout history, and as we have come to admire it."[19] Consistent with this critique, law and economics is sometimes characterized as a "reactionary movement of the right."[20] This critique is not wholly accurate; over time, liberal law and economics scholars (for example, at Yale Law School)

---

16. Oliver Wendell Holmes, *The Path of the Law*, 10 Harv. L. Rev. 457, 469 (1897).

17. Thomas S. Ulen, *The Unexpected Guest: Law and Economics, Law and Other Cognate Disciplines, and the Future of Legal Scholarship*, 79 Chi.-Kent L. Rev. 403, 416 (2004).

18. Owen M. Fiss, *The Death of the Law?*, 72 Cornell L. Rev. 1, 2 (1986).

19. *Id.* at 16.

20. Gary Minda, *The Jurisprudential Movements of the 1980s*, 50 Ohio St. L.J. 599, 602 n.10 (1989).

have emerged, as well. Examples include Guido Calabresi and Stanford Law professor Douglas Melamed.

Law and economics has also evolved over time, and its modern proponents generally reject the idea that efficiency is the only legal norm to be considered, instead embracing some degree of reform and market intervention. Even Ronald Coase, who is generally recognized as one of the architects of law and economics' conservative "Chicago school," was not "an unqualified defender of an unregulated market."[21]

G. Critical Legal Studies[22]

The sources of critical legal studies (CLS) are broad and varied, including Marxism, feminist jurisprudence (discussed below), critical theory, structuralism, and literary criticism. The CLS movement began in the late 1970s when a group of scholars developed The Conference on Critical Legal Studies. The CLS movement has been described as questioning whether the law is—or even can be—neutral and objective. Some of the better-known CLS scholars are Duncan Kennedy, Roberto Unger, David Kennedy, and Mark Tushnet, all of Harvard Law School, and Martha Fineman of Emory University School of Law.

Critical Legal Studies is related to, but distinct from, Critical Race Theory (CRT). The CRT movement began when some scholars became concerned that the CLS movement was not sufficiently and meaningfully taking issues of race into account. CRT "seeks to use the law as an affirmative tool to improve the lives of people of color."[23] One technique for doing so is to demonstrate how the existing legal system has served to disempower underrepresented racial constituencies. Cornel West, formerly of Harvard Law School, Mari Matsuda of the University of Hawaii, Richard Delgado of the University of Alabama, Kimberlé Crenshaw of the University of California, Los Angeles and Columbia Law School, the late Derrick Bell of New York University, and Cheryl Harris of the University of California, Los Angeles are well-known CRT scholars.

---

21. The Canon of American Legal Thought, *supra* note 9, at 361.

22. For additional discussion of several critical theories, consult Chapter 4 of this *Manual*.

23. Dorothy A. Brown, Critical Race Theory: Cases, Materials and Problems 1 (2003).

CLS scholarship is critical of both mainstream legal thought (discussed below) and law and economics (discussed above). In addition to being a legal movement, CLS is an intellectual, social, and political movement. One goal of CLS is to show how both mainstream legal thought and law and economics justify domination and privilege and serve to maintain the status quo while using discourse that claims to be neutral in both process and outcome. CLS scholars endeavor to show the diversity of culture with respect to race, class, and gender and argue that abstract, neutral values fail to capture this richness and diversity. Thus, for the critical scholar, "law is a social discourse."[24]

Critical scholars—whether CLS or CRT—may also bring to light unstated assumptions or highlight tensions that may exist beneath the surface of the law, revealing patterns or inconsistencies that may not previously have been understood or explored. In addition, as the word "critical" would suggest, this body of scholarship can fairly be described as existing to provide political or moral critique of a legal system or a body of law, rather than serving a primarily interpretive function. The critique, rather than any reform that might result, could be considered the main point of the scholarship.

Although criticisms of CLS have been common in society more broadly in the last several years, such criticisms are not new. In the 1980s, Duke Law School Dean Paul Carrington suggested that members of CLS be banned from legal academia as being too "radical" and "subversive."[25] Others have critiqued CLS as "crude Marxism" or "empty nihilism."[26] Consistent with these critiques, CLS is sometimes called "a radical movement of the left."[27] Harvard Law professor Roberto Unger has challenged the idea that this is what CLS is—or should—be. Unger describes a different vision for CLS: "A movement able to act transformatively... must reject the false dilemmas of conservative reform or textbook revolution."[28]

Other critiques relate to the "critical" part of CLS: some have said that CLS lacks a positive thesis, serving only to criticize without offering constructive proposals for reform. It is thus sometimes seen as "largely oppositional," deriving its sense of purpose and identity from its opposition to other schools of

24. Edward L. Rubin, *The Practice and Discourse of Legal Scholarship*, 86 Mich. L. Rev. 1835, 1866 (1988).

25. Paul D. Carrington, *Of Law and the River*, 34 J. Legal Educ. 222, 227 (1984).

26. Minda, *supra* note 20, at 603.

27. *Id.* at 602 n.10.

28. Roberto Mangabeira Unger, The Critical Legal Studies Movement 116 (1986).

thought.[29] Others have claimed that CLS scholars are "united only in a shared antagonism."[30] These critiques are not entirely fair, as CLS scholars may also suggest governmental reforms, propose new methods of interpretation, and propose using law's authority for positive societal transformation. Roberto Unger's book *What Should Legal Analysis Become* is one example.[31] Unger argues for a reconstruction of legal analysis as part of the process of making the legal system more democratic. Another example is Harvard Law professor Mark Tushnet's book *Taking the Constitution Away from the Courts.*[32] Tushnet advocates for a "populist" approach to constitutional law that he believes will be more effective than leaving the Constitution to be protected primarily by the court system.

H. Feminist Jurisprudence

Feminist jurisprudence has its origins in the women's liberation movement of the 1960s and developed as a legal school of thought in the late 1970s. The term "feminist jurisprudence" was first used in a 1978 article by Professor Ann Scales.[33] Key scholars in feminist jurisprudence include Martha Minow of Harvard Law School, Catharine MacKinnon of the University of Michigan, psychologist Carol Gilligan of New York University, and Robin West of Georgetown University.

Feminist legal scholars are diverse in their approaches but are united in claiming that mainstream legal theory fails to acknowledge and respond to the experiences of women. Part of feminist legal theory is the idea that legal concepts that may seem to be gender-neutral generally reflect a male viewpoint and the male experience. Feminist legal theory attempts to tell the story of the law from the perspective of women, examining the relationship between women and the legal system, and the social and legal biases women have faced over time.

This school of thought is also associated with the idea that law is neither autonomous nor discrete, but instead reflects social and political influences, at

---

29. Duxbury, *supra* note 13, at 305.

30. Minda, *supra* note 20, at 615.

31. Roberto Mangabeira Unger, What Should Legal Analysis Become? (1996).

32. Mark Tushnet, Taking the Constitution Away from the Courts (2000).

33. Ann C. Scales, *Towards a Feminist Jurisprudence*, 56 Ind. L.J. 375, 375 (1981).

least some of which have historically involved the political and social subordination of women. Some feminist jurisprudence is focused on the concept of difference; rather than seeking what may be an unattainable ideal of consensus, the feminist scholar might argue that the legal system should focus on the reality that different groups have different experiences with the legal system.

Feminist legal thought has been criticized as "anti-male, anti-law, and anti-theory."[34] Although these critiques are overstated, feminist jurisprudence does claim that women approach problem-solving differently from men and does propose changes to the law and legal systems to address inequities toward women that have arisen over time.

I. Queer Theory

The term "queer theory" was first used in 1991 by Teresa de Lauretis, Distinguished Professor Emerita of the History of Consciousness at the University of California, Santa Cruz.[35] The origins of queer theory are, however, a bit older. French philosopher and historian Michel Foucault's four-volume study titled, *The History of Sexuality*, originally published in 1976, is often credited as the movement's starting point. In this work, Foucault examines the social, political, and power dynamics inherent in modern understandings of sexuality.

Like CLS, queer theory can be understood as both a political movement and a philosophical movement. Honoring equality and inclusivity are core principles of queer theory, which embraces all persons regardless of whether they are members of the sexual majority or the sexual minority. Anti-subordination, anti-discrimination, and the social construction of sexual behavior are some of the themes that might be explored in queer theory scholarship. Queer theorists also challenge heteronormativity, including what might be seen as traditional conceptions of gender norms. Queer theorists include Professor Ruthann Robson of the City University of New York (CUNY); Eve Kosofsky Sedgwick, who was also a poet and artist; Professor Judith Butler of the University of California, Berkeley; and Professor Gayle Rubin of the University of Michigan.

---

34. Minda, *supra* note 20, at 602.

35. Teresa de Lauretis, *Introduction to Queer Theory: Lesbian and Gay Sexualities*, 3 DIFFERENCES: AM. J. FEMINIST CULTURAL STUD. (SPECIAL ISSUE 2) iii, xvii (1991).

J. Empirical Scholarship

Although law and economics, discussed earlier, has been credited with the significant increase in empirical legal scholarship over time, empirical scholarship merits discussion even apart from law and economics. Whereas law and economics is a topic of scholarship, empirical scholarship is a technique that may be employed in legal scholarship. To use an "empirical" approach is to employ methods associated with observation, experience, or experimentation.

Empirical scholarship employs the scientific method to explain real phenomena and has the following essential characteristics:

> Theorizing about those real phenomena so as to derive hypotheses about them; testing to see whether the assertions made are correct; revising the theory in light of the tests; doing a new round of tests so as to assess the revised theory; and so on.[36]

An empirical scholar might also engage in model-building or apply or summarize a model that was created by another legal scholar. Empirical legal scholarship can be seen as grounded in the much older concept of empiricism.[37] For the empiricist, dispassionate observation is the key to proper inquiry; any attempt to manipulate the process of fact-gathering will necessarily result in distortion.

University of Virginia Law professor Douglas Laycock and Yale Law professor Robert Ellickson are two of the best-known empirical scholars. Robert Ellickson's famous work investigating how farmers and cattle ranchers in Shasta County, California handled property damage due to wandering cattle culminated in his book, *Order Without Law: How Neighbors Settle Disputes*.[38]

Empirical legal scholarship requires training and skills that may not be accessible to all legal scholars. For example, empirical legal scholarship requires a level of comfort with statistics and statistical techniques that many legal scholars lack. It also requires data that has historically not been generated in the field of law in the way that it has in other fields of study.

---

36. Ulen, *supra* note 17, at 407.

37. THE OXFORD COMPANION TO PHILOSOPHY 226 (Ted Honderich ed., 1995).

38. ROBERT C. ELLICKSON, ORDER WITHOUT LAW: HOW NEIGHBORS SETTLE DISPUTES (1991).

K. Interdisciplinary Legal Study

Like empirical legal study, interdisciplinary legal study is characterized more by its techniques than its content. Interdisciplinarians draw insights from other fields—whether psychology, economics, sociology, or something else entirely—to illuminate some area of law or to propose a solution to some legal problem. In the words of Cardozo School of Law professor Stanley Fish, interdisciplinary work means "expanding one's discipline by listening to others."[39]

For the interdisciplinarian, law can be better understood by applying methods, insights, and objectives from another academic discipline. As Yale Law professor Jack Balkin has noted, every discipline contributes its own vocabulary, its own "heroes and villains," and even its own way of asking questions.[40] Interdisciplinary approaches are thus typically "law and" approaches, which might include law and literature, law and religion, or even law and economics, which was discussed above.

Interdisciplinary study has been criticized as being impractical and even irrelevant in the training of future lawyers.[41] Interdisciplinarian and Emory Law professor Barbara Bennett Woodhouse has challenged this conception; looking specifically at her own field of family law, she has shown that interdisciplinary study is actually quite practical.[42] Because court opinions center on the best interest of the child, the psychological parent, and equitable distributions at divorce, all ephemeral concepts, she argues that students must know something about psychology, economics, sociology, religion, and history to decipher these terms and to represent their clients effectively.

Some have expressed a concern that law might lose its own identity through fusion with other disciplines.[43] Another related concern is that inter-

---

39. Geoffrey W. Castello, *Almost a Pragmatist*, 26 Seton Hall L. Rev. 967, 981 (1996) (reviewing Stanley Fish, Professional Correctness: Literary Studies and Political Change (1995), and Stanley Fish, There's No Such Thing as Free Speech and It's a Good Thing, Too (1994)).

40. J.M. Balkin, *Interdisciplinarity as Colonization*, 53 Wash. & Lee L. Rev. 949, 955 (1996).

41. *See, e.g.*, Harry T. Edwards, *The Growing Disjunction Between Legal Education and the Legal Profession*, 91 Mich. L. Rev. 34, 36 (1992).

42. Barbara Bennett Woodhouse, *Mad Midwifery: Bringing Theory, Doctrine, and Practice to Life*, 91 Mich. L. Rev. 1977, 1979 (1993).

43. Stanley Fish, *Being Interdisciplinary Is So Very Hard to Do*, 1989 Prof. 15, 17.

disciplinary study lacks its own, unique foundational knowledge and rules.[44] Still others worry that interdisciplinary scholarship is too frequently superficial and marked by dilettantism.[45] These critiques are worth considering—and guarding against. Successful interdisciplinary work requires significant, long-term collaboration with—and communication among—scholars from the various disciplines that are represented rather than a limited and truncated exchange.[46] It also requires a sense of mutual respect.

L. Mainstream Legal Scholarship

Many of the schools of thought presented in this Chapter respond to—and critique—what is seen as "mainstream" legal thought. This phenomenon naturally raises the question, "What, then, is mainstream legal thought?" Although it is not clear that a single mainstream view exists, legal process theory, rights theory, and law and interpretation likely would be in contention for the title of "mainstream" legal thought. Another term sometimes used to describe mainstream legal thought is "liberal legalism."[47] "Liberalism," as the term is used in this context, is typically associated with capitalism even though modern proponents of liberalism generally accept at least some market interventions as being valid. Liberalism tends to be focused on individual rights, both civil and political.

The Legal Process School emerged in the 1950s. As the name would suggest, this school of thought is associated with claims that neutral decision-making can be achieved through a reasoned, objective process. Thus, for the legal process scholar, law can be understood as providing fair mechanisms for dispute resolution. Legal process scholars believe in the power of the legal system to serve as a stabilizing force, when supported by an appropriately objective judicial decision-making process.[48] The rise of legal process scholarship in the

---

44. Charles W. Collier, *Interdisciplinary Legal Scholarship in Search of a Paradigm*, 42 Duke L.J. 840, 840–42 (1993).

45. Ethan Kleinberg, *Interdisciplinary Studies at a Crossroads*, 94 Liberal Educ. 6, 8 (2008).

46. *See* Francis J. Mootz, III, *Desperately Seeking Science*, 73 Wash. U. L. Q. 1009, 1010–11 (1995) (discussing the implications of interdisciplinary work in the context of law and linguistics).

47. Minda, *supra* note 20, at 618.

48. Black's Law Dictionary 1076 (11th ed. 2019).

1950s was, at least in part, a response to concerns that realism could support "moral relativism" and, taken to an extreme, the kind of fanaticism and fascism that the world had seen in Nazi Germany and elsewhere during World War I.[49]

Law as interpretation and modern rights theory emerged in the 1980s. These theorists operate under the principle that, while the law itself may be indeterminate, adjudication can be objective because judges operate within the constraints of legal norms, rules, and conventions. These scholars appeal to democratic values and democratic processes in describing how the law can and should work.

Some of the names commonly associated with so-called "mainstream" legal thought include Bruce Ackerman, Ronald Dworkin, John Rawls, Owen Fiss, Lon Fuller, Henry M. Hart, Albert M. Sacks, and Herbert Wechsler.

M. Evaluating a Prospective Article

Incorporating an established legal philosophy makes an article neither more nor less desirable, but instead simply represents a choice on the author's part to apply a particular lens to their analysis. Yet, it can be helpful to identify whether an article includes analysis representing one or more of the schools of thought presented in this Chapter. To the extent that an article reflects an established school of thought, an editor should be prepared to evaluate whether it does so successfully.

With these goals in mind, there are a few steps an editor can take when reviewing an article for publication. First, determine whether the author intends for their article to be associated with a particular school of thought. If the author is an established legal scholar, consider reviewing the author's other articles—or, if the author is a professor, the classes they teach—to determine whether the author is generally associated with a particular school of thought. An author who teaches a class on feminist jurisprudence or law and economics, for example, is likely to incorporate those ideas in their scholarship.

The sources the author cites can be another important clue. The names that are included in each section of this Chapter are by no means exhaustive, but they do provide a starting point in identifying some of the scholars whose work is commonly cited for each school of thought. An author who cites Ronald Coase heavily may very well be writing a law and economics piece.

---

49. Kuklin & Stempel, *supra* note 3, at 158.

The themes the article reflects are another source of information. An article that is heavily focused on the extent to which a particular law, argument, or approach is morally sound may very well be grounded in natural law.

As a second step, once you have identified any school (or schools) of thought an article represents, you will want to evaluate whether the article makes a strong contribution to this school of thought, such that you would like to publish it. This can be an intimidating prospect for an editor who is new to the field of legal philosophy. Faculty advisors and other members of your school's faculty can be essential resources for this task but begin with your own analysis. If you have identified CLS themes in an article, for example, you might review the short summary above and then consider exploring some of the resources identified in section O below to learn more about CLS. Then consider consulting with your faculty advisor, a professor who teaches a CLS course, or a professor who teaches jurisprudence, to discuss your impressions of the article and get some additional context for your evaluation of its merits.

N. Conclusion

This Chapter has introduced some of the major schools of thought in modern American jurisprudence. As you consider the merits of articles that are submitted for publication, you may find that they reflect one—or more—of the philosophies referenced here. Since editors often seek to include articles representing a balance of perspectives, being able to recognize—and name—the philosophy an article best represents can be helpful.

O. Reading List

The following sources provided background information for this Chapter. Many of these books and articles were written with law students in mind, and they may be useful for further exploration of any of the topics referenced in this Chapter.

BLACK'S LAW DICTIONARY (11th ed. 2019). This source not only provides a clear, concise definition of each of the major concepts covered in this Chapter, but also includes dated quotations for many, illustrating when and where the concepts have been used in important works of legal scholarship.

ANALYTIC JURISPRUDENCE ANTHOLOGY (Anthony D'Amato ed., 1996). For each concept covered, this anthology provides brief explanatory text followed by excerpts from many of the most famous law review articles discussing each school of thought.

DOROTHY A. BROWN, CRITICAL RACE THEORY: CASES, MATERIALS AND PROBLEMS (2003). This book not only introduces CRT but connects it with many of the courses typically taught in the first year of law school.

THE CANON OF AMERICAN LEGAL THOUGHT (David Kennedy & William W. Fisher III eds., 2006). This volume contains what the authors have identified as the twenty most important works in American legal philosophy. Each is preceded by a short biographical essay introducing the author.

Richard Delgado, *How to Write a Law Review Article*, 20 U.S.F. L. REV. 445 (1986). The most pertinent portion of this article for purposes of this Chapter is part II, Varieties of Law Review Articles.

NEIL DUXBURY, PATTERNS IN AMERICAN JURISPRUDENCE (1995). This book explores the connections between, as well as the differences among, the various schools of thought represented in this Chapter.

JEROME HALL, FOUNDATIONS OF JURISPRUDENCE (1973). This book is especially helpful for its examination of the debate between proponents of natural law and legal positivism.

LAURA KALMAN, LEGAL REALISM AT YALE (1986). This book illustrates how the emergence of legal realism at Yale was, at least in part, an effort for Yale to differentiate itself from Harvard. For this reason, the book uses the Harvard casebook method as a point of comparison, throughout.

Laurie Rose Kepros, *Queer Theory: Weed or Seed in the Garden of Legal Theory?*, 9 LAW & SEXUALITY 279 (2000). This article includes a wealth of examples of and citations to queer theory.

BAILEY KUKLIN & JEFFREY W. STEMPEL, FOUNDATIONS OF THE LAW: AN INTERDISCIPLINARY AND JURISPRUDENTIAL PRIMER (1994). This book is probably the most accessible on this reading list and could be easily read over a few days. If you find that you are interested in this material and want to learn more, consider this as a first source.

Gary Minda, *The Jurisprudential Movements of the 1980s*, 50 OHIO ST. L.J. 599 (1989). This article explores the connections between, as well as the differences among, law and economics, CLS, and feminist legal thought.

Martha Minow, *Archetypal Legal Scholarship: A Field Guide*, 63 J. LEGAL EDUC. 65 (2013). Although still quite concise, this article provides a more in-depth description of many different kinds of legal scholarship than Professor Delgado's article listed above.

THE OXFORD COMPANION TO PHILOSOPHY (Ted Honderich ed., 1995). As the title suggests, this volume is broader than legal philosophy, but does include entries for most of the topics covered in this Chapter.

FREDERICK SCHAUER & WALTER SINOTT-ARMSTRONG, THE PHILOSOPHY OF LAW: CLASSIC AND CONTEMPORARY READINGS WITH COMMENTARY (1996). This book provides the most comprehensive analysis of any source on this list and would be useful for a "deep dive" into any philosophy discussed in this Chapter.

Marin Roger Scordato, *Legal Theory and Linguistic Reality: A Critical Examination of Modern Legal Scholarship*, 2 J. CONTEMP. LEGAL ISSUES 257 (1989). This article focuses on natural law and legal realism.

Thomas S. Ulen, *The Unexpected Guest: Law and Economics, Law and Other Cognate Disciplines, and the Future of Legal Scholarship*, 79 CHI.-KENT L. REV. 403 (2004). This article provides the most comprehensive discussion of empirical scholarship of any source in this Chapter.

LLOYD WEINREB, NATURAL LAW AND JUSTICE (1987). This book focuses on the debates between positivism and natural law.

Robin West & Danielle Citron, *On Legal Scholarship*, CURRENT ISSUES IN LEGAL EDUC. 16 (2014), https://www.aals.org/current-issues-in-legal-education/legal-scholarship/ [https://perma.cc/LW9K-MS4J]. This article helps to answer the question of why legal scholarship is an important contribution to the field of law—and to the pursuit of knowledge about law.

KEY TAKEAWAYS

- The boundaries between schools of thought are porous; thus, a legal scholar may be associated with more than one philosophy.
- Understanding the historical context in which a school of thought arose can be helpful in assessing the quality of articles and making informed decisions regarding article selection.

- Recognizing the philosophy an article represents can assist an editor in balancing perspectives.
- Reviewing a prospective article for its philosophical content requires a thoughtful, multi-step analysis; campus resources, along with those in this Chapter, may assist editors in completing this process.

6

Working with Law Librarians

Andrew W. Lang and Annalee Hickman Pierson

LEARNING OBJECTIVES

After reviewing this Chapter, editors will be able to

- explain the various roles, responsibilities, and expertise of librarians at law schools;
- evaluate the journal's needs and identify common forms of library support to address those needs; and
- develop strategies to work with librarians to improve journal workflows and publication processes.

Few departments are more integral to the overall operations of a law school than the academic law library. Law librarians impact every part of a law school's academic output by supporting faculty scholarship, helping students answer complex research questions, creating research strategies, providing vital study spaces, paying for database subscriptions, and obtaining necessary materials for journal cite-checking. Law libraries are so fundamentally important that they are even built into the ABA's requirements for law school accreditation[1] and are weighted in the *U.S. News & World Report* rankings.[2]

1. Am. Bar Ass'n Section of Legal Educ. & Admissions to the Bar, 2021–2022 Standards and Rules of Procedure for Approval of Law Schools ch. 6 (2021), https://www.americanbar.org/content/dam/aba/administrative/legal_education_and_admissions_to_the_bar/standards/2021-2022/2021-2022-aba-standards-and-rules-of-procedure.pdf [https://perma.cc/ 2QMH-WJ24].

2. Robert Morse, Kenneth Hines, Eric Brooks, Juan Vega-Rodriguez & Ari Castonguay, *Methodology: 2022 Best Law School Rankings*, U.S. News & World Rep. (Mar. 29, 2021), https://www.usnews.com/education/best-graduate-schools/articles/law-schools-methodology.

Yet despite the vast resources and support law libraries provide, most law students only scratch the surface of what their libraries are offering. Law students who are members of a journal tend to be more familiar with their libraries than their peers, primarily due to the rigors of checking footnotes. But many still miss out on the numerous ways librarians can make their journal experience more efficient and sustainable. Journal members are key library constituents, accounting for a significant amount of library usage, which means that librarians are usually eager to work with journals to streamline operations. Essentially, better cooperation and communication between journal members and librarians present a win-win for everyone involved.

Throughout this Chapter, we will be describing services that librarians provide to law journals.[3] We recognize that not all law libraries are sufficiently staffed to offer all services discussed, so journal members should always communicate with their librarians to identify which services are available at your institution.

A. An Introduction to Law Librarians

An academic law library's greatest resource is its employees. Professional law librarians come from a wide range of backgrounds. At many academic institutions, the law librarians hold both a master's degree in library science and a law degree; some even have extensive practice experience as attorneys. What sets them apart is expertise in legal research and a robust commitment to the academic side of the legal profession.

The librarians who work with law students generally fall under the umbrella of "Public Services." Titles and specific responsibilities can vary widely by institution, but the most common position is some variation of "Reference Librarian." The defining feature of a reference librarian is providing reference services, such as on-demand assistance for patron questions, often

---

3. For a discussion of how common each of these law library services for student journals are, see Dana Neacsu & James M. Donovan, *Academic Law Libraries and Scholarship: Communication, Publishing, and Ranking*, 49 J.L. & Educ. 433 (2020); Melissa M. Hyland, Supporting Legal Scholarship: Exploring Law Library Services for Student-Edited Law Reviews (Apr. 2017) (unpublished M.S.L.S. thesis, University of North Carolina at Chapel Hill), https://cdr.lib.unc.edu/concern/masters_papers/hx11xk03m [https://perma.cc/GNB5-EYVH]; Benjamin Keele & Michelle Pearse, *How Librarians Can Help Improve Law Journal Publishing*, 104 Law Libr. J. 383 (2012).

at a reference desk or by phone, email, video chat, or webchat. The reference desk is part of the frontlines of most library operations and is one of the most common points of contact for journal members struggling to find materials to check footnotes, but much librarian work occurs elsewhere.

Librarians are also deeply immersed in research support for law faculty, which can range from simple document delivery to manuscript formatting to literature reviews, archival research, and database construction. The chances are high that any article a law review selects for publication already has librarian fingerprints all over it. This experience also means that librarians are especially well-equipped to track down materials and recognize the sources that faculty members typically use. Librarians' experience helping faculty prepare their articles also renders them an invaluable resource for student-authors seeking to write publication-ready papers.[4]

Because they support faculty research efforts, librarians are typically well-versed in citation manuals and can provide suggestions for how to cite difficult or unusual sources. Some librarians even research and publish their own scholarship, while others serve as editors of books, journals, and other professional publications. Although the library is often seen as a repository of information, many librarians are also actively involved in creating and publishing this information.

Finally, another significant responsibility for many law librarians is legal research instruction, which can take place in both formal and informal settings. Formal instruction may include required first-year research and writing courses and elective upper-level legal research courses. Informal instruction may include training for student organizations, guest lectures in doctrinal and seminar law courses, and standalone research workshops. These instructional experiences make librarians well-suited to assist with journal orientation and training.

Unlike some other information professionals, law librarians are platform-neutral and primarily interested in finding the best way to obtain the information the journal requires. In contrast, vendor representatives from research databases often reach out to journals to set up training sessions and provide catering or other incentives. It is good to build relationships with vendor representatives, but always remember that their primary interest is in attracting more users to their platforms, which may not always offer the

---

4. Chapter 12 of this *Manual* addresses journal members who are writing their own scholarly papers.

resources the journal needs. But when journal members have questions about the intricacies of a specific database, the vendor representative for that platform will have more specialized insights to share. Law librarians develop broad expertise across all the platforms and databases in the library's subscriptions, making them experts at identifying the tools that will help journal members locate material efficiently and in the desired formats.

B. Core Law Library Services for Law Reviews

Librarians provide a wide range of support beyond simply helping students find materials for checking footnotes. This section covers the core services that many law libraries provide.

1. Assigning a liaison librarian for support, training, and institutional knowledge

Because journals are such an important constituency, librarians like to encourage frequent contact and coordination. Depending on staffing levels, some libraries will designate specific librarians to serve as journal liaisons for support, training, and institutional knowledge. This liaison librarian can be the go-to person that journal members contact when questions arise. While student leadership turns over every year, liaison librarians can serve as a locus of institutional memory, as their relationship with the journals persists across time. They better understand the services offered to the journal and the skills that the editors need to complete their work. They can prepare various training sessions and possess expertise in source retrieval and checking footnotes; they may also have previous experience with copyright and working with publishers.

2. Helping find material for checking footnotes

As mentioned above, most journal interactions with librarians occur in the context of the source retrieval and cite-checking process. This interaction may even start *before* the journal's first footnote-checking assignment, during new editor orientation.[5] Providing good, librarian-led instruction about how to find material cited in the articles early in the process may help journal

---

5. For more information about what should be covered in an orientation program for journal members, see Chapter 11 of this *Manual*.

members avoid hiccups down the line, and librarians are usually pleased (with enough advance notice!) to participate in orientation sessions.

In an orientation session, librarians can demonstrate how to find common sources, such as PDFs of the official reporters for cases, newspapers, books, law review articles, statutes, regulations, and legislative history. They can also offer training on subject-specific databases for specialized law journals.

Librarians can demonstrate how to use the library catalog to find items. Many students will not have used the library's catalog and physical collections much during their first year of law school. Librarians can offer useful suggestions about navigating the idiosyncrasies of the institution's catalog, including where and how to access the catalog for other campus libraries (like the general library, medical library, etc.) if there are separate library catalogs. Some items in the collection may have usage restrictions. For example, multi-volume treatise sets may not circulate, which means patrons cannot borrow those items or remove them from the library space.

Outside of formal orientation sessions, librarians can help journal members track down elusive sources. Because these questions usually need a quick response, the journal should familiarize all members with the library's reference department and their points of contact, which may include the reference desk, a phone number, an email account, or a virtual chat platform. This advice holds true at other libraries as well; if journal members are having trouble finding sources at another library, always remember to consult the reference librarians at those libraries.

3. Coordinating interlibrary loans

When the journal needs an item that is not available at the institution, librarians can coordinate interlibrary loans (ILL). Many sources journal members need to retrieve may be found in or through one of the institution's libraries (either the law library itself, the main university library, or a specialty library on campus like a business library, medical library, etc.). Journal members may find the source physically and need to make scans of it or may find it electronically through a library subscription. However, journal members may also run into sources that the institution does not have access to; in those instances, journal members will need to work with librarians to request the sources through interlibrary loan.

The ILL process differs at every institution, so journal leadership needs to communicate with librarians about their expectations and workflow. A key question is who should be eligible to request an ILL for the journal. Often, journals have centralized workflows where they designate one or more editors to review and submit ILL requests on behalf of the journal. This process should ensure that requests are being placed only for items legitimately not available at the institution and that multiple requests for the same item are not being submitted.

Regardless of the specific workflow, the two keys to using ILL successfully and efficiently are time and details. Time is needed for ILL materials to arrive, especially if requesting a physical copy of a source, such as an entire book. Physical sources may take weeks to arrive by mail, so editors should try to identify potential ILL sources as early in the editing process as possible.

In regard to details, give as many as possible. Crucial details include author, title, publisher, edition, and translation information. Some libraries use forms to manage ILL requests, which will specify the required information. Without the requisite information, the library may not be able to place an ILL request, so requests should be as thorough as possible.

If only a portion of the source is needed, the librarian may be able to request a scanned copy of just the necessary pages, rather than the whole book; consequently, the requested material will usually arrive electronically within days instead of physically within weeks. Receiving an electronic download instead of a physical copy is also efficient because journal members can quickly check the source utilizing optical character recognition (OCR). OCR allows members to find relevant quotes quickly by using the ctrl+f keyboard feature to substantiate information in the text.

For physical ILL materials, editors will want to pay close attention to the due dates because it is not always easy to renew items borrowed from other institutions. When dealing with ILL materials, it is advisable to make scans early and keep them in a shared location like a library hold shelf or a cloud-based storage system because replacing lost ILLs can be expensive.

4. Formatting citations for sources

Once journal members have retrieved the sources and substantiated the author's assertions, members will need to ensure all the citations are formatted correctly according to the journal's required style manual. Librarians can also be helpful in this process. The key to accurate formatting is being able to correctly identify the source type. For example, citation manuals have different formatting rules for consecutively versus non-consecutively paginated journals. Librarians are experts at finding materials and researching sources, allowing them to help journal members quickly identify source types. Many also may have extensive personal and professional experience using citation manuals from writing their own scholarly articles and assisting faculty members with their research. Thus, they may be able to help journal members find the proper citation rule or at least be able to help them feel confident that the citation manual is silent on a particular source and perhaps suggest ways to create a citation format based on a hybrid of two citation rules.

5. Permalinking resources for archiving websites

Internet sources can create issues for cite-checking as URLs may have changed since the author last accessed an online source. One tool to address this issue is permalinking, which is even encouraged by citation manuals. At many institutions, access to permalinking tools, such as Perma.cc, is provided through and managed by the law library. Be sure to ask the librarians about the available resources; they may be able to create and manage institutional accounts and provide training on best practices for permalinking.[6]

6. Preserving materials on an institutional repository

Once the editing process is complete and the issue is ready for publication, librarians may want to preserve materials digitally on the school's institutional repository. Most law school libraries maintain institutional repositories of the school's academic output. Generally, these will include copies of faculty publications, student-edited law reviews and journals, and documentation of other events related to the intellectual life of the law school.[7] Moving the journal to an open-access model through publishing materials in the school's institutional repository is a great way to improve the journal's accessibility and reach by expanding the scope of individuals who may be able to find it through general web searching.[8]

---

6. For more information about permalinking, please review Chapter 18 in this *Manual.*

7. In fact, according to a 2016 survey, the second most widely included type of material in institutional repositories is student-edited law reviews and journals. Kincaid C. Brown, *Law School Institutional Repositories: A Survey*, 25 Trends Interactive 21, 22 (2016).

8. For additional information about open-access models, please review Chapter 16 in this *Manua*l.

Beyond the print and digital issues of the journal that are created each year, journals also produce ephemeral content that is of interest, especially to archivists. For example, if the journal hosts symposia or guest lectures, the library will likely want to preserve related content, such as event schedules, invitations, advertisements, promotional materials, and even presentation recordings. This content may end up in the archives rather than in the public-facing institutional repository, but preserving this material creates a record of the intellectual life of the journal and law school, capturing activities that may otherwise be lost or overshadowed.[9]

7. Explaining journal rankings, impact factors, and citation metrics and identifying and evaluating quality law review articles

Librarians can offer training to explain to student editors the ranking of their journal according to the Washington & Lee Law Journal Rankings[10] and the factors that impact that ranking. As a general rule of thumb, when the journal publishes articles that are subsequently cited a lot, the journal will have a higher ranking. Librarians can also help editors identify and evaluate quality law review articles by checking the prospective authors' current citation metrics from previous works on Westlaw, Lexis, HeinOnline, and Google Scholar. Knowledge in these areas will help editors increase the prestige of their journal and its impact.

8. Consulting with student-authors about preemption checks, research, and submitting for publication

Journal members may need to write a paper as part of membership in the journal. Either individually or through group training sessions, librarians can help student-authors find a topic, conduct a preemption check, narrow

9. For more information on digitally archiving materials in an institutional repository, see the Chapter 16 in this *Manual*.

10. *See W&L Law Journal Rankings*, WASH. & LEE SCH. L., https://managementtools4.wlu.edu/LawJournals [https://perma.cc/WRR4-9BRA] (last visited Jan. 8, 2022). For additional information about this ranking system and citation metrics, see Chapter 16 in this *Manual*.

the topic to a thesis, and find research to support the thesis.[11] Many first-year legal research and writing classes approach the subject as a practicing attorney would but do not teach students *academic* legal research and writing. Writing a journal paper requires a student-author to expand their research beyond Westlaw and Lexis to additional platforms, such as HeinOnline, Google Scholar, and SSRN. Librarians can help student-authors use these platforms effectively.

Additionally, librarians can give student-authors information and advice for submitting the paper to other journals for publication consideration. Some law schools even pay the fees for student-authors to submit to a few other journals. Interested student-authors should consult their librarians for more information.

C. Ongoing Library Administrative Support for Law Reviews

The preceding section covered the most common ways that librarians can support the work of journal members, but this is not an exhaustive list. When developing or refining the journal's workflows, it is helpful to remember that librarians also offer ongoing administrative support. This section highlights four common areas of support.

1. Creating journal-level library accounts

Depending on journal workflows and policies, the law library may create a library patron account for the journal so that all library materials can be checked out under that account. A journal account can be beneficial if editors are looking to centralize the source retrieval process. If the library can lend materials to a journal account and hold them in a centralized location, journal members can avoid situations where another patron borrows the resource the journal members need or where needed books are not reshelved. Lending materials to a journal may also shield individual editors from overdue fines.

11. Chapter 12 of this *Manual* addresses working with student-authors.

2. Allocating library space for journal use

The law library may allocate library space for journal use. Such a space could be a study desk, carrel, office, or even a hold shelf. These designated spaces allow journal members to leave library materials in one secure place for other members to use for their journal work, helping to prevent miscommunication and situations where one editor walks off with material that others need. Additionally, housing physical ILL materials in one place is helpful for two reasons: first, journal members can use the ILL materials in the library and not take the items off-campus, and second, librarians can access the ILL materials in case they need to extend the due date or reclaim the materials if the deadline cannot be extended.

3. Providing library equipment for source retrieval

At many institutions, the bulk of source retrieval and scanning will be performed in the library, using library scanning equipment like standing copiers, flatbed scanners, or orbital/overhead scanners. The library may also lend storage devices like flash drives for large file scanning projects. Journal members will want to familiarize themselves with the available equipment and consult library employees if issues arise.

Some libraries may hold material in non-print and non-electronic formats such as microfilm or microfiche. These collections include items like court filings, superseded statute sets, and sometimes legislative history materials. If the library possesses holdings like these, the library will have special equipment for viewing the materials, and librarians will be able to give journal members instructions on how to use these devices.

4. Acquiring library materials and databases for the library collection that support journal needs

Because journal members are some of the law library's most active patrons, the library will consider journal needs, at least to some extent, when purchasing materials and database licenses for the library collection. Purchasing decisions typically happen without much input from students, but if the journal is relatively new, it would be a good idea to speak with librarians about the scope of the library's collection. For specialty law journals, the library may purchase popular treatises and databases in that field. That way, ILL does not need to be used for the same material each year. It is important to remember that it is less likely that library materials will be bought on-demand and more likely that the journal's needs will be considered as one factor when the law library makes collection decisions.

D. Less Common Law Library Services for Law Reviews

Beyond the core services and ongoing administrative support, a law library may be able to provide other, incidental services, including the following:

1. Plagiarism checking

During journal work, questions of plagiarism or unattributed text may arise. While editors will need to refer to the journal's policies and consult with the journal's faculty advisor, librarians may be able to assist with plagiarism checking. Librarians can often provide a list of different plagiarism detection tools and support subscriptions to them, like LexisNexis's SafeAssign or Turnitin, which can be used through Canvas.[12] Librarians can advise on article selection to help student editors identify papers with potential substantiation issues. Librarians can also discuss best practices for avoiding plagiarism when student-authors are working on their own papers. Accusations of plagiarism carry serious academic consequences, so it is best to take a cautious and thorough approach in checking for it.

2. Assisting with publication contracts

Depending on the administrative resources available through the law school, the law library may preserve copies of the publication contracts with authors or with the company responsible for publishing and printing the journal. If the library is performing this service already, editors should contact the librarians to see if the library can serve as a repository for this documentation, which may prove helpful to future editors. Librarians can also help editors find example publication agreements from other journals.[13]

---

12. *See* Keele & Pearse, *supra* note 3, at 393–95.

13. *See, e.g.*, Jamie J. Baker, *How Law Librarians Can Assist with Law Journal Publication Agreements*, 30 T.M. Cooley L. Rev. 245 (2013).

3. Advising on copyright

Librarians may be able to advise editors on copyright issues related to the journal's publication contracts and suggest books with applicable copyright discussion and examples.[14] Standard practices have shifted in this arena, especially with the emergence of open access publishing and institutional repositories. Librarians often can recommend ways to ensure that publication contracts strike a balance that preserves the rights of all interested parties.[15]

4. Improving discoverability for archived materials

Librarians may help to improve the discoverability of journal materials stored in databases, institutional repositories, or journal websites. For example, librarians may consult on the metadata used when archiving.[16] They may create QR Codes for the journal articles for easier discoverability by the public.[17] They may also promote the materials through search engine optimization (SEO).[18]

E. Final Thoughts

Although this Chapter provides a broad overview of the kinds of services law libraries can provide to support journal members, every institution is unique. Open a dialogue with the librarians early and think about the journal's goals. Does the journal want to place articles that will reap lots of future citations and boost the journal's ranking? Is the journal looking to produce more issues or an online supplement? Are board members hoping to streamline journal members' footnote checking to alleviate stress and administrative burdens? Does the journal want more of its members to produce publication-ready papers? All this and more? Law librarians can support these objectives and more.

---

14. Benjamin J. Keele, *Copyright Provisions in Law Journal Publication Agreements*, 102 Law Libr. J. 269, 269–70, 278 (2010). *See generally* Baker, *supra* note 13.

15. For an in-depth discussion of copyright as it relates to the work on the journal, see Chapter 17 in this *Manual*.

16. Keele & Pearse, *supra* note 3, at 398–402.

17. Michael N. Widener, *Driving Pedestrian Traffic to Law Journals*, 104 Law Libr. J. 569, 571–75 (2012).

18. *See* Neacsu & Donovan, *supra* note 3, at 462.

KEY TAKEAWAYS

- Law librarians are natural allies for journal members and can offer valuable support at nearly every stage of the journal publication process.
- Libraries may be able to assign a liaison librarian to your journal, assist with checking footnotes, coordinate interlibrary loans, format citations, support permalinking, preserve materials in an institutional repository, advise on journal rankings, and assist student-authors with their research.
- Because they work with journals every year, law librarians can serve as a point of continuity for journal processes and can suggest workflow improvements.

7

Common Editorial Positions and the Selection of Editors

Lindsey Gustafson

LEARNING OBJECTIVES

After reviewing this Chapter, editors will be able to

- identify the distinct roles and duties that a journal should ensure are filled by a specific editorial board position;
- prepare thoughtful descriptions of each editorial board position to help improve institutional memory; and
- create an editor selection process that is student centered, transparent, inclusive, and results in each editorial position being filled with a student who possesses the appropriate skill set for that position.

A. Introduction

A law review editorial board serves as the executive, administrative, and representative head of the student law review membership. The editorial board is the engine that runs the work of the law review: board members determine the content of issues, manage author relations, coordinate and oversee the editorial process, train new editors and staff members and monitor member work, handle the business of law review, represent the law review in dealings with the law school and the public, and usually select their own replacements.

Students are asked to fill these critical roles after only a year on law review, and they must supervise and lead peers. In addition, even the most spectacular board members typically serve in their positions for only a year. The reproducible effectiveness of the board depends, therefore, in large part on the structure and accuracy of the editorial board positions.

B. Board Position Descriptions Should Create Separate but Overlapping Roles and Be Regularly Evaluated for Continued Effectiveness.

A successful student-governed enterprise is reproducible when leadership roles are clearly and thoughtfully defined and then reevaluated regularly. Because board members typically serve only a year in their positions, the board's governing documents and traditions define the student leaders' expectations and interactions. To improve accountability and efficiency, the entire production process should be evident through board member descriptions.

The formal position descriptions should communicate to board members and others who is in charge of each stage of production, who reports to whom, and what enforcement mechanisms exist to ensure members complete their assignments timely and competently. Law review editorial boards can deepen institutional memory by creating position handbooks. These position handbooks may be as informal as a file passed from an outgoing editor to an incoming editor that helps the replacement build on the experience of the former editor.

Board leadership roles should be distinct, but that does not mean every task should be assigned to a single board member. Some tasks are better shared. For example, many boards assign article selection to a committee of the Editor in Chief, the Articles Editors, and possibly the Research Editor, or to the Articles Editors collectively with final approval by the EIC. In addition, many boards have a few board members—often the EIC and the Executive Editor—perform a final technical edit of the entire issue. And all board members—indeed all law review members—should be told explicitly that no one's job is done until the issue is published, and the EIC may assign various jobs, as necessary.

But without clear position descriptions, boards may fail to use or train their editors well, leading to inequitable workloads, delayed production, and frustrated authors. Carefully drafted position descriptions also improve the odds that the right student, with the right skills, is selected for each position. Position descriptions put board applicants on notice and inform them of the questions they may need to answer.

In addition, board members, together with faculty advisors, should regularly evaluate the workflow and dynamics of the board positions for effectiveness and efficiencies. Members should consider where work may be bottlenecking, whether some positions require more work than others, and whether routine tasks exist that are not clearly within any position's list of responsibilities. Boards should also consider whether the positions or their descriptions should be altered to meet societal changes or the needs of a changing readership. For example, many boards now place more content online or market through social media, so they assign oversight of online content to a board member. In addition, many boards are adding Diversity Editors.

C. The Board Selection Process Should Be Student Centered, Transparent, and Inclusive.

The incoming board is usually selected near the end of the outgoing board's tenure (often in March or April) but with enough time remaining to train and transition work to the incoming board.[1] During this time, leadership and responsibilities should stay clear: in most instances, editorial boards should have a definitive date of transition and share it with authors, so no one is confused about who is in charge or responsible.

Typically, board members are involved in selecting their replacements from the ranks of law review members. The outgoing board may select the incoming board after an application period and interviews. Alternatively, the incoming board may be selected by the entire membership after nominations from the outgoing board. Frequently, a faculty advisor or a member of the law school administration will be involved in the selection process. This involvement may range from a faculty advisor overseeing the process but not voting, to a faculty advisor participating in the interviews and selection discussions, to a faculty advisor being the final decision-maker after receiving student input or nominations and ensuring that the nominees meet the eligibility requirements. Whatever the process, because law reviews are student-edited, student members should play a key role in selecting the student leaders.

The selection process should be as transparent and inclusive as possible. If students are conducting the interviews, a faculty advisor or another member of the faculty or school staff should train the current editors to conduct interviews in a manner that comports with applicable federal and state laws and that is equitable to all candidates. It may not always be obvious to law students that they may ask whether a candidate has adequate time to devote to law review, but they may not ask whether applicants are married, have children, or have

1. For more information about board transitions and training new editors, see Chapters 8 and 11 of this *Manual*.

a disability. Board members should ask the same basic questions of applicants for similar positions. In addition, all voting members should attend all interviews, so no applicant is advantaged or disadvantaged.

Part of the faculty advisor's role may be to educate board members on unconscious or implicit bias, where candidates are preferred because they fit an existing culture or unconscious expectation, and affinity bias, where candidates are preferred because they look, act, or think as the voting board member does. Board members should also be careful when ostensibly evaluating applicants' "soft skills," which may be another way of justifying the selection of someone who is like the voting board member. Board members should be specifically encouraged to seek diversity of backgrounds, interests, sympathies, and talents, thereby strengthening the whole endeavor.[2]

Board candidates should be evaluated for the positions in which they indicate interest, but they must also be able to work with a larger team. Thus, questions should go beyond why a candidate is interested in and capable of filling a particular position. Candidates should discuss their leadership skills and ability to work with others productively. For example, candidates may be given an example of an interpersonal problem and asked how they would resolve it, or candidates may be asked to share what experiences they have had working productively with others to produce a product or complete a task. In deliberations, members participating in the interview should be invited to share relevant experiences they have had with candidates that speak to the candidates' professionalism and collegiality. Before finalizing the selections, board members should consider potential board candidates independently and as a unit.

Members considering a board position should discuss particular board positions with current board members. Board members may also want to provide potential applicants time to shadow current editors or review that position's description and any more detailed position handbook. The more information the board can provide about the specific demands of each position, the better. Applicants should be realistic about the demands the work will put on their time and should be ready to adjust work and personal commitments accordingly.

---

2. For more information about diversity, equity, and inclusion on law reviews, see Chapter 4 of this *Manual*.

D. Typical Board Positions Should Be Tailored to the Particular Needs of Each Law Review.

Every law review has its own combination of titles and responsibilities. For example, on some law review boards, the Executive Editor is the ultimate technical editor, while on others, the Executive Editor oversees the student-writing process. Obviously, the position titles a law review uses matter less than whether the board tasks as grouped and assigned encourage an organization that is efficient and effective.

The roles described below represent the primary, separable tasks of a law review editorial board:

- Editor in Chief;
- Managing Editor;
- Executive Editor;
- Articles Editor;
- Student Writing Editor (sometimes called Notes & Comments Editor or Student Articles Editor);
- Research Editor;
- Candidacy Editor;
- Symposium Editor;
- Communications Editor; and
- Diversity Editor.

Many boards have more than one student in some of these positions, and many have assistant editors who share the position responsibilities. Other boards may have "departments" with student department heads that may be called a "lead," "senior," "chief," or "executive" editor. Again, many boards cover the responsibilities with different combinations of titles.

1. Editor in Chief

The Editor in Chief is the chief student executive of the law review board and is ultimately responsible for the law review during their tenure. The EIC is actively engaged in determining the content of each issue, keeping authors satisfied, and reviewing the accuracy and efficiency of the entire editing process. The EIC is also the final student arbiter in decisions related to editorial style, management, and the publication process. The EIC may be given the discretion to alter the responsibilities of other law review members, as necessary. Finally, the EIC should guide the priorities of the law review during their tenure and suggest future improvements or innovations.

An EIC should be comfortable managing peers and encouraging leadership in others. This role also requires a calm problem-solver who can handle situations professionally, someone who can manage time, and someone who is able to evaluate and improve systems.

Generally, an EIC

- represents law review to faculty, administration, and external groups, such as alumni and bar associations;
- serves as the primary liaison to the law review's faculty advisor;
- sets priorities and generally coordinates all review work, in consultation with the other board members and the faculty advisor;
- supervises, directs, and monitors the work of all other board members;
- oversees membership and institutes discipline, in consultation with the faculty advisor and other senior editors;
- determines publication goals and deadlines, usually in consultation with the Managing Editor;
- presides at board and all-staff meetings and determines the meeting agenda—usually in consultation with the Managing Editor;
- approves article selection, in consultation with the Articles Editor;
- potentially conducts some initial substantive edits;
- performs a final review of each article and a detailed edit of the entire issue before publication;
- helps troubleshoot problems with authors; and
- resolves matters of style and format when recognized authorities are unclear.

2. Managing Editor

The Managing Editor is the operational head of the law review, which may involve managing internal operations and necessary business connections and interests outside the law review. The Managing Editor should lead in building and monitoring systems, managing weekly operations, supervising staff members, and helping the EIC make and implement strategic goals. Some of the tasks listed below may instead be handled by a Business Editor or Business Manager.

A Managing Editor should be an effective problem-solver, able to handle situations compassionately but professionally. The Managing Editor should also be reliable and skilled at finding efficiencies and keeping track of details.

Generally, the Managing Editor

- works closely with the EIC in creating, monitoring, and modifying the publication schedule;
- schedules board and all-staff meetings, reserves rooms, and drafts the agenda for the EIC to review and edit;
- unless the role is filled by the Articles Editor or the EIC, acts as the primary point of contact for authors throughout the editorial process;
- with the EIC, troubleshoots problems with authors and law review members;
- keeps an updated roster and maintains membership files;
- maintains the law review's governing documents;
- tracks deadlines and staff assignments, if not tracked by the assigning editors;
- creates and manages the budget, in consultation with the EIC;[3]
- plan social events; and
- participates in any stage of the editorial process, as directed by the EIC.

If the Managing Editor also serves as a business manager, they generally will

- establish and maintain necessary contracts with the publisher and distributor of the law review;[4]
- serve as the liaison with any printer or publisher;

3. For more information about law review budgets and other business-related matters, see Chapter 3 of this *Manual*.

4. For more information about selecting and working with publishers and printers, see Chapter 15 of this *Manual*.

- maintain copyright agreements;[5]
- serve as a liaison to the law library;[6]
- maintain the subscription database; and
- oversee billing and reimbursements.

3. Executive Editor

The Executive Editor is the position whose duties vary the most across law reviews. But most often, the Executive Editor is the senior technical editor, and as such, has substantial responsibility for the technical accuracy of the final volume. The Executive Editor works closely with other editors responsible for discrete portions of the editing process, like the Articles Editor and the Student Writing Editor. The Executive Editor emphasizes and ensures accuracy and timeliness. Because other editors should already have done so, the Executive Editor does not check the substance of citations unless they spot an apparent error. Frequently, the law review board will have multiple Executive Editors and assign each Executive Editor responsibility for an entire issue.

An Executive Editor must be skilled at detailed editing. They should also be familiar with the entire editing process and adept at encouraging other editors to meet their responsibilities.

Generally, the Executive Editor

- oversees either the entire publication process or the final steps of the editing process;[7]
- works with the EIC to perform a final edit of each article and ensure technical accuracy and consistency of form throughout the issue;
- may insert final page numbers, headers, and footers;
- may perform desktop publishing;
- may work with the EIC and review final page proofs from the printer; and
- may work with the EIC or the Managing Editor to schedule deadlines and publication dates.

---

5. For more information about copyright agreements, see Chapter 17 of this *Manual.*

6. For more information about working with law librarians, see Chapter 6 of this *Manual.*

7. For more information about the editing process, see Chapter 14 of this *Manual.*

4. Articles Editor

The Articles Editor reviews unsolicited content from outside authors and, in consultation with the EIC, extends publication offers. The Articles Editor may also solicit non-student-authored content. At some law reviews, the Articles Editor may review articles submitted by students at other schools. The Articles Editor, along with the EIC, performs or oversees the substantive edits of the articles and often oversees the technical edits and acts as a point of contact for the authors until the articles are passed to the Executive Editor or EIC. The Articles Editor often supervises staff members' work on the piece (such as cite-checking) and must enforce deadlines with students and authors.

An Articles Editor should be an efficient reader who is able to accurately assess the value of submitted articles and think creatively about how best to build the substance of the issue. An Articles Editor should be a thoughtful, thorough, but appropriately deferential substantive editor. Finally, an Articles Editor should be personable and responsive to authors and other law review editors.[8]

Generally, the Articles Editor

- oversees the article selection process, in conjunction with the EIC;
- extends publication invitations and solicits articles;
- performs or oversees the substantive edits of the articles;
- oversees the article's technical editing and passes the article to the Executive Editor or EIC;
- inputs or oversees the input of suggested edits; and
- acts as a point of contact for the authors, which may include sending author contracts and article edits and managing author concerns and needs.

5. Student Writing Editor

The Student Writing Editor supervises the student scholarship process from topic selection to submitting a publishable piece.[9] Because of this responsibility, the Student Writing Editor is actively involved in training new members. The Student Writing Editor also oversees the editing of all student

---

8. For more information about working with authors, see Chapter 13 of this *Manual*.

9. For more information about supervising student-authors, see Chapter 12 of this *Manual*.

work accepted for publication. This role, therefore, involves the training and close supervision of peers and the editing of their writing, which can be a challenging responsibility.

A Student Writing Editor shares many of the responsibilities of an Articles Editor, but because the Student Writing Editor edits and supervises students, they must show an increased capacity to lead and supervise peers. A Student Writing Editor also often teaches and should demonstrate a capacity to diagnose a student's writing problems and offer appropriate guidance.

Generally, the Student Writing Editor

- sets the schedule for student-authors;
- oversees and often conducts training on students' scholarship;
- assists student-writers in selecting article topics;
- supervises and participates in evaluating and supporting student scholarship throughout the writing process;
- performs substantive edits of student scholarship accepted for publication;
- oversees the technical editing of student scholarship and passes the scholarship to the Executive Editor;
- inputs and oversees the input of suggested edits; and
- acts as a point of contact for student-authors.

6. Research Editor

Some law reviews have a Research Editor, or a Research Editor and a Technical Editor, whose responsibility is to oversee the substantive and technical accuracy of accepted pieces. Research Editors may participate in the initial substantive edits, suggesting where the author may need additional support. Research Editors may also review articles after they have been cite-checked by staff members, ensuring the work is accurate and thorough.

A Research Editor must be able to read articles critically and thoroughly for their substantive and technical accuracy.

Generally, the Research Editor

- maintains a high level of technical accuracy in all published work;
- participates in initial substantive edits to ensure the author's cited support is accurate and adequate;

- identifies sources that may be difficult to locate or must be ordered through interlibrary loan and works with the law library on solutions to these issues; and
- reviews cite-checkers' work for technical accuracy and thoroughness.

7. Candidacy Editor

Some law reviews have a Candidacy Editor who works with the EIC and faculty advisors to manage students' entry into law review.[10] Candidacy Editors may manage the write-on competition, help support students who have been invited to join the law review but are not yet full members, and answer questions from transfer students and others interested in joining the law review. If the Managing Editor does not maintain the membership files, the Candidacy Editor may do so. Although this role is described separately here, on many law reviews, these tasks are handled instead by a Research Editor or a Diversity Editor.

A Candidacy Editor should have strong interpersonal skills and should be able to inspire and encourage new members.

Generally, the Candidacy Editor

- acts as a point of contact for students with questions about how to join the law review;
- manages the write-on competition, often in conjunction with the EIC;
- supports or mentors new staff members who are completing the writing requirement;[11]
- may organize or provide training to new staff members of the law review;[12] and
- works closely with the law school administration to manage other aspects of candidacy or membership.

---

10. For more information about selecting new members, see Chapter 10 of this *Manual.*

11. For more information about the student-writing requirement, see Chapter 2 of this *Manual.*

12. For more information about training new staff members, see Chapter 11 of this *Manual.*

8. Symposium Editor

Many law reviews regularly organize and sponsor symposia. These symposia may be "live," where the law review publishes articles that are associated with a conference, or they may be "dead," or "paper," where the law review publishes articles on a particular topic without an accompanying conference. The Symposium Editor is primarily responsible for organizing the symposium and soliciting articles. The Symposium Editor works closely with the EIC, faculty advisor, any faculty member assisting with the conference or issue, and the law school administration. Much of the Symposium Editor's responsibilities depend on the nature of the support provided by the law school.

A Symposium Editor should be good at a wide range of tasks, including conceptualizing an event on a relevant topic, planning and executing an event, managing problems professionally, encouraging authors, and conducting competent substantive edits of submitted symposium articles.

Generally, the Symposium Editor

- decides, in conjunction with the editorial board and sponsoring faculty, the symposium topic and dates;
- prepares a detailed schedule for planning and holding the symposium;
- works with faculty and administration on a proposed budget and tracks expenses;
- works with the EIC and sponsoring faculty to issue invitations or call for proposals;
- reviews the participants or submitted proposals and sets the symposium program;
- arranges accommodations and transportation as necessary for symposium participants;
- handles other logistics associated with the symposium;
- may plan social events to be held in conjunction with the symposium;
- is the point of contact for all symposium participants;
- may work with the law school administration to publicize the symposium;
- may work with the law school or local bar association to coordinate CLE credit for participants; and

- acts as the Articles Editor for the Symposium, accepting articles, performing substantive edits, and supervising the technical editing until the issue is turned over to the Executive Editor or EIC.

9. Communications Editor

All law reviews have communication tasks, both with its members and its readership. In addition, many law reviews have added content on their website or pushed it out through social media. A Communications Editor can manage all aspects of law review communication: messaging on social media, managing content on the website, and publicizing law review events. This position may also be called a Web and Publication Editor, Forum Editor, Online Content Editor, or Internet Presence Editor.

A Communications Editor should be familiar with and adept at social media and willing to push out law review content through an online format, where appropriate.[13]

Generally, the Communications Editor

- shares necessary law review information with the entire membership;
- works with the EIC, Symposium Editor, and law school administration to publicize law review events;
- manages any online content, which may require selecting and editing student writing, such as blog entries; and
- manages online companions and other companion materials.

10. Diversity Editor

Many law reviews have a Diversity Editor, whose role is to monitor and encourage diverse participation in the law review and a diversity of voices in the published articles.[14] The Diversity Editor may be actively involved in planning and promoting the write-on competition to ensure diverse representation among the candidates. The Diversity Editor may also work closely with the Articles, Student Writing, and Communications Editors to encourage diversity

---

13. For more information on using social media to enhance an article's scholarly impact, see Chapter 16 of this *Manual*.

14. For more information about diversity, equity, and inclusion matters, see Chapter 4 of this *Manual*.

in published materials. The Diversity Editor may consult with the Symposium Editor on topics or diverse participants. Finally, the Diversity Editor may work closely with the law review administration so that the law review becomes part of school-wide diversity, equity, and inclusion efforts.

A Diversity Editor should have strong interpersonal skills and a dedication to understanding diversity, equity, and inclusion issues.

Generally, the Diversity Editor

- works with the EIC to further diverse voices and issues in published work and law review membership;
- helps design fair and equitable new member selection processes, which may include helping to plan a write-on competition;
- may help review unsolicited articles and solicit articles;
- may consult with the Symposium Editor to ensure the symposium either furthers or is sensitive to issues of diversity, equity, and inclusion; and
- coordinates with law school administrators about issues of diversity, equity, and inclusion.

KEY TAKEAWAYS

- Because law reviews are student-edited, student members should play a key role in selecting the student leaders through a fair and equitable process that encourages diverse voices and contributions.
- Law reviews should ensure that the responsibilities of each board position are carefully and thoughtfully described and regularly reviewed, with the goals of enhancing efficiency and accuracy of law review processes and covering all major tasks for the year.
- Board positions and titles vary across law reviews, but each review should ensure that every major duty is covered by at least one position.
- Board positions are often overlapping given the complexity of the publication process and the need to ensure that multiple people can perform most functions.

- The EIC typically has the discretion to alter other members' responsibilities to ensure the law review operation runs effectively and the publication process stays on track.

8

Effective Editorial Board Transitions

Austin Martin Williams

LEARNING OBJECTIVES

After reading this Chapter, editors will be able to

- recognize the pitfalls and consequences of ineffective board transitions;
- determine the tools and practices they should employ to ensure that appropriate materials, insights, and accounts are preserved and shared with incoming editors; and
- develop a transition schedule that will provide the time and structure necessary to ensure that incoming editors can effectively lead in their new roles.

A. Introduction

An effective editorial board transition is critical to the journal's success. Unlike peer-reviewed or professional journals, the editorial boards of student-edited law reviews and journals are constantly changing.[1] Each year, a new set of students steps into roles held only briefly by their predecessors. As with any organization, continuous turnover can lead to a lack of continuity and knowledge transfer, which can significantly hinder the next editorial board.

1. *See* Richard A. Wise, Lucy S. McGough, James W. Bowers, Douglas P. Peters, Joseph C. Miller, Heather K. Terrell, Brett Holfeld & Joe H. Neal, *Do Law Reviews Need Reform? A Survey of Law Professors, Student Editors, Attorneys, and Judges*, 59 LOY. L. REV. 1, 9 (2013); Benjamin J. Keele & Michelle Pearse, *How Librarians Can Help Improve Law Journal Publishing*, 104 LAW LIBR. J. 383, 403 (2012); Cameron Stracher, *Reading, Writing, and Citing: In Praise of Law Reviews*, 52 N.Y.L. SCH. L. REV. 349, 363, 365 (2007); Christian C. Day, *The Case for Professionally-Edited Law Reviews*, 33 OHIO N.U. L. REV. 563, 573 (2007).

While new editorial boards may come in with their own vision, goals, and priorities, they also have a responsibility to maintain—and, if necessary, complete—the work started by previous boards. Without a proper transition plan, editors may neglect to pass down critical information, leading incoming boards to waste time and effort redeveloping materials or handling matters on an ad-hoc basis instead of following a consistent set of policies and procedures. While few organizations experience the same turnover as student-edited journals, few organizations have the benefit of the incumbents overlapping with their replacements for such a significant period. Depending on when elections occur, outgoing and incoming editors may have several months to transition materials and review practices and procedures.

As this Chapter will explain, several steps are essential to ensuring a successful board transition. First, editorial boards must employ proper knowledge-management techniques to ensure that critical documents, insights and understandings, contacts, and accounts are preserved and shared in a way that incoming boards can easily take over without having to redevelop these materials. Second, editorial boards should develop calendars and checklists that incorporate the knowledge that they have developed so that new editors know how and when to complete essential tasks and responsibilities that will keep a journal on track. Third, to provide adequate time to review materials and transfer responsibilities, outgoing editors should start the transition process shortly after editor elections are completed. By employing proper transition practices, outgoing boards will be able to hand over their duties and responsibilities on time so that they can focus on post-graduation activities, and incoming boards will be able to hit the ground running.

B. Pitfalls of Unsuccessful Transitions

While incoming editors may be familiar with the editing and cite-checking process, they may be less familiar with the administrative functions that they will assume. Some may have prior experience serving in student organizations, but nothing is quite like leading a law journal. While editing articles is a big part of the management process, editors will also assume functions that you would expect from the leaders of a small company.[2] Law journals produce a

2. For more information about the business of running a law review, see Chapter 3 of this *Manual*.

product for customers—such as legal research vendors, libraries, and attorneys—and they often engage in development activities, such as meeting with alumni and stakeholders. Simply put, incoming editors cannot rely solely on their previous journal experience to succeed in their new roles.

Incoming editors risk being locked out of email, financial, websites, software, publishing, and social media accounts if outgoing editors do not share username and password information or properly transition the designees for these accounts. In addition, failure to provide updated contact information can lead to delays in reaching critical outside contacts, such as authors, publishers, and vendors. Moreover, not sharing past editorial board work product, such as manuals, procedures, templates, and training materials, could lead the incoming editors to spend time searching for these materials or recreating them from scratch. Any of these examples can impact critical business operations and cause major delays in the publishing cycle.

While delays of a few days or weeks may seem harmless, they can have lasting impacts on the journal. Outgoing editors will want to focus their time on preparing for the bar exam and the next phase of their professional careers. Spending time addressing questions and locating documents after their tenure takes time away from these important activities. Incoming editors will want to spend time carrying out the critical functions needed to publish a successful volume of the journal while also spending time on some of their own initiatives, like a name change, cover redesign, or website revamp. Any delays caused by ineffective transitions will slowly start to add up and potentially impact the journal for years to come.

C. Key Documents, Information, and Checklists

When thinking about what journals should have in place for transition materials, editors should think of it the same way companies do when onboarding and offboarding employees. Most businesses and organizations will have a formal set of steps or procedures that employees will follow when leaving their employer. Likewise, companies also have a set of onboarding procedures and materials for new employees to follow when starting a new job. Board transitions are no different.

Just as outgoing employees must transfer accounts, provide status reports on current projects, and ensure that all files are stored in appropriate places, so do outgoing editors. In the same vein, incoming employees will be expected to go through a series of checklists to ensure they have access to the appropriate accounts and files. They will be expected to learn the status of current projects and ongoing initiatives. To facilitate effective onboarding and offboarding, journals need to ensure that they are following proper knowledge-management techniques. Outgoing editors need to provide incoming editors with calendars and checklists to help the new editors understand and perform their duties and responsibilities, like when and how to submit their annual budget request or reserve a venue for the annual symposium.

1. Knowledge management

Throughout a journal's life-cycle, a tremendous amount of knowledge is produced by way of documents and files, policies and procedures, insights and understandings, contacts, and account information. This knowledge must be captured in a way that it can be used and shared with current and future editors. To capture and preserve information effectively, journals must have practices and policies in place that identify what is captured, how it is saved, where it is saved, and most importantly, how it is handed off to the next board. What follows are examples of the types of information that boards will routinely produce during their tenure and the steps they should take to ensure that information is captured, made accessible, and transferred to the appropriate parties.

a. Online web platform

Every journal should have a web platform or system to collate information in one place. While editors may be inclined to rely solely on a journal's email account to serve this purpose, even a well-organized email account cannot provide the necessary organization and context needed to serve as the journal's information hub. This platform could be a wiki (e.g., Google Sites), a website (e.g., WordPress), a course management system (e.g., Canvas), or even a project management tool (e.g., Trello). This platform should serve as the main knowledge bank of the journal. Ensuring that incoming editors have access to this platform is critical to ensuring a successful board transition.

b. Document storage solution and retention policies

For journals to save and transfer essential materials, they must have a document storage solution and a set of policies and procedures for what the journal should retain. Some journals may use a course management system like TWEN or Canvas to store journal documents. Other options are networked drives or cloud storage solutions like Box, Dropbox, OneDrive, or Google Drive. No matter the platform, journals should follow a few key principles.

First, journals should adopt consistent folder and file naming conventions so incoming editors can find materials easily. A consistent and logical naming convention (which can be captured in a written policy or procedure) will make it easier for incoming editors to find important documents. When developing naming conventions, journals should consider how they will identify different versions of the same document by using a combination of the last edit date in the file name (e.g., edited_2021-12-31) and a version number (e.g., v01, v02, etc.). If a document is under review, journals will want to note in the file name if a document is a "draft" or "final." In addition, journals should organize files so that they can determine which final versions are current (e.g., current bylaws) versus final versions that are no longer in effect but should be retained for the journal's archives (e.g., previous bylaws). Proper file organization and using standard naming conventions to ensure proper version control can eliminate wasted time searching for or reproducing documents like training materials, publishing templates, manuals, and other archived materials.

Second, journals should be careful about how they assign file ownership and permissions. Simply sharing files from one person to the next can cause issues if the original file "owner" retains access long after their tenure on the journal. Ownership privileges over files in a cloud storage provider often give the owner the ability to set access rules and permissions for those files. If the original owner does not transfer the ownership rights to another person, then future editors may not be able to access, download, or share the files. A better solution is for the files to be held by an institutional or journal account instead of being tied to a specific individual. In addition, it is ideal if a law school staff member assigned to support the journal or a faculty advisor has ownership of or the highest permission levels to the journal's files.

Third, while you may be tempted to acquire your own third-party cloud storage solution, check with your law school's IT department first. Many institutions provide access to Google Drive through G Suite or OneDrive through Office365. While some subtle differences exist between the different cloud storage providers, all should meet a journal's basic needs—the ability to collaborate on documents and access them remotely. Using a platform that your institution supports will provide more stability, ensure an account is properly backed up, and make it less likely that an editor's departure will lock future users out of the account. Going out on your own increases the risks that the institution will not be able to support you if technical issues arise with the cloud storage provider and of current editors getting locked out of an account.

Finally, while a journal can have the best cloud storage solution and file organization system in place, the systems will be ineffective if the journal fails to retain the right documents. A retention policy will help editors determine what can be deleted and what should be retained for long-term use.

Your law school or university likely has a document retention policy, so you should find and review it, as it binds the journal. The journal will likely want to create a more tailored list for its operation, but still consistent with the school's policy. In the journal's policy, be sure to address what documents must be retained, where they are maintained, and how long they are retained. Documents that should be addressed in a journal's document retention policy include the following:

- manuals, policies, and procedures;
- position descriptions;
- meeting agendas and minutes;
- training materials;
- write-on competition problems and submissions;
- financial information and records;
- contracts;
- publishing templates;
- subscriber lists;
- communication templates (e.g., email templates, letterhead, etc.);
- published articles and backfiles;
- unpublished student-written articles;
- archived materials (e.g., "on file with" the journal sources cited in published articles);
- copyright agreements;
- mastheads; and
- honors and awards given by the journal.

c. Insights and understandings

In addition to documents, a journal should also capture insights and understandings. These insights and understandings might be as simple as "we contact the librarian for a training session the last week of July" or "we have hosted alumni happy hours at the following restaurants." While this type of information may not rise to the level of a policy or procedure, it can help incoming boards and should be captured in a way that it can be easily transferred. Insights and understandings could be included as part of a shared calendar or checklist, or they could be included in a wiki or an internal website.

Another possibility is to include this information in an exit memo for each board position. In an exit memo, outgoing editors could outline key aspects of their positions or decisions that they had to make throughout the year. For each listed item, they could provide information about why and how they reached the decision or provide factors or questions that incoming editors should consider when faced with similar situations. Ideally, one outgoing editor, like the outgoing Editor in Chief, and the faculty advisor would review all exit memos to ensure consistency and completeness.

d. Online accounts and passwords

Journals should also develop a plan for transferring all online accounts to the incoming editors.

The journal's most important account is its email account. The journal's email account is the primary communication tool with those outside the journal and will also be tied to other online accounts created by the journal. While editors may be tempted to use their individual school accounts or personal email accounts, creating an institutional account that the law school or university supports will ensure that outgoing editors are removed, incoming editors are added, and messages from the account will be archived for future access. The number of institutional accounts will vary based on the journal's size and needs. Some journals may need only one account (e.g., lawreview@school.edu), while others may need several accounts (e.g., eic-lawreview@school.edu and articleseditor@school.edu).

Because most software and tools are now cloud-based, each tool or service requires the user to create an online account for accessing and using these resources. While some may restrict accounts to individual users, others will allow users to create accounts with generic logins to allow several individuals to access the accounts. It will be best to use the journal's institutional email account for those that allow you to register using a generic account. If passwords for online accounts are lost or misplaced, it will be easier to retrieve this information using the "forgot password" feature if the accounts were set up using an institutional email account.

The proliferation of online accounts also requires journals to have procedures for storing and sharing passwords. Journals should consider using password managers, such as LastPass or 1Password, to avoid keeping passwords on a post-it note or in an unsecured document. If a password manager is not available, journals might consider storing passwords on a platform that requires editors to authenticate with their school accounts during the login process. At all costs, journals should avoid sending the username and the password in the same communication to lessen the chance that this information will be exposed to an outside party.

e. Financial information and accounts

Most journals will have access to funds that they can use for publishing expenses, hosting events, and paying other miscellaneous costs.[3] Outgoing editors must provide incoming editors with detailed information on the following financial topics:

- the budgeting process and the timeline for submitting the annual budget request;
- types of funds available to the journal (e.g., restricted vs. unrestricted);
- fixed costs (e.g., publishing expenses) and discretionary costs (e.g., catering);
- budget lines;
- procedures for spending funds and seeking reimbursements; and
- how to check the balance of the journal's financial accounts.

Depending on how the journal is set up, these funds could be controlled by the law school, the university, or the journal itself as an independent organization. The journal's status will play a large part in how it manages finances and accesses financial accounts. In some limited circumstances, a journal may have its separate financial accounts set up through a credit union or bank. More likely, a journal's finances will be part of the law school's or university's

3. For more about journal budgets and finances, see Chapter 3 in this *Manual.*

accounts. Outgoing editors must know how the journal's financial accounts are managed to transition these accounts to incoming editors.[4]

If set up within the law school or the university, there will be less need to transfer authority to check the balance and approve certain expenses. On the other hand, if the journal is set up as an independent organization, then someone, either a law school administrator or an editor, will be the party who has the authority to access and manage these accounts. Under this arrangement, journals will need to ensure that financial information, like account numbers, bank statements, credit cards, and checks, is kept in secure locations. Moreover, they will need to make sure that incoming editors are added to these accounts, which could require completing forms and providing personal documentation, such as driver's licenses. This transfer process can take several weeks, so outgoing editors should plan accordingly.

f. Contact information

Contact information should be stored in a way that it is easily transferable between outgoing and incoming editors. Key contacts are those individuals and entities with whom editors interact outside the journal. This contact information could be combined with a "who does what" list. The contact information for every person, department, organization, or entity that the journal works with during the publication process should be captured to make it easy to locate and update.

While contact information could be captured in a digital or physical address book, a spreadsheet, document, or wiki is also a good place to store this type of information. For each entry, you should include the contact's phone, email, and address, along with a few notes about what the contact does for the journal.

The following are examples of people, departments, and entities that you will want to make sure you have the correct contact information for

- faculty advisors;
- law school personnel who oversee or assist with administering the journal;
- law school or university IT departments;
- librarians;

4. For additional information about how a journal's status vis-à-vis the host school can impact operations, see Chapter 3 of this *Manual.*

- legal research vendors (e.g., Bloomberg Law, LexisNexis, Westlaw);
- financial institutions;
- bar associations;
- journal publishers (e.g., Joe Christensen, Inc.; Sheridan);
- individual and institutional subscribers;
- merchandise vendors;
- journal alumni;
- authors whose articles have been accepted or published; and
- donors.

The transition period is the perfect time to update and confirm that the contact information on file with the journal is accurate. Annually confirming that someone is still the primary contact for a given entity or purpose is a good practice. In addition, confirming that someone is still in place can also be a good time to introduce the incoming editor to the contact. An email introduction from the outgoing editor that connects the contact with the incoming editors can go a long way to ensuring a smooth transition.

2. Calendars and checklists

While having all of the information organized and in place is critical to a successful board transition, outgoing editors also need to provide incoming editors with guidance on how and when to use this information. Calendars and checklists are great ways for outgoing editors to convey how and when to execute important tasks and responsibilities.

a. Calendars

Calendars or a list of annual events and deadlines are excellent ways for editors to identify when certain tasks, processes, or events happen throughout a board's tenure.

Editors can create calendars to display events and other actions at the semester, quarterly, or monthly level. While the details held within a calendar will depend on the individual needs of each journal, they are flexible enough to provide editors with general guidance about when certain events happen (e.g., new staff member orientation takes place in August) or specific deadlines that must be followed (e.g., when final grades are submitted to the registrar's office).

When creating calendars, editorial boards can put everything onto a central calendar or create calendars for each position. For example, a central calendar might include information about when certain major events occur, like induction ceremonies, elections, and end-of-year celebrations. A calendar specific to each role might be appropriate to ensure that each editor meets their position's responsibilities. For example, the Research or Candidacy Editor's calendar might include all dates related new member selection process, such as information sessions, competition dates, deadlines for reviewers' scores, and the public announcement about new staff members. While a calendar will provide details about when something must get done, most of the how-to instructions should be conveyed through policies, procedures, or checklists.

While the format of calendars will depend on each journal's preference, a simple document, wiki, or journal website with months listed as headings is sufficient for the transition. Under each month, editors can list the key events, processes, or actions that should happen. Going one step further, adding links from items on the calendar to checklists or folders that contain additional information and procedures will allow editors to easily locate the information and tools they need to carry out their responsibilities. During or shortly after the transition, new editors can select specific dates and add them to their position and personal calendars.

b. Checklists

Checklists are excellent tools to employ when determining what has to get done next. Editors should create checklists for any action or process that will be repeated. These checklists can direct the order of tasks that need to get done or provide the items that are included as part of a task. For example, editors can develop a checklist for training new student-editors. As part of that list, subtopics can include selecting a date for the training, working with appropriate law school schedulers to identify a room, contacting vendors and librarians for presentations, and placing orders for catering. Then, within each task, editors can list non-sequential items or sub-tasks. For example, if the task is to contact legal research database vendors to schedule a training, items under the task could include the name of each vendor to contact. The beauty of checklists is that they free you from figuring out what needs to be done next or what should be considered when working on a specific project or task.

To make checklists even more powerful, editors should include direct links to folders and documents that the incoming editor can refer to when completing the task. For example, if the Managing Editor is responsible for submitting an annual budget to the Student Bar Association, a checklist should include a link to past submissions. By including links or details about where past materials are stored, new editors can more easily harness the knowledge of previous boards.

D. Post-Election Processes

While successful knowledge management—along with calendars and checklists—will capture all essential information in a form that will facilitate a smooth transition, it does not replace the need for outgoing and incoming editors to meet and hold training sessions to ensure a proper handoff of these materials.[5]

Once a new editorial board is in place, outgoing editors should start the transition processes by holding both group and one-on-one meetings with the incoming editors. Group meetings will give the outgoing and incoming editors the chance to get to know each other and discuss the journal from a high-level perspective. These meetings also will allow them to discuss the status of the current issue or volume, whether the outgoing board will meet its goals and objectives, and strategic initiatives that are carryovers from previous boards, like journal name changes or online publishing initiatives.

One-on-one meetings will provide the necessary structure for editors to discuss the duties of specific editorial board positions. These meetings are also great opportunities to review checklists and annual calendars to ensure that the incoming editors know what happens throughout the year. Outgoing editors typically need to meet with their incoming counterparts multiple times to cover all topics effectively. One approach is to focus each meeting on a particular topic. Holding multiple meetings over several weeks will ensure incoming editors have time to review pertinent information and ask questions. In addition, one-on-one meetings provide a venue where an incoming editor can shadow the outgoing editors and assist with the current board's work, thus getting hands-on experience before assuming leadership.

In addition to meeting with outgoing editors, incoming editors should meet with school officials who will be keys to their success. At a minimum, incoming editors should have at least one individual or small-group meeting

---

5. For additional guidance on journal member training and orientations, see Chapter 11 of this *Manual*.

with the school official who is most relevant to their role on the journal. Incoming officials include the journal's faculty advisors, relevant law school administrative staff who interact with the journal,[6] the law library director, and law librarians assigned as journal liaisons.[7] Part of the new board's success will be knowing who to contact and when to contact them, so scheduling introductions early in the transition will allow editors to be prepared when their terms begin.

A unique feature of student-edited journals is the opportunity for significant overlap between the outgoing and incoming editors. Journals can use this overlap period to their advantage by investing as much time as possible in new editor training, including shadowing. An effective transition also requires that incoming editors spend time with each other to build connections, establish their priorities, and invest in additional training they will need to excel. Chapter 11 of this *Manual* provides an in-depth discussion about how to facilitate team building and training sessions. By investing time in the board transition, incoming editors will be better prepared to lead the journal, and outgoing editors will ensure that the journal's legacy lives on after their departure.

KEY TAKEAWAYS

- Effective board transitions allow incoming editors to learn their new roles through efficient and effective knowledge transfer and shadowing.
- Editorial boards must have practices and policies that identify what information is captured, how it is saved, where it is saved, and how it is shared with the next board.
- Editorial boards should treat the day after elections as the start of the transition period and use this time to schedule group and one-on-one meetings to provide a structure for training incoming editors and introducing them to key contacts and stakeholders.

6. For additional guidance about working with law school officials during the transition process, see Chapter 3 of this *Manual*.

7. For additional guidance about working with law librarians, see Chapter 6 of this *Manual*.

9

Leadership Styles for Law Review Editors

Ashley R. Hilliard

LEARNING OBJECTIVES

After reading this Chapter, editors will be able to

- select and apply effective leadership styles for particular situations;
- recognize the importance of active listening and effectual communication with supervisors and team members;
- demonstrate skills associated with being a great follower; and
- design and implement tactics to resolve common challenges that editors face.

A. Introduction

Although many students associate "law review" with "editing," law review also provides many students—and especially editors—with leadership opportunities. In addition to being an academic journal, the law review is also an organization and a business.[1] And the heart of an organization or business is its people. For the law review to function smoothly, editors must develop and exercise a range of leadership skills.

Leadership is more than simply being in charge. Rather, leadership is a skill set that an individual must learn and develop. "Breaking out of the 'lawyerly comfort zone' and becoming a leader means embracing self-reflection,

---

1. To explore issues related to the law review as a business, review Chapter 3 in this *Manual.*

education and training, feedback, and practice."[2] Simply put, leadership is "a process by which an individual or a group influences others to achieve positive and ethical change."[3]

A first step in becoming an effective leader is to learn about different leadership styles and determine which style, or combination of styles, might work best for you and the organization. Effective, practical leadership requires more than just following the same model repeatedly. Rather, it requires the leader to identify, choose, and implement "the right thing at the right time. Leadership can be learned, and 'the best leaders are the best learners.'"[4]

This Chapter first presents six leadership styles by examining their characteristics and presenting practical examples pertinent to editors. It then assists readers in choosing the best approach given the circumstances. Next, the Chapter discusses the powerful relationship between being a good leader and a good follower and why developing both skill sets is critical to the journal's success. Finally, this Chapter suggests various leadership tactics that, when paired with the appropriate leadership style, can prevent challenges from arising and help editors resolve the issues that do arise.

B. Six Leadership Styles

An editor's personality and the structure and dynamics of the law review influence the leadership style the editor adopts with staff and student-authors. Although many theories and models of leadership exist, in 2000, researcher Daniel Goleman surveyed and studied 3,871 executives and then identified

---

2. Eric Sigurdson, *The Science of Leadership: The Legal Industry and an Integrated Approach to Modern Organizational Leadership*, Sigurdson Post (Feb. 29, 2019), http://www.sigurdsonpost.com/2019/02/28/the-science-of-leadership-and-the-legal-industry-an-integrated-approach-to-modern-organizational-leadership-theories-competencies-and-styles-for-legal-leaders-on-the-front-line/#_ftn3 [https://perma.cc/D629-KWT2].

3. Donald J. Polden, *Leadership Matters: Lawyers' Leadership Skills and Competencies*, 52 Santa Clara L. Rev. 899, 903 (2012); *id.* at 901–04.

4. Sigurdson, *supra* note 2; *see* James Kouzes & Barry Posner, The Leadership Challenge: How to Make Extraordinary Things Happen in Organizations (6th ed. 2017); *see also* Deborah Rhode, Lawyers as Leaders (1st ed. 2013); Deborah Rhode & Amanda Packel, Leadership for Lawyers (2d ed. 2017); John Zenger & Joseph Folkman, The Extraordinary Leader: Turning Good Managers into Great Leaders (2009); Roger Gill, Theory and Practice of Leadership (2d ed. 2009); Joseph Rost, Leadership for the Twenty-First Century (reprint ed. 1993).

six different leadership styles.[5] These styles are summarized below, along with examples of how each style might look in the law review setting.

1. Democratic leadership

Democratic leadership on a law review occurs when the leader—whether the Editor in Chief or Senior Student Writing Editor—leads by consensus after seeking input from each team member.[6] Specific examples of democratic leadership within a law review include seeking input from all articles editors before accepting an article for publication, taking a vote of all editorial board members before recommending changes to the law review's bylaws, and having a group discussion with all student writing editors before selecting the winner of this year's best student article award.

Adopting a democratic leadership approach can help generate new ideas and build morale, trust, respect, and commitment among the editorial board and staff team. Democratic leadership can also empower all members to invest in processes and complete assignments at a high level. Articles editors faced with a large queue of submissions will understand that—if they review the articles and come to the meeting with input and opinions—they will be heard, which means that their hard work will be rewarded.

While democratic leadership can be effective in many situations, it may not be appropriate or effective in all situations. For example, if not implemented appropriately, democratic leadership could lead to endless meetings and discussions. It can also cause people to "hide," hoping they will not be held accountable for group decisions.[7] Sometimes, circumstances require a fast decision, meaning that one person must decide without the benefit of input. Other times, the sensitivity of a topic may mean that the leader is not free to seek broad input.

---

5. Deborah L. Rhode, *Leadership in Law*, 69 STAN. L. REV. 1603, 1623 (2017); Daniel Goleman, *Leadership That Gets Results*, HARV. BUS. REV., Mar.–Apr. 2000, at 78, 82.

6. Rhode, *supra* note 5, at 1623.

7. *Id.* at 1625.

2. Affiliative leadership

The touchstone of affiliative leadership is "people come first."[8] Leaders who adopt an affiliative approach seek satisfaction and harmony amongst the team and work to build relationships by offering constant, positive feedback and celebrating team accomplishments.[9] Many seek to avoid conflict at all costs.

While the affiliative approach can promote high levels of communication, team spirit, organizational identity, and trust because editors support their team members' emotional needs, it also comes with challenges. When used exclusively to reward good work, too much praise can result in poor performance going unaddressed, thus impacting quality.[10] To maximize team performance, an affiliative leader should consider incorporating constructive feedback that addresses areas for improvement. Most leaders and supervisors want their team members to be proud of their work and understand their role in the organization. But many affiliative leaders soon realize that it is impossible to make everyone happy all the time. And as peer supervisors, some student leaders may find this approach emotionally overwhelming.

Many editors might feel comfortable defaulting to the affiliative style because it caters to goals centered around team satisfaction and harmony. But no style will fit all situations, so editors should strive to develop the ability to apply other styles as well. In addition, those who prefer the coercive style, which is described below, might feel awkward adopting affiliative approaches without guidance and practice.

3. Authoritative leadership

Many characterize an authoritative leader as a "visionary."[11] Individuals who adopt an authoritative style lead by conveying their expectations up front and motivating others to fulfill these expectations by illustrating how each person's work fits into the larger picture.[12] With this guidance, law review

---

8. Bruna Martinuzzi, *Leadership Styles and How to Find Your Own*, AM. EXPRESS (July 22, 2021), https://www.americanexpress.com/en-us/business/trends-and-insights/articles/the-7-most-common-leadership-styles-and-how-to-find-your-own [https://perma.cc/3B2M-UVG2].

9. Rhode, *supra* note 5, at 1624.

10. *Id.* at 1625.

11. Martinuzzi, *supra* note 8.

12. Rhode, *supra* note 5, at 1624.

members are then free—within reason—to choose how they will meet those expectations and contribute to the vision. For example, suppose the EIC states that one goal for the year is to publish all issues on schedule and with as many well-known authors as possible. In that case, the Managing Editor can set and monitor the publication timetable, and the Articles Editors can exercise a fair amount of autonomy in selecting articles.

While this style may seem appealing, it may be more problematic to implement on a law review where all leaders are peers, unlike in other organizations where the leaders often have vastly more experience than others.[13] For example, an authoritative lead editor with a vision for a social justice law journal may divide the other articles editors into teams for article selection and direct them to select from a group of articles about police brutality. An editor with a law enforcement background may feel that others, including the lead editor, lack the professional experience to recognize sound analysis on this subject. So while the group might understand the charge, conflict may still emerge.

4. Coaching leadership

As the name implies, a leader who adopts a coaching style seeks to develop each team member's full potential. Goleman and others suggest that the coaching approach is the most effective, yet least common, leadership style.[14]

While similar to democratic leadership in that leaders tend to encourage team contributions, "coaches" tend to focus more on nurturing each team member's strengths by providing general guidance but not micromanaging.[15] "Coaching leaders excel at delegating; they give ... challenging assignments, even if that means the tasks [will not] be accomplished quickly. In other words, these leaders are willing to put up with short-term failure if it furthers long-term learning."[16]

This leadership style requires patience and time, and editors with a one-year term may not be able to use this style as their primary approach. That said, because the law review is an academic endeavor within an institution devoted to learning, putting on the coach hat as frequently as possible can

---

13. *Id.*
14. *Id.* at 1627.
15. Martinuzzi, *supra* note 8.
16. Rhode, *supra* note 5, at 1627.

have an array of positive benefits.[17] For example, the EIC of an animal law journal aiming to enhance each staff member's cite-checking skills might require each team member to provide a corresponding citation rule for each reviewed footnote in their assigned article. While this additional step may require extra time, this coaching technique forces team members to research and investigate rules they may not be familiar with and allows the EIC to coach them through their inquiries.

As with the authoritative style, editors may be uncomfortable coaching peers with similar or different characteristics or backgrounds—including race, age, gender, educational background, socio-economic background, viewpoint, or political affiliation. However, a leader who can grapple with that discomfort can provide team members with mentorship and practical skills.

For example, assume that an editor is assigned to work with a group of new members cite-checking an article. After meeting individually with each member, the editor discovers that one team member is extraordinarily detail-oriented. Another seems more comfortable focusing on processes, and the third is adept at legal research. The editor has an opportunity to give assignments and build team rapport so that each person can play to their strengths while learning skills from the other. The "coach" is on the sideline and is not leading from the front. Instead, the assignment is structured so that the team members learn from each other, with input and suggestions from the editor-coach. "In the long run, this leader focuses on creating strong teams that can communicate well and embrace each other's unique skillsets in order to get work done."[18]

5. Coercive leadership

Coercive leadership is a style that is rarely used but can be effective in extreme situations.[19] Leaders following this style tend to issue top-down orders and demand immediate compliance, which impedes flexibility and discourages motivation.[20]

---

17. *Id.*

18. Braden Becker, *The 8 Most Common Leadership Styles & How to Find Your Own*, (July 16, 2021), https://blog.hubspot.com/marketing/leadership-styles [https://perma.cc/R7ND-J3ME].

19. Goleman, *supra* note 5, at 82.

20. *Id.*; *see* Rhode, *supra* note 5, at 1623 ("Coercion, the style frequently associated with positions of power, is typically the least effective.").

Coercive leadership works best when trying to fix a major organizational problem or implementing a dramatic organizational shift.[21] For example, an incoming EIC may be faced with leading a journal in crisis mode because the prior board failed to publish all issues in its volume. While it may be standard policy for the Managing Editor to communicate with subscribers, the incoming EIC could adopt coercive leadership by reaching out to subscribers directly, explaining the situation, and offering a remedy, such as a 50% discount for one year, to avoid losing their business. In the short term, the Managing Editor is stripped of this responsibility, but the shift could conserve the journal's client base for the long term.

If we consider another example, suppose two senior editors have left the review for reasons related to academic integrity. The journal likely has policies and guidelines to replace these editors, but the immediate vacancies are disrupting the journal's publication timeline. In an effort to stay on track, a senior editor may step in to disperse the departed editors' workload amongst the rest of the editorial board, even though assigning work to other editors might not have been that senior editor's role. This act would not prevent new editors from being appointed under the bylaws, but it would allow the journal to keep on schedule while the bylaws process plays out.

Overall, a coercive approach can impact team climate and morale negatively and should be employed sparingly and with caution. Coercive leaders also fail to provide positive reinforcement, which can further damage relations with team members. Because coercive leaders shy away from collaboration, their "do as I say" approach leaves staff editors in the dark about the leader's vision for the journal.[22]

But there is a time and place for coercive leadership. When used appropriately, "the coercive style can break failed business habits and shock people into new ways of working."[23] Using the example above, let's assume that while reaching out to disgruntled clients, the EIC discovers that the Managing Editor responded only to correspondence received via physical mail because the Articles Editor is the only board member with access to the journal's email account. An EIC using the coercive style will jump in—often without asking questions about how the problem arose—to solve the issue so the organization can move past the problem. In this case, the EIC might act quickly to fix this

21. Goleman, *supra* note 5, at 82.

22. *Id.*

23. *Id.*

poor business practice by providing the Managing Editor with access to the account. But while the problem is resolved, the other editors might be offended that they were not consulted or allowed to explain the situation before the EIC acted. Thus, once the issue is resolved, the EIC should consider switching styles, maybe to the coaching or affiliative approach, to unpack the source of the issue and provide constructive feedback so a similar problem can be avoided in the future.

In sum, coercive leadership can work well in emergency situations and can be an effective last-resort strategy for handling problematic journal members. "But if a leader relies solely on this style or continues to use it once the emergency passes, the long-term impact of [their] insensitivity to the morale and feelings of [the team] will be ruinous."[24]

6. Pacesetting leadership

Running an organization using the pacesetting leadership approach can be akin to a relay race or the classic Tour de France cycling competition. Because these pacesetters tend to possess more direction and authority than the rest of the team (or peloton), they institute high standards at the outset, exemplify them, and expect other members to fall in line while maintaining the pace. Those unable to keep up are quickly replaced for the sake of the team's winning streak.

While this style provides a regime for other members to follow, like coercive leadership, it tends to overwhelm and pressure others to maintain a status of excellence, thus hindering individuals' drive for success. Contrary to an authoritative leader who shares their vision with the team, a pacesetter often leaves others in the dark by failing to state the goals clearly.[25] Essentially, those seeking support from their leader are in distress when left without instruction.[26] Similar to coercive leaders, who often act without explaining their reasons, an information void left by the pacesetter has a negative impact on morale and stifles members' creative contributions. Instead of providing more direction or changing the routine to fit the team's needs, the pacesetter either steps in to complete the task or replaces this person with someone who is more their speed.

---

24. *Id.* at 83.
25. *Id.* at 86.
26. *Id.*

The pacesetting style functions best with small teams composed of self-motivated, proactive, experienced individuals who possess the desire and ability to complete work on time or ahead of schedule. For example, an EIC might be able to use this approach to manage a team of returning senior editors who are familiar with the journal's goals, policies, and procedures. But an editor who adopts this style as their primary leadership style will likely burn out the team and sow seeds of resentment. They may also find themselves performing others' job responsibilities instead of empowering the other editors or members to perform to the best of their ability and with more discretion.

C. Choosing the Best Approach

Leading a peer group can be complicated and challenging. During an academic year, individual editors or the editorial board may be asked to

- assign work—some of it tedious and inconvenient—to other students without favoritism or perceived favoritism;
- direct the work of students who might have more business or editing experience;
- discipline fellow students (and sometimes friends), including removing them from the law review;
- express disagreement with other editors and potentially the faculty advisor; and
- make a decision when consensus cannot be reached.

While you will need to decide how best to handle each issue, you will also need to determine which leadership style will fit best to prevent these issues and to handle these issues if they arise.

Most individuals find that adopting a single leadership style is less effective than learning multiple styles and when to use each. An effective leader knows when and how to use which style. And the best fit will vary from organization to organization. One size does not fit all. An effective leader should aim to be sensitive to the needs of the law review and how their style and actions impact others.[27]

27. Rhode, *supra* note 5, at 1628.

Leadership is a skill. People are not simply born with leadership skills. Developing the skill takes time and effort. Read blogs, articles, and books about leadership. Observe other leaders and evaluate their styles. Talk with others about what styles they use and under what circumstances. Skill building also requires some degree of trial and error. If you adopt a particular style in a specific situation and that style didn't seem effective—or if you receive criticism—stop and evaluate. Your leadership toolkit will grow and evolve, and over time, you'll become more comfortable and gain more confidence in your ability to select the best style for the situation.

Your leadership style will set the tone for your team. The style you adopt can empower team members and encourage them to communicate effectively and respectfully with you and others—or can create resentment and strife. When considering your leadership style, remember that the focus should be on your team members and the organization.

Editors should also remember that one benefit of leadership is the opportunity to build positive and lasting relationships. If you take time to get to know those with whom you are working and help them build their skill sets and reach their own goals, you are creating a network that you can tap into for the remainder of your professional career. And you may make personal friendships that last long beyond law school. You will also find that those you supervise have a lot to teach you. Take advantage of their knowledge and talents to build your own.

D. The Leader as Follower

Leading a group requires confidence, but part of that confidence involves following the direction and guidance of others. We often overlook the value of following because we spend so much time focusing on developing and improving our leadership skills.

Some of the leadership styles discussed above focus on a leader's ability to communicate down the masthead.[28] But a leader must often work with or report to a supervisor to ensure critical information is shared and organizational goals are met.

---

28. *See* Kelsey Miller, *Managing up: How to Lead When You're Not the Boss* (June 18, 2019), https://www.northeastern.edu/bachelors-completion/news/blog-managing-up [https://perma.cc/T9EH-KXEG].

Just as a leader should aim to use approaches that strengthen team morale and effectiveness, the leader should also strive to maintain a healthy relationship with their supervisor, whether a faculty advisor or a senior editor.[29] Leaders who nurture a relationship with their supervisor and take steps to improve their supervisor's efficiency end up contributing to the overall success of the organization.[30] This concept, known as "managing up," not only helps build the supervisor-supervisee relationship but allows the supervisee to use this connection to anticipate their supervisor's needs and the needs of the organization.[31] In a nutshell, the best relationships depend on effective communication.

Effective communication takes hard work, especially if the individuals prefer different leadership styles that do not mesh easily. In the beginning, take time to learn as much about the preferred communication and leadership styles of everyone you work with regularly, whether as the supervisor or supervisee. By doing so, you will become more aware of other leadership styles and better able to appreciate what others can contribute to the group.[32]

As they say, "Birds of a feather flock together." In other words, individuals with similar leadership and communication approaches tend to work better together and gravitate toward each other. But working only with those who share your preferences may lead to missed opportunities and mistakes that could have been avoided by consulting with a more diverse group.[33]

E. Leadership Tactics

While selecting a leadership style is important, law review leaders can also adopt tactics that can help prevent certain issues from arising in the first place.

---

29. Luke Burton, *15 Managing up Techniques You Can Use Every Day in Student Affairs*, PRESENCE (Aug. 22, 2019), https://www.presence.io/blog/15-managing-up-techniques-you-can-use-every-day-in-student-affairs [https://perma.cc/W9T5-BL9Z].

30. Miller, *supra* note 28.

31. *Id.*

32. Lisa Rabasca Roepe, *How to Manage Different Workplace Personalities*, SHRM (May 12, 2020), https://www.shrm.org/resourcesandtools/hr-topics/people-managers/pages/managing-different-personalities-.aspx [https://perma.cc/GZ63-DP73]; Brett Relander, *How to Merge Differing Management Styles into a Cohesive Team*, ENTREPRENEUR (Aug. 4, 2015), https://www.entrepreneur.com/article/248074 [https://perma.cc/X8VQ-8ZNY].

33. Roepe, *supra* note 32.

This section suggests tactics new editors should consider implementing to improve journal operations.

1. Understand the law review constitution, bylaws, and other policies

"Knowledge is power in leadership."[34] While editors are encouraged to be creative and innovative, they must stay within the confines of their organization's constitution, bylaws, and other law review and school policies. As discussed in Chapters 2 and 3 of this *Manual*, editors must locate these policies, review them carefully, and seek clarification from the faculty advisor or other key law school administrators. They must then strive to follow and implement them during their tenure.

Understanding these foundational documents will allow editors to fulfill their leadership duties by communicating critical information to members at the right time. As just a few examples, the editors will be able to inform members when and how to register for academic credit, set writing timelines to ensure members qualify for financial aid, and develop timekeeping procedures to document that journal members have completed sufficient hours to earn academic credit.

Understanding the law review constitution and bylaws will also allow journal leaders to help others predict issues that might arise. For example, most constitutions or bylaws include provisions to remove editors or members. Take that as a sign that editors or members may act in ways to trigger removal procedures. Then consider how you can help that issue from occurring during your year. As with most leadership matters, the key is communication. Ensure that journal editors and members understand their responsibilities and the consequences that may attach for failing to fulfill those responsibilities.

Also, developing the ability to read, understand, and implement policies is a skill and a sign of professionalism. By showing the faculty advisor and other law school administrators that you have read and are following key policies will enhance both your personal reputation and the journal's reputation.

---

34. Rhode, *supra* note 5, at 1629.

2. Listen

While leaders may have the skills to jump in and take control, a good leader knows it's impossible to run a journal alone. A critical skill in working with others is listening. A leader often has their own ideas about how to proceed. But because the journal is full of talented individuals, other editors and members also have ideas about a variety of journal-related matters. Leaders should objectively listen to all ideas and avoid shutting down those that initially seem irrelevant. Listening intently may reveal an underlying strength in a seemingly weak idea or uncover a hidden pitfall in an otherwise strong suggestion. One strategy to improve listening skills is for the leader to speak last, not first, on any issue.

Listening is also a critical skill when moderating internal conflicts. Even though you, as the leader, may need to make a tough decision, the "losing" person or side will be more likely to accept the decision with grace and move forward as part of the team if they feel like you took time to hear their perspective in advance. In this context, listening often involves allowing others to vent, which might cause you to feel uncomfortable. Remember that you need not respond to every point someone raises; instead, ask them what remedy they seek and why—and then continue to listen. Also, asking questions instead of making statements can help show that you are listening instead of defending a specific position.

3. Establish and maintain deadlines

By the end of their first semester, most law students begin to realize the importance of deadlines. Deadlines are pivotal in keeping the wheels of justice constantly in motion. Unsurprisingly, they appear in almost every part of the legal process. For example, for most civil complaints, the opposing party is given thirty days to file an answer and respond to the pleading. In a criminal case, a defendant must assert their notice and intent to appeal a trial decision within days after the verdict is entered. Law journal editors must incorporate deadlines to produce a journal that is published on time.

To set these timelines, learn each step in the publication process (from article selection to final page-proof review) and speak with outgoing editors, the faculty advisor, and any law school staff assigned to work with the law review about how much time each step in the publishing process typically takes. Then work backward from your desired publication date. Be sure to build in time along the way for the inevitable delays that might occur: the author or an editor working on a piece becomes ill, the author includes rewrites that will send the piece back to cite-checking, or a key source must be ordered through interlibrary loan.

Communicate these deadlines early and often, use them to prioritize work, and select a leadership style that will allow you to keep the team motivated and working hard to stay on course. A journal that misses its publication deadlines is not one that will attract top authors, as their careers often depend on the journal appearing when it is supposed to.

4. Team check-ins

Team check-ins are another practical tactic to consider—especially for those who favor a coaching or democratic leadership approach. A leader may want to divide journal members into cite-checking teams that include individuals with various legal writing and editorial skills so they have an opportunity to learn from one another. To advance individual skills and stay on deadline, the leader may want to schedule regular team check-ins where staff members share issues and feedback with team leaders. Team check-ins can take place weekly, bi-weekly, or at whatever frequency is necessary to meet each deadline and the overall cadence of the editing process.

Check-ins allow the team members and leader to get to know each other better (rather than working in isolation), which in and of itself can help prevent conflicts. They also allow the leader to gauge whether team members understand their assignment and how it relates to overarching journal processes and goals, which can make members feel like important contributors instead of mere cogs. And check-ins can help leaders see when members are tired, frustrated, or not putting in enough effort and course-correct before a deadline is blown.

5. Retrospective meetings with returning members

While some people choose not to live in the past, we can often learn from the past. For law review leaders, it is important to examine the past to identify areas for improvement. Similar to the team check-ins discussed above, scheduling retrospective meetings with returning journal members is another practical tactic to consider. At the beginning of each semester, consider holding individual or small-group meetings with returning members to seek their input on processes, climate, and content. These members are not part of board meetings, so their input might otherwise be lost. By tackling old problems, you can provide the journal with a clean slate on which to operate more effectively.

6. Performance improvement plans

A final tactic is to consider developing individual performance improvement plans for underperforming members. While some may view performance plans as disciplinary, they can be constructive tools for professional growth and assessment. Although a pacesetting leader might tend to remove a member from a project or recommend a subpar grade, a coaching leader might strive to improve the team member's skills by articulating benchmarks the team member must meet, the schedule on which the benchmarks must be met, and resources the member can use (whether training materials or consulting with another person) to meet the benchmarks. The coach would frame this plan in terms of skill building instead of remediation or punishment.

Of course, the team members' attitude and receptiveness are key. A person who is offended and defensive likely won't accept the challenge to improve. But others might be grateful for the guidance and additional opportunity. If the member accepts the challenge and succeeds, the staff member will gain new skills that will benefit the journal. While this tactic may require additional focus and attention from both the leader and the member, helping an existing member succeed is often more palatable than losing or attempting to replace the member.

F. Handling Other Sticky Situations

As discussed earlier, it is important for editors to understand and get to know those they supervise and those to whom they report. This understanding provides context and perspective to ideas and can also be useful when conflicts arise. The next discussion examines common sticky situations that editors should be prepared to handle.

1. Faculty advisors

Contrary to popular belief, great minds do not always think alike. No matter what leadership style you choose, your style may conflict with that of your faculty advisor. And that is okay! Similar to the role you play as a peer supervisor, your faculty supervisor is there to help and provide feedback; they do not want to see you or the journal fail. When differences of opinion or style emerge, engage—don't withdraw.

To help develop a positive working relationship, consider setting up standing appointments or check-ins with your faculty advisor to report on the journal's progress and any issues that you are struggling to resolve. Regular meetings allow your faculty advisor to serve as a resource. Faculty advisors have the benefit of experience and likely have seen past editors address similar situations. Regular meetings also create another professional building block and networking opportunity where the faculty advisor can see first-hand how you handle issues and potentially recommend you for opportunities that require similar skills.

2. Negative peer feedback

Because you are working primarily with peers, even though your name may appear higher on the masthead than another member's, editors are likely to face trials when other members perceive themselves to be as equally or more qualified. The non-editor may challenge your approach or authority. Or they may tell you or others that you are not performing your role well.

Although it may be difficult, especially at first, embrace this negative feedback. Think about whether the feedback is actually true (even in part). Listen to the other person's perspective; ask questions to understand their position more deeply and completely. And truly be open to change. If you are flexible and exhibit a growth mindset, your team will be inclined to protect you and give you constructive input to assist your performance (as opposed to gossiping behind your back or becoming disgruntled and not completing assignments).

For example, if a staff member feels like the editor constantly picks distasteful articles and voices this concern to the editor, the best approach is for the editor to welcome the feedback as a gift. Also consider creative solutions, like inviting the member to participate in the article selection process for the next publication. This solution may be impractical for journals utilizing a lead articles selection process, as that process is often limited to one or a few senior editors and has a significant impact on the ideological dynamic of the journal. Still, for other journals, this type of solution creates both a learning opportunity for the editor and a networking opportunity for both parties, thus turning a seemingly negative situation into a positive team-building endeavor that will benefit both students and the journal.

3. Ethical issues

Leaders must make ethical decisions on a daily basis. On a law review, a leader may also face ethical issues involving favoritism, competition, and professional isolation. Peer supervision can produce the same ethical issues that tend to arise when dealing with friends in the workplace—perceptions that the friends get better assignments, higher compensation (translate to grades or awards), and more access to the leader and "inside information."

Leaders are key in determining organizational climate. Studies show that leaders tend to be responsible for 60% of workplace misconduct.[35] If the leader does not exemplify high levels of ethics and integrity, the rest of the team will lose trust and confidence. By promoting unethical practices, a leader also runs the risk of these poor practices trickling down to the staff.

For example, a leader may decide to "cut corners" by deleting critical citations from an author's article to preserve length or meet a deadline. A staff member who observes this conduct might then emulate the conduct and remove citations from their own student article—which, if the piece is ever accepted for publication—could result in charge of plagiarism and reputational damage.

Ideas to build an organization with high ethics include surveying members once a semester about processes and climate. Creating an ombuds position might also help: a member with a concern could approach the ombuds for advice and input, and the ombudsperson could provide feedback to the editorial board. Another idea is to create ethics exercises and use them as ice-breakers in team meetings throughout the year. These steps may help the journal identify potential or perceived ethical issues more quickly and develop effective solutions to ensure that the organization remains strong.

4. Editor isolation

When a peer is elevated to leader, a power differential emerges. The leader's relationships with classmates and friends change. They often cannot share sensitive information and must create professional boundaries to effectively supervise—and potentially discipline—those with whom they take classes and play intramural sports. As such, peer leaders can often feel isolated.

---

35. Dori Meinert, *Creating an Ethical Workplace*, SHRM (Apr. 1, 2014), https://www.shrm.org/hr-today/news/hr-magazine/pages/0414-ethical-workplace-culture.aspx [https://perma.cc/L448-CELQ].

Asking faculty advisors and past editors to develop training sessions and materials for new editors about leadership challenges is something to consider. Another idea is for senior editors to routinely touch base with other editors informally. Still other ideas include regular social gatherings for editors and finding peers with similar positions on other journals who can understand the editor's challenges and with whom the editor can safely share their true feelings.

KEY TAKEAWAYS

- An effective leader can identify which leadership style works best for them, their team, and their organization in different situations and also understands that others may not share their same preference in leadership style.
- Clear and frequent communication is required for effective leadership.
- Good leaders listen and also learn how to be good followers.
- Leaders should get to know their team members and welcome honest and constructive feedback.
- An effective leader exemplifies high ethical standards.
- Problems will arise but implementing smart tactics will help editors avoid some issues and identify others before they disrupt journal operations.

10

Selecting Journal Candidates

The Purpose and the Process

Wes E. Henricksen

LEARNING OBJECTIVES

After reviewing this Chapter, editors will be able to

- critique the various selection methods journals use to determine eligibility for membership;
- recognize how selection criteria can lead to the underrepresentation of POC, women, first-generation, part-time, and evening students on journals; and
- explain how selection committees can address diversity and equity issues while ensuring that the process yields highly qualified candidates.

A. Introduction

Journals play an important role in producing and publishing legal scholarship, which helps shape the development of the law.[1] They also play an important role in enhancing the careers of student members, which helps shape the legal profession.[2] Therefore, journals must tailor their selection methods to ensure

1. *See* Charles E. Hughes, *Foreword*, 50 YALE L.J. 737 (1941); Douglas B. Maggs, *Concerning the Extent to Which the Law Review Contributes to the Development of the Law*, 3 S. CAL. L. REV. 181 (1930).

2. *See* JEFF DEAVER, THE COMPLETE LAW SCHOOL COMPANION: HOW TO EXCEL AT AMERICA'S MOST DEMANDING POST-GRADUATE CURRICULUM 170 (1984); Max Stier, Kelly

that those who have the greatest chance of contributing to the law and the profession are selected to join.

Journals have historically addressed this need by crafting merit-based selection criteria. But no uniform approach has emerged. Instead, criteria and formulas vary greatly, even at the same journal over time. Accordingly, although most journals select new members based on merit-based criteria, what counts as merit at one journal—such as finishing the first year ranked in the top ten percent of the class—may be given no weight at another journal.

Also, merit-based criteria do not always adequately address the overarching aim of ensuring that those with the greatest chance of contributing to the law and the profession are selected. Consider the following: Imagine that a journal selects all or most of its new members based on first-year student grades. By using this process, most, if not all, positions will be filled by students whose first-year grades put them above a specific threshold, such as the top six percent cut-off used by the University of Miami.[3] Although students selected will be top-performing academically, this restrictive selection method will miss students who would be a great fit for journal but did not earn top grades in all their first-year classes.

For example, some students who are excellent writers and editors, and could therefore contribute enormously, may have aced their first-year legal writing course but may not have scored as well on their timed doctrinal essay exams. Students who fit this description include those who excel at writing and editing if given enough time to complete the assignment, but who do not perform as well under the strict time constraints of essay and multiple-choice exams. These excellent writers might be passed over in a pure or primarily grade-on selection process.

A pure or primarily grade-on process would also exclude transfer students who performed exceedingly well at their original school. In addition, the journal would be excluding upper-level students who needed a semester or two to acclimate to law school. Many first-generation students enter law school without the benefit of a mentor to guide them, so they must navigate the complexities of law school on their own. While many first-generation students end up excelling, it may take some time.

M. Klaus, Dan L. Bagatell & Jeffrey J. Rachlinski, *Law Review Usage and Suggestions for Improvement: A Survey of Attorneys, Professors, and Judges*, 44 STAN. L. REV. 1467, 1487–88 (1992).

3. *Membership*, U. MIAMI L. REV. (last visited Jan. 22, 2022), https://lawreview.law.miami.edu/membership [https://perma.cc/7CJ8-XSWR].

Finally, and perhaps most importantly, a restrictive grades-only selection method virtually ensures the journal will be composed largely of relatively privileged law students. Students who come from more privileged academic and economic backgrounds and likely know others who have completed law school have an enormous advantage over students who lack such contacts and connections. Thus, a grades-only approach would almost certainly result in a homogenous, non-diverse membership. Indeed, several authors have lamented this result at many journals.[4]

Accordingly, journals should carefully and consciously tailor their selection methods to ensure meritorious and fair criteria that will result in members who are most likely to contribute to the law and profession. The selection criteria should address not only work ethic and writing and editing skills, but inclusiveness and diversity as well. Studying the different ways journals have crafted selection methods shows that many options are available.

This Chapter will give a brief overview of different membership selection methods. First, the Chapter will discuss the different ways journals choose members. Second, the Chapter will discuss ways that journals have often overlooked certain students who, although they are likely to contribute to the journal's mission and goals significantly, are nevertheless underrepresented on journals. These students include first-generation, part-time, evening, POC, women, and other underprivileged or disadvantaged students. Finally, the Chapter will suggest how journals can ensure that their selection criteria address diversity and equity issues while ensuring that the members selected are most likely to contribute to the law and the profession.

B. Methods of Getting onto a Journal

Historically, law schools nearly uniformly used first-year grades as the sole criteria for selecting members. In the 1960s, however, journals began implementing a writing competition to select applicants for their actual writing

4. *See generally, e.g.*, Lauren A. Graber, *Are We There Yet? Progress Toward Gender-Neutral Legal Education*, 33 B.C. J.L. & Soc. Just. 45 (2013); Mark A. Godsey, *Educational Inequalities, the Myth of Meritocracy, and the Silencing of Minority Voices: The Need for Diversity on America's Law Reviews*, 12 Harv. Blackletter L.J. 59 (1995). For more information about diversity, equity, and inclusion on law reviews, see Chapter 4 of this *Manual*.

and editing skills rather than their performance on exams.[5] Today, most law schools and journals generally use some combination of first-year law school grades, performance in a writing competition, and submission of other materials or exercises. Additionally, some journals offer membership opportunities to students who independently submit a publishable article or participate in a separate competition for transfer students.

When a student earns membership on a journal purely through first-year grades, it is called "grading-on." A student invited purely based on their performance in the write-on competition is "writing-on." A student chosen based on a combination of grades and performance in the write-on competition is "combining-on."

Some journals also accept members who submit a publishable student casenote or comment; this process is called "noting-on." Finally, some journals—most often specialty journals—offer membership to all who apply, regardless of grades, competition, or other criteria. This process is called "walking-on." Below is a brief overview of each selection method.

1. Grade-on

Grading-on is the oldest method of gaining membership to a journal. Historically, grades were how most, if not all, journal members were selected.[6] From the journal's perspective, the advantage of this selection method is that it is effortless. It simply involves coming up with a cut-off threshold, such as the top 10 percent of students, and inviting those above the threshold to join.

Although the write-on competition has played a greater role in recent decades, most flagship law reviews and specialty journals still offer membership opportunities to students through a pure grade-on avenue.

For example, in a recent year, the Boston College Law Review selected fifteen members through grade-on and five members through write-on.[7] This decision meant that journal membership was offered to the top 15 students in the first-year class at Boston College Law School. The remaining students gained membership by scoring in the top five in the write-on competition.

---

5. Kristin Booth Glen, *When and Where We Enter: Rethinking Admission to the Legal Profession*, 102 Colum. L. Rev. 1696, 1722 n.100 (2002).

6. Lorenzo A. Trujillo, *The Relationship Between Law School and the Bar Exam: A Look at Assessment and Student Success*, 78 U. Colo. L. Rev. 69, 91 (2007); Roger C. Cramton, *"The Most Remarkable Institution": The American Law Review*, 36 J. Legal Educ. 1, 5 (1986).

7. Graber, *supra* note 4.

The New York Law School Law Review likewise chooses most of its members through grade-on. An invitation to join the New York Law School Law Review is extended to the top 15 percent of students, based on class rank, at the end of their first year, and to the top 10 percent of students, including those who transferred in and evening students, at the end of the second year.[8]

The University of Chicago Law Review has a more nuanced approach to the grade-on selection method. It extends grade-on invitations to the top 20 students based on first-year class rank.[9] However, to get a grade-on invitation, the student must rank in the top 20, participate in the write-on competition, and score in the top 60 percent of the competition. In addition, another 30 students are selected based solely on their performance in the write-on competition.[10] While grade-on invitations are often contingent upon participating in the write-on competition, what makes The University of Chicago Law Review's approach unique is its double threshold: top 20 rank and top 60 percent performance in the competition.

The Stetson Law Review presents another approach. It extends a grade-on offer to join the law review to students who rank in the top four percent of their first-year class (cumulative) and receive a 3.25 or above in Research & Writing I.[11] It has a second grade-on round after the spring semester. At that time, the Stetson Law Review extends grade-on offers to any student who ranks in the top seven percent of their class (cumulative), regardless of their performance in Research & Writing I and II.[12]

Accordingly, although the grade-on selection criteria appear simple at first glance, journals often add nuances by considering other factors such as performance in the write-on competition, the first-year legal research and writing course, or an editing exercise. Some also require and consider personal statements.

---

8. *Law Review*, N.Y. L. Sch. (last visited Jan. 22, 2022), https://www.nyls.edu/academics/specialty-areas/law-review-and-journals/law-review [https://perma.cc/239P-9U8W].

9. *Becoming a Member*, U. Chi. L. Rev. (Apr. 22, 2019), https://lawreview.uchicago.edu/sites/lawreview.uchicago.edu/files/v87%20Letter%20to%201Ls%20FINAL.pdf [https://perma.cc/KH63-M4VA].

10. *Id.*

11. *Stetson Law Review—How to Become a Member*, Stetson U. Coll. L. (last visited Jan. 22, 2022), https://www.stetson.edu/law/lawreview/student-resources.php [https://perma.cc/MYZ9-PZ84].

12. *Id.*

2. Write-on

In the 1960s, journals began phasing in a new way of assessing candidates: the write-on competition.[13] Today, the write-on competition typically involves the main assignment and one or more additional components, such as an editing exercise or a personal statement.

a. The main assignment: Casenotes and comments

At most law schools, the core component of the write-on competition is the main assignment. In the main assignment, candidates must write a persuasive or objective paper in which the student analyzes a legal issue. This assignment can be called a brief, memorandum, or essay. For our purposes, we shall call it the "submission paper."

The journal provides candidates with detailed instructions on the submission paper requirements. Many journals hold one or more mandatory orientation sessions for those who want to participate in the write-on competition or be considered for journal membership. Other journals may offer on-demand videos in lieu of live programs that walk students through the type of submission paper they must prepare.

These instructions include the following:

- what issue the students must analyze, or whether they must find their own issue;
- what authorities the students can rely on in preparing their submission paper;
- formatting requirements, including page limits or word counts and whether to use footnotes or endnotes;
- the submission deadline; and
- rules regarding collaboration and seeking help.[14]

Submission papers are normally graded blindly, identified only by a number that the graders cannot associate with a particular candidate. Candidates are cautioned not to share their numbers with anyone else, whether on the journal or not. The score assigned to a submission paper is typically based

---

13. Cramton, *supra* note 6, at 6.

14. Wes Henricksen, Making Law Review: A Guide to the Write-on Competition 32 (2d ed. 2017).

on several criteria, such as soundness of the legal analysis, persuasiveness, use of authorities, grammar, punctuation, and adherence to the competition instructions.[15] Often, journals have two or more graders review every submission paper to ensure each paper is given a fair assessment. At some journals, most editors read all papers while one or two editors are assigned to grade citation form.

The two frequently used submission papers are the "casenote," which analyzes a single case, and the "comment," which analyzes a particular area of the law.[16] Professor Elizabeth Fajans and Professor Mary R. Falk's book titled *Scholarly Writing for Law Students* provides a comprehensive discussion about different submission papers.[17]

The differences between these two kinds of submission papers are important. Let us turn first to casenotes. A casenote must analyze the law and reach an original conclusion about why the court decided the issue correctly or incorrectly. As articulated by Professors Fajans and Falk,

> a successful casenote always looks beyond a court's articulated reasons for its decision and beyond the dissent's articulated reasons for disagreement. It is, therefore, never sufficient to argue that the majority is correct for the very reasons the majority advances, nor is it sufficient to argue that the majority is wrong for the very reasons advanced by the dissent.[18]

When designing and preparing a write-on competition problem involving a casenote submission paper, journal members should be aware that casenotes may be framed in several different ways. As categorized by Professors Fajans and Falk, a candidate could, for example, argue that the result was incorrect because the court failed to look at the larger social context or because the court's interpretation is at odds with the goals of the statute. Conversely, the candidate could argue that the result was correct, but that the court failed to propose a

---

15. *See, e.g.*, *Case Note Scoring Rubric*, *in* Mitchell Hamline Law Review, 2020–2021 Writing Competition Handbook 24–25 (2020), https://mitchellhamline.edu/law-review/wp-content/uploads/sites/37/2020/05/MHLRWriteOnHandbook_2020.pdf [https://perma.cc/T76A-5KRF].

16. Henricksen, *supra* note 14, at 33.

17. Elizabeth Fajans & Mary R. Falk, Scholarly Writing for Law Students: Seminar Papers, Law Review Notes and Law Review Competition Papers 5–13 (5th ed. 2017).

18. *Id.* at 10.

clear standard for future guidance. These are merely representative examples; Professors Fajans and Falk provide additional examples in their book.[19]

The structure of a casenote is "virtually unvarying": "introduction, background, analysis, conclusion."[20] The introduction "describes the case and its holding very briefly and plainly states the writer's thesis."[21] The introduction also "provides a roadmap: 'Part I describes X; Part II analyzes Y.'"[22] The background section should include a summary of the facts of the case, its procedural history, and the court's reasoning, as well as that of any concurring or dissenting opinions.[23]

The analysis section accounts for the majority of the submission paper and contains the substance of the writer's claim. For example, it states why the court got it right or wrong and what the correct outcome should have been. The conclusion is a short summary of the analysis and may also address issues raised by the writer's claim.[24]

Although less common, some write-on competitions require students to draft a comment. A comment, unlike a casenote, analyzes an area of law rather than any particular case. As with casenotes, a candidate could take a variety of approaches to the topic.[25] Professor Richard Delgado has identified "at least ten" distinct subcategories of comments:[26]

- the *case cruncher*, which analyzes case law that is in flux or is suffering from split decisions and applies public policy to identify a solution;
- the *law reform article*, which scrutinizes a black letter law that results in unjust decisions and proffers a change to avoid the negative result in the future;
- the *legislative note*, which critically dissects and evaluates the merits and deficiencies of proposed or enacted legislation and, if warranted, suggests changes to achieve the desired result;

---

19. *Id.* at 10–11 (footnotes omitted).
20. *Id.* at 12.
21. *Id.*
22. *Id.*
23. *Id.*
24. *Id.*
25. HENRICKSEN, *supra* note 14, at 35.
26. Richard Delgado, *How to Write a Law Review Article*, 20 U.S.F. L. REV. 445, 446–47 (1986).

- the *interdisciplinary article*, which demonstrates how the integration of other disciplines, such as psychology or sociology, can enhance the law's ability to deal with the specified issue;[27]
- the *theory-fitting article*, which explores new developments in an area of law and proposes a new legal theory that arises from the development;
- the *discussion of the legal field*, which spotlights different aspects of the legal profession, including new or changing legal terminology and legal education;
- *revisiting a pre-existing legal debate*; for example, "[i]n an influential article in the *W Law Review*, Professor X argued Z. Critics, including Professor Y, attacked her view, arguing A, B, and C. This Article offers D, a new approach to the problem of Z";
- the *legal history article*, which details the development of a legal rule from inception to current use;
- the *comparative law article*, which evaluates how other legal systems handle a specific legal issue and then contrasts that system with how the United States legal system approaches the same issue; and
- the *empirical research* article, which reports the results of a study that uses data derived from actual observation or experimentation.[28]

Like casenotes, comments include an introduction, a background section, an analysis section, and a short conclusion. These sections are identical to those of a casenote, except that the comment deals with an area of the law rather than critiquing the outcome of a particular case.

b. The citation or proofreading exercise

Many write-on competitions include a citation and proofreading exercise. This exercise typically consists of pages of body text and footnotes (or it may simply contain footnotes) containing dozens of intentionally planted errors. The student's job is to find the errors and correct them, using the editing symbols provided to the student in the competition materials. Students are typically instructed to use the *ALWD Guide*, *The Bluebook: A Uniform System for Citation*, or some other citation manual as a guide for correcting the cita-

27. *Id.* at 446–48.

28. *Id.*; *see also* FAJANS & FALK, *supra* note 17, at 6–8.

tions. Students may also be instructed to use *The Redbook: A Manual on Legal Style* when editing text.

These exercises often test everything from typos and misspellings to extra spaces and whether a particular comma should be italicized. Like other parts of the write-on competition, the editing or proofreading exercise was historically paper-based. But in recent years, more journals have shifted their write-on competitions, including the editing or proofreading exercise, to electronic form.

c. The personal statement

Some journals also require write-on students to submit a personal statement that competition graders then use to assess candidates' writing and editing abilities. The journal will often provide detailed instructions about what topics or questions a candidate should address. For instance, the prompt might ask students to discuss why they want to be on the journal or why they might be a particularly good fit for a specialty journal. Other competition instructions give a more open-ended prompt, such as, "Tell us about yourself."

d. Write-on variations

Journals structure their write-on competition differently, with each presenting a distinct mix of different components, such as the main assignment, editing exercise, and personal statement. For example, the write-on competition at the University of San Diego School of Law (USD) is a ten-day competition immediately after spring finals.[29] The USD write-on competition "has two components: (1) a two-issue closed memorandum, and (2) about twenty Bluebook citation corrections."[30] The competition does not include a personal statement. The editors judge candidates "according to writing style, legal analysis, organization, and Bluebook accuracy."[31] The San Diego Law Review accepts about 35 to 45 students every year. Students in the top 2.5 percent based on first-year class rank receive grade-on invitations, while the rest are invited based entirely on their write-on competition performance.[32]

---

29. *Academic Journals*, U. San Diego Sch. L. (last visited Jan. 22, 2022), https://www.sandiego.edu/law/academics/journals/sdlr/competition.php [https://perma.cc/GH7Q-4XEB].

30. *Id.*

31. *Id.*

32. *Id.*

The California Law Review, on the other hand, accepts all members via a write-on competition. The law review does not extend grade-on invitations or consider grades in any way when selecting members. The write-on competition at the University of California, Berkeley includes a comment, an editing packet, and a personal statement.[33] The California Law Review offers a separate write-on competition for transfer students.[34]

The Emory International Law Review, like many specialty journals, selects members out of its law school's general write-on competition. The Emory competition includes submitting a casenote, a Bluebook citation quiz, and a personal statement.[35] The Emory International Law Review selects members based on the following formula:

- 40% casenote;
- 30% Bluebook citation quiz;
- 20% personal statement; and
- 10% first-semester grade point average.[36]

Of course, the line between writing-on, grading-on, and combining-on is often vague. Many students who "write-on" are, in fact, likely combining-on because grades are considered, even if only a little bit. The Emory International Law Review's selection criteria above show a case-in-point. Likewise, many students who grade-on must nevertheless participate in, or even score well in, the write-on competition.

3. Combine-on

Most journal members likely obtain their position through a combination of criteria. This combine-on process is analogous to the law school admissions process because it involves measuring multiple quantitative scores to come up with a single composite number or ranking to determine who receives an offer. The law school admissions process considers a candidate's undergraduate

---

33. *Write-on*, Cal. L. Rev. (last visited Jan. 22, 2022), https://www.californialawreview.org/about/write-on [https://perma.cc/FY9B-ZXF4].

34. *Id.*

35. *Emory International Law Review: Write-on Frequently Asked Questions*, Emory Int'l L. Rev. (last visited Jan. 22, 2022), https://law.emory.edu/eilr/write-on.html [https://perma.cc/Q294-QVZ9].

36. *Id.*

GPA and LSAT scores, while the journal's the combine-on process considers a candidate's first-year grades and write-on competition score.

Journals weigh the various criteria differently. For example, the Michigan Law Review reviews students' performance in four categories: (1) a write-on competition submission; (2) grades from the six required first-year courses, plus legal practice; (3) a personal statement; and (4) a note proposal.[37] The review does not impose a GPA cut-off, so students are eligible to apply for membership as long as they are in good academic standing after the first year. The Michigan Law Review does not disclose how it weighs these four criteria. But the editors do clarify that "[a]n applicant's performance in the Writing Competition is a more significant factor in the selection process than [their] GPA."[38]

The Rutgers University Law Review selects most of its members through a pure write-on process involving a student comment and a citation exercise. Once these write-on members are selected, the Rutgers University Law Review may then select "additional staff members based on the combined average of the submission's grade and the author's grade point average."[39] The journal does not indicate how much relative weight is given to each criterion. Likewise, the Buffalo Law Review selects 20 out of approximately 30 members based on a combination of first-year grades, a Bluebook exercise exam, and a write-on casenote submission paper.[40] Although the Buffalo Law Review does not disclose the exact formula used to calculate the combine-on score, its website states the following: "Each year some students with straight A's who complete the competition are not offered admission. Likewise, each year we accept some students with few A's."[41] This system makes sense, given that "[b]eing a member of the law review requires more than the mere ability to garner an A on an exam."[42]

---

37. *Michigan Law Review Applicant Packet*, Mich. L. Rev. (Apr. 1, 2014), http://michiganlawreview.org/wp-content/uploads/2014/09/applicant-packet.pdf[https://perma.cc/75E4-SUHK].

38. *Id.*

39. *Staff Selection*, Rutgers U. L. Rev. (last visited Jan. 22, 2022), https://rutgerslawreview.com/about/staff-selection [https://perma.cc/6Y6Y-DHM2].

40. *Becoming a Member of the Buffalo Law Review*, Buff. L. Rev. (last visited Jan. 22, 2022), http://www.buffalolawreview.org/membership.php [https://perma.cc/33WU-NQFE].

41. *Id.*

42. *Id.*

4. Note-on

Some journals offer students an opportunity to gain membership by submitting a full-length, publishable student casenote or comment. The Michigan Law Review offers the opportunity to note-on. To be eligible, students must submit a publishable casenote and meet other criteria such as having at least two semesters remaining in law school and being the sole author of the casenote; the student must not have written the note for class credit.[43] The student may also be a member of another journal at Michigan Law and need not give up that editorial position; instead, they may join the Michigan Law Review as an associate editor and serve in both positions simultaneously, as long as the student can carry out their work on the Michigan Law Review effectively.[44]

Other journals that offer the note-on avenue to membership include Columbia Law Review,[45] Florida State University Law Review,[46] Hofstra Law Review,[47] University of Illinois Law Review,[48] and Virginia Law Review.[49]

5. Walk-on

Through the "walk-on" process, "all students are invited to become members."[50] Flagship journals rarely offer walk-on opportunities. But some specialty journals offer membership to any student interested in joining. While

---

43. *Michigan Law Review Note-on Policy*, Mich. L. Rev. (last updated Apr. 2020), http://michiganlawreview.org/wp-content/uploads/2014/06/Vol.-119-Note-On-Policy-.pdf [https://perma.cc/F4EX-S6QG].

44. *Id.*

45. *Publishable Notes Program*, Colum. L. Rev. (last visited Jan. 22, 2022), https://live-columbia-law-review.pantheonsite.io/publishable-notes-program [https://perma.cc/4H8V-CXEL].

46. *Prospective Members*, Fla. St. U. L. Rev. (last visited Jan. 22, 2022), https://www.fsulawreview.com/about-us/prospective-members [https://perma.cc/2TWT-KYPE].

47. *Membership Selection*, Hofstra L. Rev. (last visited Jan. 22, 2022), https://www.hofstralawreview.org/about/membership-selection [https://perma.cc/8KLN-3JCV].

48. *Membership*, U. Ill. L. Rev. (last visited Jan. 22, 2022), https://publish.illinois.edu/lawreview/about [https://perma.cc/C3SN-K4X4].

49. *Becoming a Member*, Va. L. Rev. (last visited Jan. 22, 2022), https://www.virginialawreview.org/becoming-a-member [https://perma.cc/V3JD-BD2W].

50. Frederick Ramos, Note, *Affirmative Action on Law Reviews: An Empirical Study of Its Status and Effect*, 22 U. Mich. J.L. Reform 179, 191 n.46 (1988).

some specialty journals take every student who desires to join, others do not consider walk-ons full members until they write a publishable casenote.[51]

Some journals refer to "walking-on" whenever they offer membership to a student who was not required to complete the write-on competition. That is, some journals call grading-on "walking-on." For example, the various journals at the University of Miami School of Law offer grade-on options at different thresholds for each journal. However, they call that process walking-on.[52]

At Yale Law School, however, the only competitive journal is the Yale Law Journal. The school's other eight journals, such as the Yale Journal on Regulation, Yale Law & Policy Review, and Yale Journal of Law & the Humanities, are noncompetitive, offering any student interested the opportunity to walk on.[53]

C. Ways to Ensure the Selection Criteria Address Diversity, Inclusion, and Equity

As discussed in Chapter 4 of this *Manual*, diversity and inclusion considerations are key components of managing a journal. However, many journals' selection methods run counter to these considerations and result in members being selected based on criteria that do not necessarily correlate with success on the journal. These selection methods also exclude some highly qualified candidates who have a lot to contribute. Accordingly, how journal candidates are selected can impact diversity and inclusion.

The selection methods used by many journals have historically resulted in POC, women, and first-generation law students being underrepresented.[54]

---

51. *Id.*

52. *2012 Competition Instructions*, U. MIAMI L. REV. (last updated June 5, 2012), https://lawreview.law.miami.edu/wp-content/uploads/2012/06/Competition-Instructions.pdf [https://perma.cc/KW2P-W9HB]; *see also 2020 Writing Competition Rules and Instructions*, U. MIAMI L. REV. (last updated June 17, 2020), http://lawreview.law.miami.edu/wp-content/uploads/2020/07/2020-Law-Review-Writing-Competition-Rules-and-Instructions.final_.pdf [https://perma.cc/WJ42-R3UU].

53. *Interview with Asha Rangappa, Associate Dean of Yale Law School*, TOP L. SCHS. (July 2010), https://www.top-law-schools.com/asha-rangappa-interview.html [https://perma.cc/87RJ-WG4A].

54. *See* Godsey, *supra* note 4, at 61 (POC law students); Graber, *supra* note 4, at 57 (women law students); Nancy Leong, *A Noteworthy Absence*, 59 J. LEGAL EDUC. 279, 288 (2009) (women law students); Adriane Kayoko Peralta, *The Underrepresentation of Women of Color in Law Review Leadership Positions*, 25 BERKELEY LA RAZA L.J. 69, 84 (2015) (first-generation law students).

Thus, journals should evaluate their selection method and implement new methods that counteract this undesirable result. Because most journals use anonymous selection systems, those in charge of selecting the next cohort of journal members often assume the selection process is unbiased. In truth, cultural biases of the journal submission graders and educational obstacles faced by POC, women, and first-generation students have resulted in the underrepresentation of highly qualified students who, if selected, would contribute significantly to the journal.[55]

Journals can implement several measures to ensure that a more diverse pool of candidates has an opportunity to join. Below are a few suggestions for how journals can ensure the selection criteria address diversity, inclusion, and equity.

1. Broadcast the opportunity

One of the greatest obstacles to POC, women, part-time evening, and first-generation law students joining a journal is the failure to appreciate the importance of journal membership and its potentially enormous impact on the student's career. A common refrain is, "As a first-generation law student, I had no idea what journal was, let alone how to join. If I could go back in time I never would have skipped the write-on competition." This situation happens disproportionately to POC students and those from underprivileged or disadvantaged backgrounds.

Accordingly, the journal has a responsibility to educate the first-year students on the importance of journal service and its potential impact on future career options. The journal should also demystify the entire process of how members are selected, including how the write-on competition works, how it is assessed, and on what basis selection is made. Journal editors in charge of this educational process should not assume that students already know about the journal or how its members are selected. Start with the basics and explain what journal is, what a member's responsibilities are, including time and project requirements, how certain employers view journal service, and how members are chosen. The journal might

- send a class-wide or school-wide email announcement;
- hold in-person information sessions at different times to accommodate different student schedules (e.g., day and evening);

55. Godsey, *supra* note 4, at 61–63.

- offer to meet with different affinity groups like APALSA, BLSA, LLSA, MELSA, SALSA, OutLaw, neurodiverse law student groups, and first-generation groups to discuss journal membership opportunities and answer questions;
- visit first-year legal writing courses;
- ask Career Services counselors to speak with each first-year student about journal service during any mandatory counseling sessions;
- set up information tables set up in the common areas;
- include postings in the law school newsletter on or announcement screens or boards in heavy-traffic areas;
- host an open house in the journal office; and
- post videos and information, including FAQs about membership, on the journal webpage.

Ideally, the journal would do all of the above.

2. Ensure that the opportunity is inclusive

Broadcasting the opportunity is important but is not enough. In addition to knowing about the journal and the write-on competition, the opportunity must actually be available to candidates. Several hurdles hold back certain students and create artificial and unnecessary barriers to entry. These include barriers involving logistics, qualifications, and perceptions of the journal and the selection process.

a. Logistics

Competition organizers should schedule the competition to accommodate the greatest number of students and not unduly prejudice those with greater workloads or out-of-class responsibilities. For example, the write-on competition should occur when the greatest number of students are available. Many schools hold the competition immediately after spring final exams. This period can be one of the best times to hold the competition—but only for students who are not working and not in a summer session or program that starts right after spring finals. For students who work, the journal should recommend—well in advance—that they request time off to coincide with the competition.

Other law schools hold the competition during spring break or later in the summer. Other schools offer multiple windows to enter the competition. One size does not fit all when planning competition logistics. Still, everything about the competition, from the dates and times it is administered to the manner of submission, should be crafted to ensure the greatest number of students can participate. For example, requiring students to submit hard copies of papers will impose hardships on candidates living or working out of town or who are in town but have caretaker or job responsibilities.

As a final point, the journal should announce competition dates as far in advance and as widely as possible so that potential candidates can plan and adjust their schedules, if necessary.

b. Qualifications

A major barrier that keeps many students—and at some schools, most students—out of the running for journal is the minimum grade or class rank threshold. Clearly, grades may play a role in selecting some journal members. Although some journals, like the California Law Review, refuse to look at students' grades as part of the selection process, most journals still offer some or all positions based either entirely or partly on grades. This criterion excludes all students below the minimum threshold, regardless of writing ability, editing skills, work ethic, and other qualifications for the position.

The literature makes clear that grades are a poor proxy for qualifications to be a journal member or editor.[56] Grades also artificially keep out many students who would contribute significantly to the journal, to the law, and to the profession. This issue has also been examined and reported on.[57] Accordingly, the journal should craft selection criteria to include as many students as possible and not exclude participants based on purely academic or other unreliable measures of journal membership fitness.

c. Perceptions/sense of belonging

Even if the opportunity is broadcast to all and barriers are removed to open the opportunity to as many students as possible, some students will still be excluded because they are led to believe they do not belong on journal. In

---

56. *See, e.g.*, Christian C. Day, *The Case for Professionally-Edited Law Reviews*, 33 Ohio N.U. L. Rev. 563, 572 (2007); Michael Vitiello, *Journal Wars*, 22 St. Mary's L.J. 927, 931–32 (1991).

57. Godsey, *supra* note 4, at 86, 89–90; Morrison Torrey, *Actually Begin to Satisfy ABA Standards 211(a) and 212(a): Eliminate Race and Sex Bias in Legal Education*, 43 Harv. C.R.-C.L. L. Rev. 615, 617 (2008).

particular, women and POC students have decided not to try out for journal because they did not feel it would be a good fit for them. For example, an African-American student at George Washington Law School reported the following: "Many blacks and other minorities have not applied to these publications. There's a feeling [that we] wouldn't be warmly greeted."[58] As one author noted, "[s]uch widespread perceptions cause many minority students to feel unwanted and unwelcome, and ultimately, to become discouraged from 'trying out' for law review."[59]

To help create a sense of belonging for candidates, the journal should incorporate into its public communications an explicit message that it is open to all students and everyone is welcome. Of course, the journal needs to ensure the statement is true.

3. Address diversity explicitly in the selection process

Journals should address diversity and inclusion directly in the selection process. Steps might include setting up a diversity committee to review applicants' personal statements, including a diversity statement in the competition materials, and considering other factors that correspond with diversity and inclusion.

The New York University Law Review sets up a Diversity Committee to review applications. As part of applying for a journal, all candidates must submit a personal statement. There are a variety of topics students are invited to write about, including diversity and inclusion considerations. Candidates are also allowed, but not required, to submit a redacted resume with their competition materials. Of the 52 students selected to join the New York University Law Review, 40 are selected blindly based only on the competition materials. The Diversity Committee selects twelve students based on a review of their materials, including the personal statements and resumes.[60]

The Fordham Law Review selects some members based on an optional Diversity Statement, which students can submit with their competition materials. The Fordham Law Review selects about 20 members based solely on first-year grades and 30 based on the writing competition. However, to be eli-

58. Anne Kornhauser, *Quotas or Outreach?: GW Law Review Implements 'Diversity Criteria,'* Legal Times, May 15, 1989, at 3, 6.

59. Godsey, *supra* note 4, at 75.

60. *Membership Selection*, N.Y.U. L. Rev. (last visited Jan. 22, 2022), https://www.nyulawreview.org/about/membership-selection [https://perma.cc/NL8J-8JSV].

gible to write-on to the Fordham Law Review, students must rank in the top 33 percent of the class. The Fordham Law Review also selects up to 10 additional members based on the optional Diversity Statement, in conjunction with their other submission materials. Students selected based on the Diversity Statement need not have a specific GPA or class rank.[61]

The Rutgers University Law Review uses another approach. Journal applicants in Rutgers's Minority Student Program ("MSP") are invited to indicate this on a card included with their submissions. The MSP is "a nationally-acclaimed and highly successful post-admissions program that serves students of any race or ethnicity who are members of groups that are underrepresented in the legal profession, and who have faced discrimination or overcome social and economic hardships."[62] The MSP card is kept in a sealed envelope until all submission packets are graded. At that point, the review determines whether MSP cardholders are underrepresented in the acceptance pool. If the proportion of MSP cardholders accepted onto a journal is equal to or greater than the proportion of MSP cardholders who applied, no additional offers are made. If the proportion is lower, additional applicants who submitted MSP cards are extended offers in rank order until the accepted proportion roughly equals the overall ratio.[63]

Some journals have created an editorial board position called Diversity Editor. The purpose of the Diversity Editor is to "ensure that the Law Review remains committed to its mission of increasing the representation of diverse identities among its membership, leadership and authorship."[64] Journals that have introduced the Diversity Editor position include the California Law Review and the Wayne Law Review.[65]

When crafting the write-on competition and packet, journal members should carefully consider how topic selection might disproportionately impact certain groups of people. For example, a case about a police shooting might

---

61. *Membership Selection*, Fordham L. Rev. (last visited Jan. 22, 2022), http://fordhamlawreview.org/about-us/membership-selection [https://perma.cc/H4SQ-FDWF].

62. *Minority Student Program*, Rutgers (last visited Jan. 22, 2022), https://law.rutgers.edu/minority-student-program [https://perma.cc/2KNX-RNAW].

63. *Staff Selection*, *supra* note 39.

64. *Wayne Law Review Announces 2021–22 Editorial Board*, Wayne St. U. (Apr. 16, 2021), https://law.wayne.edu/news/wayne-law-review-announces-2021-22-editorial-board-42417 [https://perma.cc/ CN6D-4SDF].

65. *See id.*; *Diversity, California Law Review*, U. Cal. (last visited Jan. 22, 2022), https://www.californialawreview.org/about/diversit/ [https://perma.cc/B2V4-8PL7].

trigger some and cause them to withdraw from the competition. Accordingly, write-on competition topic selection should be carefully and thoughtfully selected, ideally with input from a diversity committee, Diversity Editor, or a diverse group of faculty advisors.

Finally, it is important to note that before creating board positions or changing a selection method, the journal editors need to check their bylaws and other official documents. They also should check with their faculty advisor before starting to change the process. All changes to the journal selection process should be made by following the required procedures and after obtaining all necessary authorizations.

D. Conclusion

In conclusion, because journals play an important role in publishing legal scholarship, developing the law, and enhancing the careers of student members, the selection methods must be carefully tailored to address several concerns. First, it is important that the students chosen have the greatest chance of contributing to the law and the profession. Some selection methods include write-on, grade-on, and note-on, and selection based on other factors, such as diversity. Second, it is important to ensure that the selection methods are open and fair to all students. Finally, it is critical that those who have been historically underrepresented on journal be given access to membership to help ensure that future editorial boards are diverse and inclusive.

KEY TAKEAWAYS

- Journals should carefully tailor their membership selection methods to help address several concerns, including selecting members qualified to perform journal work and who reflect the diversity within the student body.
- Selection methods include write-on, grade-on, and combine-on, and each may be adjusted in ways that ensure a more equitable and representative selection of candidates.
- Journal members can take several steps to ensure the selection criteria address diversity, inclusion, and equity.

11

Orientation and Training for Editors, New Staff Members, and Returning Staff Members

Carolyn V. Williams

LEARNING OBJECTIVES

Orienting and training journal staff members and editors is essential to increase the journal's overall productivity and performance.[1] These processes can help establish clear standards and reduce the risk of disputes.[2] And they can promote successful, productive, and collaborative working relationships amongst the journal members.[3]

After reviewing this Chapter, editors will be able to

- identify topics and teaching methods for new staff member orientation and training;
- recruit partners to help present training programs;
- facilitate effective training for incoming editors and staff members to learn expectations, acquire knowledge to fulfill their responsibilities, and build rapport; and
- foster continuing growth of returning staff members.

1. *See* Martin Luenendonk, *10 Tips for an Effective New Employee Job Orientation*, CLEVERISM (Sept. 23, 2019), https://www.cleverism.com/10-tips-effective-new-employee-orientation/ [https://perma.cc/LU8N-7WQQ].

2. *Id.*

3. *See id.*

A. Training New Editors

Once new editors are selected and receive guidance from outgoing editors about their respective positions' expectations, deadlines, and responsibilities,[4] the new editors may need further training and knowledge from other sources. By participating in board retreats, incoming editors can build camaraderie, clarify their objectives for the year, and set goals to attain them. New editors should also consider requesting people outside the journal to provide training on additional topics the outgoing editors may not have covered.

Retreats are usually all-day affairs and, unlike board meetings, are times to focus on high-level strategy. The objective of a retreat is to remove leaders from their busy day-to-day schedules and gather in a setting that allows them to tap into their creativity to tackle "big picture" items. Retreats incorporate lots of unplanned time—time "intended to allow (and sometimes force) you to zoom out, reflect, come up for air, relax, and refuel."[5] This break from "busyness" is crucial for regaining the ability to be productive and creative.[6]

The agenda for a retreat is much looser than the agenda for a business meeting because retreats focus on strategic, innovative brainstorming rather than tasks to be accomplished. Retreat agendas involve discussions like how the board wants to improve the journal or its status. What goals should the journal have for the year? What obstacles existed the prior year, and how can the editors avoid or resolve those problems?

Before coming to the retreat, editors should read scholarship critiquing the journal process to understand the big-picture issues and suggested solutions.[7] During the retreat, editors can use technology to promote brainstorming. Inexpensive alternatives include using Google Jamboard, Mural, or similar programs so the group can submit ideas anonymously on "post-it notes" to a commonly accessible screen.

---

4. For more on the transition of knowledge from the outgoing editors to the incoming editors, see Chapter 8 of this *Manual.*

5. Regan Bach, *Creating "White Space:" The Key to Increased Creativity and Productivity*, Noteworthy—The Journal Blog (Feb. 2, 2019), https://blog.usejournal.com/creating-white-space-the-key-to-increased-creativity-and-productivity-50af0d1c2811[https://perma.cc/KMA9-WGR8].

6. *Id.*

7. *See, e.g.*, Barry Friedman, *Fixing Law Reviews*, 67 Duke L.J. 1297 (2018), https://scholarship.law.duke.edu/cgi/viewcontent.cgi?article=3936&context=dlj [https://perma.cc/DW2Y-MCG6].

If possible, the retreat should occur before the end of the spring semester, but only after the incoming editors have met with their outgoing counterparts, as described in Chapter 8 of this *Manual*. Logistically, retreats can occur anywhere: at the journal offices, another venue at the law school, at someone's home, or in a sponsoring law firm's conference room.

Because retreats incorporate opportunities for participants to get to know one another and relax, it's customary to include team-building activities, meals, and outings. If time permits, consider playing trivia or another group board game, going to an escape room, or completing an obstacle course together. If your law school or journal budget does not allow for purchasing meals or participating in activities, consider asking Westlaw, Lexis, or a local law firm to sponsor them—but consult with the journal's faculty advisor first.[8] These organizations often budget small expenditures to gain access to journal members and showcase their businesses. If they do sponsor an event or meal, chances are that they will want to send a representative to talk to or mingle with the new editors.

Additionally, different law school departments might want to arrange training sessions for editors. For example, the legal writing faculty might be willing to present an advanced class to student writing editors about giving feedback on writing.[9] Or a law librarian might be willing to teach an advanced research class for the research editors.[10] A well-published faculty member might agree to talk to articles editors about strategies for working with authors or choosing articles.[11] The IT staff may be able to help train editors who have to hold a symposium or training remotely; that same IT staff may be able to help editors tasked with redesigning or upgrading the journal's website or by suggesting new technology tools that the journal could utilize for specific tasks.

Taking these steps to bring new editors up to speed will increase their efficiency and allow them to lead the journal more effectively.

---

8. For additional information about fundraising and sponsorships, see Chapter 3 of this *Manual*.

9. For additional guidance about working with student-authors, see Chapter 12 of this *Manual*.

10. For more information about working with law librarians, see Chapter 6 of this *Manual*.

11. For tips on author relations, see Chapter 13 of this *Manual*.

B. Training New Staff Members

The new board will then be responsible for training the new staff members.

1. Orientation

Orientation to a law review occurs when new staff members learn the journal's policies, various staff member responsibilities, and any other concepts they need to succeed on the journal.[12] Typically, one specific editor, or perhaps a returning staff member, assumes responsibility for organizing and planning orientation and then serves as the "moderator" during the program. The responsible editor or returning staff member should consult with others involved with the journal, especially the Editor in Chief and faculty advisor, before finalizing and distributing the program.

The elements of an excellent orientation include the following:

- touring the journal office (if it occupies physical space in the law school) and other spaces dedicated to journal work (like designated shelves or carrel in the law library);
- introducing new members to editors and continuing staff members;
- providing the training needed to develop skills members need to complete their job responsibilities;
- reviewing the key deadlines for the year;
- communicating the details of initial projects (e.g., their first cite-checking responsibilities or the deadline for their own article topic) and expectations;
- conducting team-building exercises;
- explaining the bylaws and other important law review and law school policies;[13] and
- answering any questions new members have.[14]

---

12. *See What Is Orientation?*, HRZONE (last visited Jan. 29, 2022), https://www.hrzone.com/hr-glossary/what-is-orientation [https://perma.cc/N883-ADM7].

13. For information about policies and accreditation standards that impact law reviews, see Chapter 2 of this *Manual.*

14. *See Job Orientation: How to Create a Job Orientation Program Template*, BETTERTEAM (last visited Jan. 29, 2022), https://www.betterteam.com/job-orientation [https://perma.cc/ZV2P-V2MW].

The next sections address how to achieve these goals.

a. Timing and format

When planning a new staff orientation, the first task is to select a date and format. Orientation usually occurs right before school starts in the fall, immediately before staff members typically begin their cite-checking duties and drafting their student articles.

It's preferable to have an in-person orientation so new staff members can meet and socialize with their peers. Sometimes that isn't feasible, so ensure the journal has access to a video-conferencing platform that accommodates the number of staff members, editors, and other trainers who will join throughout the orientation. Even if trainers have participated on a video-conferencing platform, it takes practice to host, share screens, and run applications within the platform. Host a technology run-through with all individuals presenting so they aren't learning as they present.

The most successful orientations have elements of both a business meeting and a retreat. In addition to planning task-oriented agenda items such as learning nuances of citation, the role of the student writing department, or the important deadlines, leave time for recharging and socializing. Journal members need to build relationships with each other to ask for help, build a professional network, and facilitate communication when members are in high-stress situations that come with working on a journal. Most find that building relationships is easier during an in-person orientation. Staff members can chat over coffee during breaks, sit with new people at lunch, and strike up a conversation with someone waiting for a ride home.

If you are conducting a virtual orientation, you will need to be more intentional in creating space for socializing. It's awkward for everyone to be in a virtual meeting "get together" with more than a few people because, predictably, two or three people monopolize the conversation and everyone else just listens. Instead, build in time for a virtual trivia game in which the questions and answers tell the new staff members about one another. Host a virtual karaoke competition at the end of the day. Randomly assign staff members to breakout rooms where they participate in a "speed meeting" interview: give them five minutes to find out a few interesting facts about the other person; when everyone rejoins the main room, have a few students share a fact or two about their colleague. Assign teams to play online games on the virtual platform. If your budget permits, send e-cards so participants can purchase lunch or a beverage to enjoy at a set time during the meeting. In sum, get creative about socializing online.

Inevitably, the time you have to socialize depends on how long orientation runs. Some orientations are a full day; others span two or three days. You may want all the introductions, tours, and team building on one day, a reception or similar event that night, and a citation review course the second day. That way, most editors participate only one day. (Of course, the editor who planned the orientation and the Editor in Chief should participate in as much of the program as possible.) Or you may want to complete the task-oriented items—the citation review, review of the schedule and deadlines, and details of the initial projects—at the law school on day one and meet off-site the next day for team-building exercises.

If choosing a virtual format, shorter is better. Split the sessions into no more than one-hour chunks, with plenty of rest time in between. You might consider having some presenters record their presentations for staff members to watch asynchronously. On-demand videos might be ideal for introducing the editors or taking staff members on a virtual tour of the journal offices. Even if most of the orientation will be in-person, consider if these introductions could be recorded to shorten the time.

You may also consider spreading orientation over the semester or year. Each month, you could hold a training meeting that deals with a different citation topic. Or you may want to have short presentations or videos to correspond with the stages of writing a student article that staff members watch as they progress through the writing process.

b. Recruiting outside help

As with new editor orientation, tap into your school's resources. Often, law school faculty are willing to present on certain subjects. A legal writing professor could share tips on writing a scholarly article or advanced citation rules, or a law librarian could teach how to narrow a topic for a student article or find unique sources cited by authors. Westlaw and Lexis representatives are typically willing to demonstrate advanced research resources. Faculty or published judges could provide an overview of scholarly writing and how the legal community uses legal scholarship.

When inviting presenters, the organizing editor should give each the time, date, and place of the training; the intended audience (i.e., new journal members); the specific time allotted for the presentation (e.g., 11:30 a.m. to 1:00 p.m.); the title and scope of the session; and other topics the training will cover. Providing each with the agenda will help reduce overlap and unwanted surprises. As you consider the agenda and presenters, strive to invite a diverse group to participate. And if someone you invite cannot participate and you don't have a backup in mind, ask that person for recommendations about who might also be a good person to present on that topic. Another option would be to ask the person to record their presentation instead of appearing live, although students tend to be more engaged with in-person presenters.

Ask presenters if they intend to use slides or other technology and whether they anticipate having handouts. A best practice is to request copies of the handouts by a date certain in advance so you can share them with new staff members. It's also good practice to request the final slides before the presentation so you have a backup in case technology fails. Before sharing the slides with participants, be sure to get the presenter's permission. If you plan to record the session for absent members or archival purposes, obtain each presenter's written permission in advance. Finally, remember to place a copy of all training materials in the journal's archive for future boards.

In addition to finding presenters, look for sponsors. Local law firms often want to make good impressions on journal students they hope to recruit as summer associates. Those law firms might happily sponsor breakfast, snacks, lunch, or reception with incoming new members, especially if they could send law firm representatives to network with the new members. Start by asking any firms that gave job offers to editors. Firms or the journal's publisher may also sponsor prizes for games or competitions at orientation or pay for an off-campus activity. Westlaw, Lexis, or Bloomberg will often donate money for meals or prizes in exchange for a time slot to present.

An important caveat is not to approach any potential donor without first consulting with the journal's faculty advisor and coordinating with your law school's alumni and development office. That office will know whether the school has recently asked that person or organization for a gift or if the school is preparing to seek a large gift.[15]

c. Learning about the journal and meeting the team

A large part of orientation is learning the places, people, and programs new staff members will need to know to succeed. As for the place, if the journal occupies physical space, give the new members a tour, especially if you won't be holding orientation there. This tour can be in-person or virtual. Make sure they know the unspoken rules like not leaving food in the refrigerator over the

---

15. For additional information about working with your school's alumni and development office, see Chapter 3 of this *Manual.*

weekend or just where to kick the printer to get it to work. Let them know the code to get in or who to contact to get access through their student ID cards.[16]

Invite key people to meet the new staff members. Key people include editors, returning staff members, and faculty advisors. Also include law school employees who help the journal regularly—such as the journal's faculty advisor, IT staff, the business office staff, law librarians, and the administrative assistant to the journal. You may want to show a welcome video from those who cannot attend in person. The new staff members should understand each person's role and responsibilities and how staff members will or will not interact with those key people.

All journal departments (articles, student writing, production/operations, symposium, technology, etc.) should describe their responsibilities and functions. The overview should include any opportunities for new staff members to volunteer to get more involved. Some journals have committees that accomplish journal tasks not specifically assigned to one editor, such as the fundraising committee, the write-on committee, or the journal's end-of-year banquet committee. Explaining those committees that the new staff members can participate in and encouraging them to get involved is one way to get them even more invested in the journal's success.

Give new staff members an overview of the schedule and expectations. Share key deadlines for the year and where to find them posted online. Explain where to find the bylaws and any particularly useful provisions for staff members, such as how student manuscripts are chosen for publication, lists of expectations for staff members, and reasons for dismissing a staff member from the journal.[17] Advise them of any other important journal policies, such as its policy on plagiarism.[18] Clarify if and how journal participation is graded and the requirements for staff members to earn academic credit.

d. Cite-checking instruction

The cite-checking process is one major topic that editors should cover during new staff member orientation. Explain the process of receiving articles to cite check, how corrections should be noted, and the deadlines to submit

---

16. For a discussion of journal office space, see Chapter 3 of this *Manual.*

17. For a discussion of law review constitutions, bylaws, and other governing documents, see Chapter 3 of this *Manual.*

18. For ideas about which specific policies to share with new members, see Chapter 2 of this *Manual.*

assignments. Additionally, include instruction on legal citation. Before thinking about the content of that instruction, journals should critically think about the citation manuals the staff members use to learn and craft citations.

Although a few state-specific citation manuals (e.g., *The New York Law Reports Style Manual*), specialty legal citation manuals (e.g., *Guide to Foreign and International Legal Citations*), and agency-specific citation manuals (e.g., the *Office of the Solicitor General Citation Manual*) exist, two legal citation manuals are meant to be used by journals nationwide: the *ALWD Guide to Legal Citation*[19] and *The Bluebook*.[20] The biggest difference between the two for purposes of scholarly writing is that students typically learn the "blue pages" of the latter (the rules for practitioners) during their first year and aren't exposed much to the more expansive "white pages" that include the rules for scholarly writing. The ALWD Guide integrates the academic formatting used for journal articles within the appropriate citation rules. It also has diagrams that illustrate the basic components of citations; "Fast Formats" that preview and refresh recollection of standard citation forms; "Sidebars" that explain the "why" of legal citations and provide helpful background; and "Snapshots" of actual source material that show where to look for needed citation components.

Editors should consider allowing staff members to choose the manual with which they are most comfortable. The citations that result from using both manuals are exactly the same. The ALWD Guide authors are so confident of the consistency that its rules include citations to specific Bluebook rules or examples that the ALWD Guide explicitly breaks down. This appendix also makes it easy for ALWD Guide users to cross-reference rules for others who may be using The Bluebook.

As for the content of the citation instruction, new members' citation education before joining the journal probably focused exclusively on citation format for practice documents, not for legal scholarship. Thus, new members arrive with three types of gaps in their citation knowledge.

First, orientation should include instruction on points of citation that differ between practice and academic documents:

- **Placement:** Although new staff members understand what footnotes look like from reading legal scholarship, it may be helpful to

---

19. Carolyn V. Williams & ALWD, ALWD Guide to Legal Citation (7th ed. 2021) [hereinafter ALWD Guide].

20. The Bluebook: A Uniform System of Citation (Columbia L. Rev. Ass'n et al. eds., 21st ed. 2020).

cover where to place footnotes within a sentence and in relation to punctuation.[21]

- **Typeface:** In scholarly writing, some citations include large and small capital letters (called "small caps"). As just a few examples, book author names and titles appear in "small caps," as do website domain names.[22] The "small caps" typeface is not used in practice documents. And although case names are always italicized in practice documents, case names appear in ordinary type for full citations in scholarly writing while short citations are italicized.[23]
- **Short citations:** In contrast to writing practice documents, academic writers must cite a primary source in full, not by using a short citation, if the authority has not been cited within the last five footnotes.[24]

Second, in addition to instruction on rules that capture the differences between citing in practice documents and citing in scholarly works, the orientation should address the numerous rules that apply to sources that appear almost exclusively in scholarly writing. For these sources, new staff members would have had little, if any, prior exposure to the citation formats for those sources:

- **Common secondary sources:** The types of documents that appear in scholarly writing are much broader than those that appear in practice documents. Practice documents focus on primary authority—e.g., statutes, regulations, and case law—and seldom include secondary sources. Below are categories of sources that new staff will likely need training on:
  - advisory opinions;[25]
  - executive documents;[26]

---

21. *See* ALWD Guide, *supra* note 19, R. 34.1(e)FN, at 366–67.

22. *See id.* R. 1.4FN, at 5–6 (includes a chart of components that use large and small capital letters in academic footnotes).

23. *See id.* R. 12.2(a)(2)FN, at 58.

24. *Id.* R. 11.1(d)FN, at 44.

25. *See id.* R. 18.7, at 197–99.

26. *See id.* R. 18.9, at 199–202.

  - books and treatises;[27]
  - legal encyclopedias;[28]
  - American Law Reports;[29]
  - Restatements and Principles of Law;[30]
  - model codes or acts;[31]
  - uniform laws;[32]
  - interviews;[33]
  - video and visual programs;[34]
  - audio recordings;[35]
  - forthcoming works and unpublished manuscripts; and[36]
  - internet sites[37]
- **Periodical abbreviations:** If your journal does not use Appendix 5 from the ALWD Guide—which is free online[38]—as a shortcut to constructing periodical abbreviations, orientation should cover the rules regarding periodicals and constructing their abbreviations.[39]
- **Graphical material,[40] Illustrations,[41] and Appendices:[42]** Although graphical material, illustrations, and appendices are common in

---

27. *See id.* R. 20.1, at 214–22.
28. *See id.* R. 22.3, at 255–58.
29. *See id.* R. 22.5, at 260–64.
30. *See id.* R. 23.1, at 268–72.
31. *See id.* R. 23.3, at 272–75.
32. *See id.* R. 23.6, at 277–79.
33. *See id.* R. 27.1–27.3, at 302–04.
34. *See id.* R. 28.1, at 312–16.
35. *See id.* R. 28.2–28.7, at 316–22.
36. *See id.* R. 29, at 328–32.
37. *See id.* R. 31, at 339–48.
38. Carolyn V. Williams, *Appendix 5: Periodicals and Looseleaf Services*, ASPEN PUBLISHING (last visited Jan. 29, 2022), https://www.aspenpublishing.com/File%20Library/Faculty-Product-Resources/Law%20School/Authors%20A-E/ALWD%207e/ALWD_App05.pdf [https://perma.cc/5G82-2YVA].
39. *See* ALWD GUIDE, *supra* note 19, R. 21, at 235–50.
40. *See id.* R. 9.1, at 40.
41. *See id.* R. 28.8, at 322–23.
42. *See id.* R. 9.3, at 40–41.

secondary sources cited in scholarly writing, they are not common in the primary sources more frequently cited in practice documents. Thus, it's worth spending training time on these topics.

Third, plan to incorporate training on some advanced points of citation that staff members likely did not encounter, or at least did not spend much time studying, during their legal writing courses:

- **Signals:** Signals are used more pervasively in scholarly writing, which also uses more types of signals; for example, it is rare to find a "*but see*" signal in a persuasive motion filed with the court. To complete their cite-checking duties, staff members must be taught the nuances that various signals convey to the reader. The training about signals is a good place to emphasize that cite-checking involves more than correcting citation format. Instead, the process requires staff members to understand the author's assertions and judge whether the cited material relates to the author's point in the precise manner conveyed by the signal (including no signal).
- **Hereinafter, *supra*, and internal cross-references:** "Hereinafter" is primarily used in academic footnotes when no author is attributed to the authority, when two or more works from the same author appear for the first time in the same footnote, or when a shortened form would help the reader recognize the source.[43] Because *supra* cannot be used as a short format for most primary sources, it rarely appears in practice documents, so students will need to understand when and how to use it in scholarly writing.[44] Internal cross-references, like "*supra*" and "*infra*," refer a reader to material in another part of the same document; they are most commonly found in scholarly writing.[45]
- **Advanced citation for case opinions:** Although new staff members may be most familiar with citing case law, orientation may need to cover more obscure topics that likely did not arise when drafting practice documents. Examples include indicating subsequent[46]

43. *See id.* R. 11.5(c), at 51–52.
44. *See, e.g., id.* R. 9, at 40–41.
45. *See id.* R. 10, at 42–43.
46. *See id.* R. 12.8, at 85–90.

or prior case history,[47] using explanatory and weight of authority phrases (e.g., "en banc," "concurring," or "per curiam"),[48] and formatting forthcoming[49] or unpublished cases.[50]

- **Advanced citation for statutes:** Like case law, new staff members are probably familiar with the basic citation format for statutes. But orientation may need to cover less common topics like session laws,[51] publication parentheticals,[52] and legislative materials.[53]
- **Citing footnotes or endnotes:** Primary sources do not commonly have footnotes or endnotes, so this topic would be helpful to cover.[54]
- **Internet sources:** An essential training topic is when to cite a source that appears online as a website versus when to cite it as the type of source it is with a URL appended. For example, it can be particularly difficult to choose how to cite interviews, speeches, letters, and videos that appear online.[55]
- **Order of authorities:** Although prior editions of the ALWD Guide and Bluebook included clear-cut rules for the order in which various authorities were listed within one signal, the current advice is to order them "logically."[56] If your journal prefers a more structured approach or has journal-specific guidance on how to interpret this logic, relay that guidance to the new staff members.
- **"Cleaned up" quotations:** Some scholars have advocated for "cleaned up" citations—omitting punctuation, such as brackets,

---

47. *See id.* R. 12.9, at 91.

48. *See id.* R. 12.10, at 91–93.

49. *See id.* R. 12.13, at 96–97.

50. *See id.* R. 12.14, at 97–99.

51. *See id.* R. 14.6, at 126–28.

52. *See id.* R. 14.2(f), at 118–19.

53. *See id.* R. 15, at 131–72.

54. *See id.* R. 7, at 34–37.

55. *See id.* Sidebar 26.1, at 297 (explaining how to choose between citing a source as an internet source or as a regular speech, interview, or other oral presentation with a URL appended); *id.* R. 27.3, at 304 (citing recorded interviews posted online); *id.* R. 28.1(f)–(g), at 315–16 (citing videos available online); *id.* R. 28.5–28.6[FN], at 318–20 (citing podcasts, audiobooks, and other audio recordings found online).

56. *Id.* R. 36.1, at 377.

ellipsis, and footnote references, that show how one source altered a quotation from the original source and adding "(cleaned up)" after the citation.[57] The Bluebook does not address the practice, and the ALWD Guide discourages it.[58] Editors should communicate your journal's preference on "cleaned up" citations to the new staff members.

Some content covered will depend on your journal's specific needs. If your journal is a specialty journal, include instruction on sources specific to your genre. For example, journals focusing on international law may want to include instruction on citing treaties, United Nations documents, and International Court of Justice publications. In addition, consider covering sources used in the journal's upcoming articles. At the very least, by late summer, the journal likely will have selected those articles it plans to publish in the first volume or two. If the topic of one article is administrative changes to federal tax law, staff members may need to know how to cite the *Cumulative Bulletin*, I.R.S. Announcements, and Treasury Regulations. And don't forget to tell new staff members about citation rules and style conventions specific to your journal, which often appear in an internal style manual or staff handbook.

Instead of creating footnotes from scratch for exercises when teaching citation, or when creating quizzes and games as described below, pull footnotes from articles submitted to or published in your journal. If you pull footnotes from recent past volumes, you have the correct answer already and can "mess them up" for quizzes. Additionally, if you do not want to create a quiz yourself or don't know where to start, Lexis has Interactive Citation Workshop (ICW) exercises for use with both the ALWD Guide and Bluebook that are accessible through Lexis's website with a student login. ICW has five modules specifically designed for journal citations: case citations; state and federal statutes; legislative and administrative sources; secondary sources; and short forms. Other useful modules include prior and subsequent case history; parentheticals; signals; and more on legislative resources and administrative resources. In addition, if the staff members use the ALWD Guide online through Casebook Connect, that source also includes citation quizzes.

---

57. *E.g.*, Jack Meltzer, *Cleaning Up Citations*, 18 J. App. Prac. & Process 143, 154–55 (2017); Bryan A. Garner, *LawProse Lesson 303: Cleaned-Up Quotations and Citations* (Mar. 3, 2018), https://lawprose.org/lawprose-lesson-303-cleaned-up-quotations-and-citations [https://perma.cc/6LNY-LFE8].

58. *See* ALWD Guide, *supra* note 19, Sidebar 39.1, at 406.

Let's face it. Many law students find learning citation difficult, too detailed, and boring. The challenge, then, is to keep the staff members' attention. Ways to pique and keep their attention include breaking learning into manageable chunks and using active learning techniques rather than lectures.

One way to break citation instruction into manageable chunks is to have staff members do some homework at their own pace before orientation. Editors can assign reading from a citation manual, practice exercises designed to teach advanced concepts, or sets of five-minute online tutorials to watch before orientation. To introduce active learning, editors could ask new staff members to complete a quiz individually before orientation and then take it again in teams during orientation to ensure they do the homework. Alternatively, editors could assign a short cite-checking exercise using part of an article before orientation and then have members compare their edits in a group during orientation. Having staff members complete a task individually and then as a team has the added benefit of allowing them to meet each other and talk through the rules together.

Another way to create manageable chunks is to simply talk about the logistics of receiving, completing, and submitting citation checks during orientation and discuss citation rules during other times—whether on a separate day of orientation or various days during the first month or semester. Editors could also create a series of short video presentations that the staff could watch on their own. Of course, because journals need staff members to ramp up quickly, spreading out the citation instruction may not be ideal.

If addressing citation rules during orientation, keep any lecture short—15 minutes at most—before incorporating an active learning activity. Active learning involves behavior and activities other than reading and listening.[59] Using active learning techniques "triples students' gains in knowledge."[60] It also helps eliminate the gender gap for female students in male-dominated fields.[61] The Socratic method is not a good example of active learning, even though one student interacts with the professor.[62]

---

59. Rafael Gely & Paul L. Caron, *Taking Back the Law School Classroom: Using Technology to Foster Active Student Learning*, 54 J. LEGAL EDUC. 551, 552 (2004).

60. Elizabeth Anne Kirley, *Are We Ethically Bound to Use Student Engagement Technologies for Teaching Law?* 7 (Deakin Law School Legal Studies Research Paper No. 17-20, 2015), https://papers.ssrn.com/sol3/papers.cfm?abstract_id=2952188 [https://perma.cc/RKJ9-4A6B].

61. *Id.* at 9.

62. Gely & Caron, *supra* note 59, at 554–55.

Using student engagement technology (SET) encourages active learning and increases the likelihood of passing a class by 150%.[63] SETs are web-based systems that allow interaction through student-owned devices (phones, laptops, tablets). Free or low-cost platforms such as Mentimeter or Poll Everywhere allow students to answer questions without having their name attached to the answer. But by monitoring the overall percentage of staff members who answer correctly, the presenter can identify knowledge gaps. Schools may subscribe to platforms like Socrative and TopHat that offer more options for quizzing or playing games. Another benefit of SET is that it can be used for online or in-person orientation.

Besides real-time quizzing, creating games for actively learning citations can tap into staff members' competitive nature, driving them to learn more. Websites like Playfactile.com let you create Jeopardy-style games using any topic. Kahoot! is another popular website on which to create learning-style games. Again, these games can be played either online or in-person. You could even have the new staff members square off against the editors to build rapport.

Whether you have quizzes or games, small prizes are always welcome encouragement. As stated above, sponsors may donate money for gift cards or scratchers or donate swag, if that is allowed by your law school. Even silly prizes like cheap plastic trophies or medals, stickers, or candy can make new staff members laugh and encourage them to participate.

Last but not least, orientation should include the logistics surrounding cite-checking. How are the articles assigned to staff members? Can they work collaboratively with other staff members on the same section? Is there a certain word-processing program (e.g., Word) they must use to make their changes to citations? Do they need to use the "track changes" or "compare" functions in Word? Are specific staff members assigned to research missing sources, or does each locate their own? Who can the staff member approach with questions? What are the deadlines, to whom do they submit the changes, and through what medium? When, from whom, and how will they receive feedback on their work?

No matter how you conduct citation training, the time spent during orientation to refresh and deepen staff members' knowledge of citation will enhance their confidence and result in better work product.

---

63. Kirley, *supra* note 60, at 2–3.

2. Instruction on writing a student article[64]

Writing a casenote or comment is a large part of staff writers' responsibilities during their first year on the journal. Some law schools require staff writers to enroll in a course taught by a professor who will teach them how to draft a scholarly article. Other law schools assign a professor or writing center staff member to teach those skills in a workshop setting—maybe over a few lunch hours—or on-demand videos. If your school falls into one of these categories, you may not need to train the staff members on this subject. But if your journal does not have a course or a recurring workshop, editors may need to organize presentations on scholarly writing.

a. Recruiting help

As noted in other sections, the journal editors do not have to do everything on their own. Talk to your journal's faculty advisor about whether they can help, and if not, who else on the school's faculty and staff can help. Legal writing faculty have particular expertise in helping students with various types of writing. Legal research professors and law librarians are well-suited to teaching specific research skills for academic writing, such as researching whether the topic has been preempted and using databases other than Westlaw and Lexis. Many journals ask commercial database representatives to present on advanced research topics. Some law schools have writing centers with resources and sessions geared toward helping students with their upper-level writing requirement. Editors should always be on the lookout for potential partners.

b. Timing and format

Once presenters are set (whether editors or others), many options exist for timing and format. Some journals incorporate student article training into the initial orientation. But that timing may not be ideal. Unlike cite-checking, staff members don't have to know all or even most aspects of writing a scholarly paper to get started. If the knowledge staff members need months down the line is presented at orientation, they will likely forget it because of the mass of information they gain and people they meet at orientation.

It may help new staff members to simply give an overview of what scholarly writing is, the writing process, and important deadlines, saving the details

64. Chapter 12 of this *Manual* addresses working with student-authors.

for another time. By spacing out discussions on topics such as finding a topic and implementing feedback on drafts, students can learn information as they need it. "Microlearning"—also known as "just-in-time learning"—focuses on learning only one skill or concept at a time.[65] Research confirms that chunking information into small topics learned just in time makes the concept easier and helps ensure learners will remember the information because they use it right away.[66] Short presentations spread throughout the first semester or year can either be in person or videotaped for students to access as they move through the writing stages.

c. Components of effective guidance

To prepare new staff members to write high-quality student articles, instruction should include the following components:

- explaining what student articles (sometimes called "casenotes" or "comments") are and characteristics they must have to meet the law school's expectations;
- selecting a topic;
- formulating a thesis;
- conducting a preemption check;
- conducting research, especially outside of Westlaw and Lexis;
- best practices for reading sources and organizing information for a scholarly article;
- organizing the paper;
- best practices for outlining and writing;
- avoiding plagiarism;
- receiving and implementing feedback;
- revising the paper; and
- avenues for publishing and submitting papers to competitions.[67]

---

65. Jay Tankersley, *Top 4 Benefits of Microlearning*, Vital Learning (July 5, 2016, 12:28 PM), https://www.vital-learning.com/blog/benefits-of-microlearning [https://perma.cc/PMV2-KE42].

66. *Id.*

67. *See Writing Center Resources: Scholarly Legal Writing*, U. Ariz. James E. Rogers C. L. Legal Writing (last visited Jan. 29, 2022), https://arizonalawwritingcenter.arizona.edu

Myriad books and articles flesh out these topics.[68] Additionally, your law library or writing center likely has compiled lists of resources to help students with scholarly papers. If you are lucky, your law school may even have an archive of videos designed to help students with notes, comments, and other scholarly papers.[69]

C. Continuing Training for Returning Staff Members

Training for returning staff members will differ from training for new members because returning staff members understand the basics of cite-checking and likely have completed their student articles. But if their duties will change, editors should communicate those new expectations.

Invite returning staff members to any team-building activities or other opportunities to socialize during new staff member orientation. But whether returning staff members attend the rest of orientation may depend on the type and quality of their prior work. You may want the outgoing editors who oversaw the returning staff members' prior cite-checking assignments to assess them. If their work was good or acceptable, you might excuse them from the cite-checking instruction portion of orientation. If their work was not up to par, consider requiring them to attend. Alternatively, instead of singling out returning staff members, consider having them complete the cite-checking assignments that the new staff members complete as a way to refresh their skills. Editors might consider meeting one-on-one with returning staff members to discuss goals for the coming year.

Likewise, unless the returning staff members did not complete a student article, they should be exempt from the writing portion of orientation.

/resources [https://perma.cc/4XPZ-NP88] (scroll to drop down menu under "Scholarly legal writing") [hereinafter *Arizona Law Scholarly Legal Writing Video Modules*].

68. Jessica L. Clark & Kristen E. Murray, Scholarly Writing: Ideas, Examples, and Execution (2d ed. 2012); Elizabeth Fajans & Mary R. Falk, Scholarly Writing for Law Students: Seminar Papers, Law Review Notes and Law Review Competition Papers (5th ed. 2017); Eugene Volokh, Academic Legal Writing: Law Review Articles, Student Notes, Seminar Papers, and Getting on Law Review (5th ed. 2016); Heather Meeker, *Stalking the Golden Topic: A Guide to Locating and Selecting Topics for Legal Research Papers*, 1996 Utah L. Rev. 917.

69. *See Arizona Law Scholarly Legal Writing Video Modules*, *supra* note 67.

Students' skills and understanding of concepts deepen as they teach those skills and concepts to someone else.[70] Thus, the best way to continue to train returning staff members is to enlist returning staff members' help in training others.[71] Returning staff members could lead some cite-checking sessions for new staff. They could collaborate on new staff members' first cite-checking assignments by completing them in tandem with the new staff members or comparing changes when both staff members complete the same section of an article. Returning staff members could also teach some topics related to writing, whether during orientation or throughout the year. They could record on-demand sessions for new staff members. Additionally, returning staff writers could lead a committee or a special project (e.g., the committee that organizes the end-of-year banquet). If those tasks are normally assigned to an editor, the returning staff writer could still be invited to work with a particular department, committee, or editor on special projects.

KEY TAKEAWAYS

- Training new journal editors and staff members will make them more confident, happy, and productive.
- Build time for team building and socializing into orientation sessions to help build rapport.
- Students do not have to do all the training. Take advantage of faculty, law firm, and commercial partners' willingness to provide knowledge and resources.
- Training is an ongoing process. After the initial orientation, hold intermittent training sessions, assess staff member work, give feedback, and give members opportunities to teach each other.

---

70. Annie Murphy Paul, *The Protégé Effect: Why Teaching Someone Else Is the Best Way to Learn*, TIME (Nov. 3, 2011), https://ideas.time.com/2011/11/30/the-protege-effect/ [https://perma.cc/FJ2C-PS92].

71. *See id.*

12

Working with Student-Authors

Kristen E. Murray and Jessica Lynn Wherry

LEARNING OBJECTIVES

After reviewing this Chapter, editors will be able to

- describe the challenges of the student-author and student-editor experiences;
- identify the stages of the writing process and the opportunities for editorial support at each stage; and
- apply techniques for giving helpful feedback with the ideal student-author–student-editor collaboration in mind.

A. Introduction

New journal staff members are likely to identify primarily as student-authors. They typically have cite-checking responsibilities to support articles in the journal's publication pipeline, but their central experience is authoring their own pieces of legal scholarship. This writing experience can be both exciting and intimidating for new members.

New student-editors who directly supervise student-authors must pivot quickly from their previous roles as student-authors and supervisees to supervisory, editorial positions. This Chapter is designed to support student-editors as they transition into supervising new student-authors. The advice offered can be applied to any student-author experience, regardless of whether the journal requires or permits "notes," "comments," or other articles.[1] Although the Chap-

---

1. JESSICA LYNN WHERRY & KRISTEN E. MURRAY, SCHOLARLY WRITING: IDEAS, EXAMPLES, AND EXECUTION 5–8 (3d ed. 2019) (discussing various types of student legal schol-

ter focuses on student-editors who work most directly with student-authors, the advice may also be useful for other editorial board members. This Chapter will discuss the typical student-author experience, consider some challenges that student-authors and student-editors may confront, suggest strategies for an ideal author-editor relationship, and offer effective feedback techniques from start to finish.

B. The Student-Author Experience

To supervise student-authors successfully, student-editors will need to understand the student-author's motivations and goals, the stages of the writing process, and what a final, publishable article looks like.

1. Motivations and goals

Student-authors bring different motivations and goals to the writing experience. Some might match student-editors' own experiences as student-authors, while others might be unfamiliar. Student-authors might also have several motivations and goals in play.

All student-authors should, at a minimum, be motivated to meet the base-level requirements set by the journal, especially if the written work product is worth academic credit or fulfills a graduation requirement.[2] As someone who has committed to an editorial position, it might be hard for a student-editor to appreciate that some student-authors seek only to meet the minimum requirements. While various reasons exist for why this might be true, we need not explore those here. What is important for student-editors to remember is that some student-authors plan to put in only the minimum effort required to earn writing credit.

Other student-authors are motivated by the opportunity to have the article published. Most journals offer that opportunity to some but not all student-authors. Some journals allow student-authors to opt out of consideration for publication, and others have a competitive selection process to determine which student-authored pieces will appear in the journal.

---

arship).

2. For a discussion about law school policies and accreditation standards regarding the upper-level writing requirement and law review, see Chapter 2 of this *Manual.*

Some student-authors may have career goals that make publication an asset or important credential. For example, they may seek judicial clerkships, for which publication is often highly valued if not required, or aspire to academic careers, where publication of scholarship is critical. Or they may wish to use their publications as credentials to demonstrate interest or establish expertise in particular fields.

Understanding different student-authors' motivations will make student-editors more thoughtful and empathetic supervisors. These motivations will be important throughout the writing process, as they will affect how the student-authors process feedback.

2. The scholarly writing process

No matter the nature of the written work product, the writing process for student-authors remains the same.[3]

The first steps are choosing a topic and identifying a thesis.[4] The editorial role may vary based on journal protocols. For example, a student-editor might take an active role, helping to identify a list of topics or cases for student-authors; a student-editor might serve as a facilitator, connecting student-authors with faculty members or law librarians who can assist; or a student-editor might simply weigh in at the end of this phase, approving student-authors' topics. Regardless, at the end of these steps, student-authors should have some idea about what they are writing.

The second step is a phase of deeper research and exploration, as student-authors learn more about their topics, refine their theses, and usually use their research to write "background" sections. Next, student-authors begin drafting "discussion/analysis" sections for their papers. A formal written outline might precede the draft. Once the full draft is written, several stages of revision usually follow.

Again, a student-editor's role in these later stages depends on journal processes. A student-editor might be offering feedback or approval at each stage and perhaps working adjacent to or in collaboration with the student-author's faculty advisor.

Presumably, student-editors are also working according to a timeline set by the journal. The student-authors are likely doing their best to adhere to this

3. Wherry & Murray, *supra* note 1, at 18–19.

4. *Id.* at 21–22.

timeline, but their journal work is likely one of many responsibilities they have. Thus, clear communication about the timeline, the accompanying deadlines, and the journal's editorial process is key to making this a successful experience for student-editors and student-authors alike.

3. Articles of publishable quality

At the end of the process, your journal will decide which student-authored articles it will publish. How does a student-editor decide if a student-authored piece is worth publishing? Mindfulness about the final written product can help student-editors give helpful feedback to student-authors throughout this process. Your journal may have specific standards, but here are a few common concepts to keep in mind:

- the novelty of the topic, generally speaking and in comparison to other student-authors working on the same volume;
- whether the journal has published on a similar topic recently;
- the depth of analysis;
- the quality of the writing as a matter of style, grammar, and syntax;
- the content and accuracy of the footnotes in the draft; and
- the student-author's adherence to internal processes and deadlines.

C. Common Challenges for Student-Authors

For most student-authors, the most significant challenge is the lack of in-depth knowledge about the topic and thesis. This lack of knowledge can make student-authors feel overwhelmed, like novices trying to master the topic and figure out what they want to say about it. Learning-while-doing is fairly standard for student-authors and can be a productive part of the scholarly writing process. But most student-authors will not intuit this common struggle. Because of this lack of knowledge, early-stage submissions may be underdeveloped, lack clarity, or otherwise be problematic. For example, student-authors may overwrite or over-outline background while giving little attention to novel analysis. Early-stage work products may also appear to over-rely on a small number of sources or over-rely on quotations.

Novice student-authors often choose topics or theses that are either too broad or too narrow. Both approaches can overwhelm student-authors; broad approaches can make student-authors feel like they will never be able to understand the subject enough, or specifically enough, to produce the paper, and narrow approaches can make student-authors feel like they cannot conduct meaningful research or find enough to write about. Student-editors may be able to identify topics or theses as too broad or narrow based on their own journal writing experiences, but as non-experts they might not be able to do so immediately. Student-authors may need some time to settle on a thesis that is neither too broad nor too narrow, and student-editors can help guide student-authors through that development stage.

Also, student-authors may change their minds midway through the writing process. This change can take many forms, whether a slight alteration to an initial thesis or a whole-cloth restart. In fact, changing their minds goes hand-in-hand with student-authors' lack of in-depth knowledge about their topics. As student-authors learn more about their topics and what they think about them, they will find opportunities to rethink their original ideas. Rethinking or restarting can frustrate student-authors who may feel as though they are wasting time. Student-authors may also feel overwhelmed by how much time, thought, and energy it takes to get their projects to where they want them to be. Student-authors often overwrite their background sections because it is easier to report and summarize what has been said than to say something new. This overwriting is not necessarily a problem, however, as overwriting can help student-authors gain mastery of a topic and understand how much background is necessary to support the paper's thesis.

For many student-authors, academic legal writing is a new type of writing. Even students who wrote a thesis or other major research papers before law school often find legal scholarship unique. Thus, another challenge is understanding academic legal writing compared to the practical legal writing they encountered in the first-year legal research and writing courses. In previous coursework, law students had specific writing prompts within a fictional factual universe. A scholarly project is unbounded and can feel overwhelming, even within a specific subject area.

Academic legal writing is often an isolating experience, and student-authors need guidance and support. Even student-authors who are part of journal staff will find themselves researching, thinking, and writing independently. Student-authors look to their student-editors for substantial support, but student-editors often find that they can offer only minimal supervision or support—or worse, advice that conflicts with other feedback. While it may be impossible for student-editors to provide as much support as student-authors want, if the student-editors are aware of this potential mismatch, they can strive to avoid misplaced reliance by communicating the limitations and boundaries of their expertise and input.

Another challenge is balancing writing deadlines with other commitments. Though law reviews typically have interim deadlines, these deadlines are often much further apart and feel less concrete compared to the writing deadlines students experienced as part of their first-year legal research and writing courses. Also, upper-level law students may be heavily involved in extracurricular activities, and many may be over-committed. Student-authors may find it easy to keep pushing off their journal work in favor of more concrete deadlines or more practical, doable tasks.

D. Common Challenges for Student-Editors

As a peer supervisor, student-editors are likely to encounter several challenges while managing and supporting student-authors. Similar to student-authors, student-editors may have limited knowledge about the student-authors' topics. Even on specialty journals, most third-year law student-editors are not likely to have mastered the topic area. The knowledge gap can make responding to student-authors' proposed topics and theses difficult, especially when a student-editor is supervising several different student-authors at once. In providing feedback to student-authors at the early stages of topic and thesis development, student-editors may mislead student-authors with false positives. Student-editors may even want to acknowledge that they are new to the editorial role and have limited experience. This acknowledgment is not intended to undermine the student-editor's role but to help the student-author understand the student-editor's perspective.

Student-editors also face challenges in balancing feedback deadlines with other commitments. The combination of time pressures and lack of knowledge might lead student-editors to give superficial feedback. One way to manage the various challenges is to develop and use checklists that help focus the student-editors' assessment and provide meaningful feedback. Thinking of feedback as a two-way conversation between student-author and student-editor can also reduce the pressure a student-editor may feel in "approving" a topic or draft. Rather than framing feedback as approval, student-editors can engage in a conversation that helps the student-author take the next steps with confidence.

Finally, student-editors may face challenges when collaborating and coordinating with faculty advisors. The best way to avoid these challenges is to have clearly defined roles throughout the process. For example, who is giving feedback at different stages of the writing process? Who makes the decision about whether the student-author has produced a credit-worthy paper? How will differences of opinion be reconciled? Clear communication throughout the process, with both the advisors and the student-authors, can mitigate problems that arise among advisors, student-editors, and student-authors. And to the extent problems do arise, open channels of communication can facilitate resolution.[5]

E. The Ideal Student-Author/ Student-Editor Collaboration

Creating an ideal supervisor experience requires planning and consistent follow-through. Student-editors should think of themselves as supportive facilitators; this mindset will allow them to respond best to common challenges. Student-authors will be figuring things out as they go, and student-editors simply will not have all the answers. Rather than set up a false expectation of expertise, student-editors can embrace their strengths and weaknesses to respond to student-authors' needs. Below are a few strategies to consider in working toward an ideal editor-author collaboration.

To the extent allowed within any academic rules requiring independent or confidential work, student-editors can create space and opportunity for conversation and peer review. Given that working on a scholarly project can be isolating, providing opportunities to discuss ideas can transform the experience and the final product. Conversations could be held as small group check-ins, with a student-editor facilitating a conversation among four to six student-authors. The student-authors might discuss their ideas and where they are in their projects, raise questions with which they are struggling, offer feedback to each other, and generally enjoy the camaraderie of knowing they are not alone as they work on their individual projects. Student-editors may

5. Consult Chapter 2 of this *Manual* for additional guidance about faculty advisors' responsibilities when academic credit is at issue.

want to set up more formal peer-review relationships, giving student-authors accountability to each other for meeting deadlines and setting up a go-to person for ongoing conversation about their papers.

To the extent possible, for each interim deadline (e.g., topic statement, bibliography, etc.), student-editors should provide student-authors with a detailed description of the goals and expectations for the interim deadline and examples. Student-authors often find annotated examples that identify strengths and weaknesses to be particularly helpful. Identifying and preparing these examples also helps the student-editors better articulate their expectations and identify strengths and weaknesses in their supervisees' work products.

Student-editors might also provide precise guidance for interim drafts that encourages student-authors to develop their analyses. For example, if the journal has a "first draft" requirement with little guidance about what that draft should contain, most student-authors will likely submit a background-heavy draft. To avoid that situation, student-editors could require something more specific, such as "first draft of analysis" or "first draft with no more than 30% background." Not only does this approach set clear expectations, but it focuses the student-author on the analysis, which is typically the most challenging part of the scholarly project. The more time, writing, and revising the student-author spends on the analysis, the better chances of a solid final paper.

In addition to setting expectations for student-authors' work, student-editors should discuss and set expectations for how to process feedback. Student-authors may have little experience receiving, considering, and applying peer feedback. Student-authors may be used to viewing feedback as "things to do" rather than as suggestions they could take or reject. To the extent feedback is intended to encourage the student-author to consider whether and how to revise their paper, that feedback should acknowledge that the student-author has autonomy about using the feedback. For more directive feedback, the student-editor should explain that distinction so that the student-author understands what is expected. For example, if the student-editor notes a grammatical error, they should cite the source and rule or page, so the student-author understands that specific change is not discretionary. Student-editors should also be open to ongoing conversations with student-authors as they work to incorporate feedback and make other revisions. Indeed, student-editors should encourage and facilitate these ongoing conversations to support and guide the student-author toward a successful paper.

Given the time most student-authors devote to their journal papers, consistent, responsive, and forward-looking support is critical to an effective editor-author relationship. In offering constructive feedback, student-editors can reinforce how the struggle is part of the writing-while-learning process. Simply acknowledging student-authors' experiences can go a long way toward helping student-authors take feedback as an opportunity to strengthen their papers.

When student-editors identify weaknesses, they should also suggest ideas for improvement. For example, suppose a paper's thesis is difficult to identify. In that case, the student-editor could suggest that the student-author write the thesis in a separate document and then compare it to the version in the paper. Or, if a student-editor notices large-scale organizational weaknesses, they could suggest the student-author create a reverse outline by pulling out the topic sentences of the paragraphs and then reading just those topic sentences to get a bird's-eye view of the paper. That technique can help uncover organizational flaws that are hard to identify by just rereading the entire paper.

Asking questions can be effective feedback in the early drafting stages. Questions can give the student-author a sense of how a reader may be struggling and provide a concrete path for further research, thinking, and writing. When possible, student-editors may also want to be flexible when it seems that a particular interim project is underdeveloped. Some drafts just may not be worth commenting on; student-editors should recognize that possibility and offer an opportunity for the student-author to revise the draft to avoid wasting time on both sides.

Finally, student-editors can ask student-authors to self-assess after each interim project. This technique gives the student-author the opportunity to step back, identify strengths and weaknesses, and start or continue a conversation with the student-editor. Accepting constructive feedback can be easier when student-authors have already identified their own weaknesses because the feedback comes as less of a criticism and more of a confirmation of their own thinking. Student-editors can also look for opportunities for knowledgeable empathy in responding to student-authors' self-identified challenges. The student-editor can affirm the student-author's concerns while giving direction for moving forward.

F. Giving Thoughtful Feedback

As discussed earlier in the Chapter, the writing process involves several stages.[6] This section will discuss challenges and strategies for each stage, with the ideal author-editor collaboration in mind.

6. Wherry & Murray, *supra* note 1, at 18–19.

1. Topic and thesis development

a. Pitfalls for student-authors

For many student-authors, choosing the topic and developing the thesis will be among the most time-consuming stages. These steps can also be the most frustrating, as some students eliminate several topics or theses before settling on something workable. The freedom to choose whatever topic they want can also intimidate many student-authors, especially if they did not experience that kind of autonomy in their first-year writing courses or have never written a scholarly research paper.

b. Suggestions for student-editors

Student-editors can share their own experiences finding a topic and developing a thesis. Setting early and frequent check-ins can also help support student-authors during this stage. A more formal training series could also be developed to help student-authors work through the topic and thesis development stage.

Student-editors may find it useful to provide a handout on how to identify a topic or thesis and a case suitable for a case note or comment. Faculty advisors and law librarians might also help develop these materials. Student-editors should provide this guidance as soon as possible to give the student-authors maximum time for brainstorming. A handout could include the following suggestions for brainstorming.[7]

TOPIC BRAINSTORM GUIDE[8]

- What am I interested in?
- What do I read first in the news? Have I read anything lately that bothers me or raises questions in my mind?
- What classes do I like the most? Why? What do I remember most from class? Was there a discussion that stuck with me?
- What questions were unanswered in class readings? Were there any questions from the notes portion of my casebooks that interested me?

---

7. *See, e.g.*, Lauren H. Uhlig, *Choosing a Successful Paper Topic*, Geo. U. L. Center Writing Center (2012), https://www.law.georgetown.edu/wp-content/uploads/2018/06/Uhlig-Choosing-a-Successful-Paper-Topic.pdf [https://perma.cc/S26N-7QH2].

8. This checklist is based on a suggested checklist in Wherry & Murray, *supra* note 1, at 39.

- Did I work on something over the summer that was interesting or that left me with questions?

Student-editors can also encourage student-authors to be intentional about brainstorming, suggesting that student-authors schedule time for it and stick to the schedule. Once student-authors feel comfortable enough with their initial topic and potential thesis, they may want to reach out to faculty experts who write about the same topic. Student-editors may be able to suggest faculty contacts for student-authors given that student-editors have had the opportunity to take more classes than student-authors.

c. Editorial feedback

In evaluating a topic or thesis, student-editors can focus on the clarity of the thesis and the likelihood that the thesis will evolve as the student-author researches and considers the subject. The feedback on topics and theses can be fairly general (because of the likely evolution) while including some sense of direction. Given student-editors' likely limited knowledge, a high-level assessment will probably be more effective than trying to review a proposed topic or thesis critically. Student-editors may want to consider less of a topic-approval process and more of a supportive conversation to help guide the student toward a workable topic and thesis.

One way to approach the feedback at this stage is to use a checklist and provide written responses to the student-author. The checklist can help the student-editor focus on the big picture and create opportunities for discussion between student-author and student-editor. Here is a sample checklist:

TOPIC AND THESIS REVIEW CHECKLIST

- Does the topic fit within the journal's limitations, if any?
- Is the thesis easily identifiable?
- Does the thesis say something concrete?
- Does the thesis seem manageable in light of the anticipated paper length and submission deadlines? If not, what suggestions do you have for refining the thesis at this early stage?
- What is your reaction as a reader to the proposed thesis?

Customizing a checklist to suit a particular journal could improve the review process. Student-editors could also ask student-authors to self-assess by completing a similar checklist.

Student-editors could collaborate with each other in providing feedback to student-authors. For example, student-editors could have a roundtable discussion to evaluate a group of student-authors' topics or theses. This approach would create an opportunity for student-authors to receive feedback from multiple student-editors, and to the extent there are common strengths and weaknesses among the group, student-editors could provide both individual and global feedback to the student-authors.

2. Research and background development

a. Pitfalls for student-authors

At the research and background-development stage, student-authors often feel lost as they attempt to learn about the relevant topic while simultaneously refining their thesis. Student-authors often feel inexpert and overwhelmed at this stage, resulting in an overly long background section.

b. Suggestions for student-editors

Providing research training can help student-authors leverage the various research sources, strategies, and tools they were not exposed to as first-year law students. For example, law librarians can provide individualized research assistance to student-authors working on a scholarly paper.[9] Scheduling a training as part of journal responsibilities could be a good way to make sure student-authors take advantage of the law librarians' expertise. Student-editors could require one-on-one meetings between student-authors and librarians as part of the writing process, group training, or a combination.

Managing research is also a critical part of this stage. The potential magnitude and variety of sources can present challenges, and many ways exist to organize research, whether electronically or in hard copy. Student-editors can share their expertise and offer advice on how to avoid common pitfalls, such as failing to identify the source of an idea or quotation properly. For example, student-editors might share spreadsheets or research plan templates as examples for student-authors to rely on or use as a starting point in developing their own approach. They might also hold a panel discussion with law faculty who regularly publish law-review articles to discuss their strategies for organizing material.

---

9. For more specific ideas about working with law librarians as part of the student-writing process, review Chapter 6 of this *Manual.*

At this stage, student-authors are considering preemption. Preemption only occurs when another author has published a paper that states the same thesis for the same reasons or when events change the premise on which a thesis is based. Student-editors can help student-authors understand preemption by explaining how rare it is and suggesting how student-authors can continue with the topic by adjusting their thesis or approach.

c. *Editorial feedback*

Student-editors often find it difficult to offer meaningful feedback at this stage unless the student-author's topic happens to be within the student-editor's area of knowledge. Err on the side of encouraging inclusiveness (of sources, content, or arguments), even if it is possible the student-author will later cut portions from the final version. At this stage, it's rare that a student-author or student-editor is equipped to make editorial choices related to the scope. Some student-authors struggle with deleting later once they realize they have too much background, but a successful scholarly project requires intentional edits to focus the paper.

The research and development stage is also when the student-editor might touch base with the student-author's substantive faculty advisor so that the student-editor and the faculty advisor are not providing conflicting or seemingly conflicting information to the student-author.

3. Drafting the analysis section

a. *Pitfalls for student-authors*

As student-authors transition to drafting, student-editors often back off and assume the student-authors are progressing. Some student-authors will thrive, while others will struggle with all or some of the challenges discussed above.

b. *Suggestions for student-editors*

During the stage when student-authors are drafting the analysis section, student-editors can offer support in at least two ways. One is to set interim deadlines that force the student-author to write something, even if it is later revised or deleted. The momentum of "just writing" can be enough to help student-authors avoid a last-minute writing marathon. For example, student-editors could require partial drafts even without reviewing them, just to keep student-authors on pace writing and revising.

Another supportive technique is to set up round-robin workshops for student-authors to check in with each other and the student-editors by describing the work they have done so far and their next steps. This check-in approach gives student-authors an opportunity to ask questions, respond to peers, and learn they are not alone in struggling through the drafting stage. Even that feeling of camaraderie can help motivate student-authors.

c. Editorial feedback

As a partial or full draft of the piece starts to emerge, student-editors might consider using checklists to provide feedback. A student-editor's checklist during this stage could be something like the following:

DRAFT FEEDBACK CHECKLIST[10]

- Is the thesis well-placed in the opening of the draft?
- Does the thesis seem valid and supported?
- Does the draft offer something practical or implementable?
- Does the draft identify any scope limitations?
- Does the draft use hypotheticals to illustrate the analysis?
- Does the analysis address counterarguments?
- Does the draft reflect any biases or assumptions?
- Does the draft ground the thesis in a broader context?
- Does the large-scale organization support the substance of the draft?
- Are the parts of the draft proportionately balanced?
- Does the draft seem to reflect rigorous research by relying on a reasonable number of seemingly authoritative sources?

Written answers to these questions with explanations (the "why" or "why not") can support and guide student-authors. Self-assessment during this stage can also be productive, again creating opportunities for student-authors to engage with their writing and discuss matters with their student-editor.

---

10. This checklist is based on a suggested checklist in WHERRY & MURRAY, *supra* note 1, at 157–58.

4. Feedback and revision

a. Pitfalls for student-authors

At the feedback and revision stage, student-authors might start to feel fatigued about the writing process and their own piece. Student-authors can also feel overwhelmed by feedback—especially if multiple supervisors are weighing in—or unsure whether or how to incorporate the feedback.

b. Suggestions for student-editors

During this stage, student-editors can support student-authors by discussing how the student-authors should evaluate and decide whether and how to incorporate feedback. As discussed earlier in this Chapter, student-authors will likely benefit from guidance about what to do with the feedback. Student-editors may want to encourage student-authors to apply feedback globally, use feedback to reread their work from a reader's perspective, and communicate disagreement about specific feedback. Student-editors may also need to remind student-authors that their paper is their own work and that, as the student-authors, they can decide whether and how to incorporate feedback.

Having student-authors participate in peer-review writing workshops at this stage can also be productive, as the student-authors can experience giving and receiving feedback. It can help to have additional peer feedback that reinforces student-editor feedback or offers an alternative view. In setting up a peer evaluation, questions could include the following:

WRITING WORKSHOP CHECKLIST[11]

- Do you understand the thesis?
- Are you interested in reading the paper based on the thesis?
- Does the thesis seem too narrow or broad?
- What would you expect to see in the paper based on the thesis?
- Does the organizational flow make sense to you as a reader?
- What questions come to mind as you read the draft?

---

11. This checklist is based on a suggested set of workshop questions in WHERRY & MURRAY, *supra* note 1, at 163.

5. Finalizing the piece

In the final stage, student-authors begin to feel relief at the prospect of finishing their project. Student-editor support includes reviewing and approving the technical aspects of the paper and explaining the publishing process—both of which can vary journal-by-journal. For example, some journals publish all student works, while most select only a few. When a journal selects only a small number to publish, student-editors may want to encourage student-authors to seek publication elsewhere and provide some guidance about that process.

6. Leveraging technology throughout the writing process

Technology can help make the writing and editing experiences seamless and paperless. Below is a non-exclusive list of ideas for ways to incorporate technology:

- use a shared Dropbox or similar cloud-based folder to store different drafts and collect sources;
- use news alerts or social media to track "hot topics" during the writing process;
- use shared Westlaw or Lexis folders so that student-editors have easy access to student-authors' sources;
- use a shared Google Doc for collaborative writing or to offer comments and editorial suggestions on drafts;
- use name-identified margin comments in a word-processing program so that multiple supervisors can offer comments within the same document;
- use learning management systems like Canvas or Blackboard to communicate with student-authors and collect drafts;
- use peer-review software such as Peerceptiv to facilitate sharing feedback among student-authors; and
- where permissible, use editing software such as WordRake to help with grammar, writing, and syntax.

KEY TAKEAWAYS

- A successful editorial experience depends on the student-editor understanding the student-author's motivations and challenges.
- The ideal student-editor–student-author collaboration involves clear expectations, meeting deadlines, and open communication.
- Student-editors can offer student-authors various methods of feedback throughout the writing process, for example, brainstorming support, peer feedback, self-reflection, checklists, and traditional written feedback.
- Leverage technology to help make the writing and editing experiences seamless and paperless.

13

Author Relations

Mark Cooney

LEARNING OBJECTIVES

After reviewing this Chapter, editors will be able to

- recognize their authors' goals, needs, and concerns;
- communicate effectively with authors, including judicial authors;
- resolve suspected plagiarism or latent author errors;
- defend edits to skeptical authors; and
- plan marketing strategies with authors or respond to criticism of their work.

A. About Your Author

First, let's meet your author.

Your author is a friend of your journal and your school. They had hundreds of publishers to choose from. Something about your school or journal prompted them to submit their article to you. The author may have submitted to dozens of journals, but one was yours.

Your author has spent months or years researching, thinking about, and writing their article. It embodies their creativity, hard work, and sacrifice, and it reflects their hope to share knowledge and advance professionally. Your author is someone who values scholarship, careful research, and the power of language. They are a dedicated person—a person willing to think, teach, question, and challenge.

These truths should shape your author relations.

As you read and evaluate submissions or edit an accepted piece, you and your fellow editors might start to view an article as yet another law-school burden. Take a step back every so often and remember that you are holding something precious to the author. You have important decisions to make. But whatever your editorial words, thoughts, or actions may be, remember that your author, the person impacted by them, is a friend of your journal and your school—a friend who has taken pains to produce something beyond the usual.

B. Working with Different Types of Authors

1. Academic authors

Academic authors are probably your most typical authors because they are motivated to produce scholarship. They have incentives (and pressures) that practitioners, judges, and students usually don't have. Because so many of their professional hours are devoted to writing law review articles, academics often get quite good at producing interesting, refined work—the type of work that makes your job a bit easier. You'll surely receive less refined efforts, and sometimes articles that shine in the text lose a bit of luster in the footnotes. But most academic authors will submit articles that are well researched, polished, and insightful.

Your relations with academic authors will likely be colored by their intimate understanding of law journals and how they work. This may be a mixed blessing. When interacting with an academic author, you'll often be interacting with a keen strategist—someone who's eager to jockey for a faster decision, a more careful (and receptive) reading, and ultimately, a coveted placement.

During the height of submission season, you'll receive a fair number of requests to expedite article reviews. The authors making these requests will inform you that another journal has already accepted their article and has imposed a tight deadline for acceptance. The author will then explain that they would rather publish with you and ask you to move their article to the top of the pile.

One unspoken message in this request is, of course, that the author's article must be top-notch or else the other journal wouldn't have accepted it so quickly. So this author hopes that you'll not only read their article immediately but will also read it with a positive bias.

Even the Scholastica website counsels authors on these strategies, and academic authors are the obvious targets of this advice.

Your journal should adopt and follow a standard procedure for handling requests to expedite. What that procedure looks like is a policy decision.

Your journal might simply refuse to play the game. If so, say that in your submissions guidelines. If your journal takes a less rigid stance, consider requesting proof of the competitor journal's acceptance. Also consider carving out student safe zones, meaning times when your journal won't consider requests even though it usually does. You and your fellow editors should not, for instance, feel compelled to do expedited reviews during finals week or the week before finals.

A 2007 survey revealed that journal editors—from the highest-ranked journals to the lowest-ranked journals—resented authors' gamesmanship in trying to "trad[e] up."[1] The surveyed editors saw authors as "calculating" and "brutal."[2] They lamented the wasted time and wondered why an author would put so much effort into such a negligible boost in prestige.[3] Some editors were surprised by the lack of author loyalty[4] and were disappointed that law professors, who should serve as positive role models for law students, reneged on agreements after receiving offers from higher-ranked schools.[5]

The consequence of this trading-up game is that you may find yourself in the inferior bargaining position, forced to sell your journal to keep an article whose author may be looking to climb another rung up the prestige ladder.[6] The transaction may end up resembling an arms-length horse trade. It may try your patience.

Editors negotiating to keep an accepted piece might rely on citation statistics, noting the number or prominence of citations to their journal. (In my law review days, editors flaunted a then-recent citation by Justice Sandra Day O'Connor.) You might emphasize your journal's institutional attentiveness to author needs or your record of timely, regular publication. You might even sway some authors by wondering aloud whether a modest trade-up will have any practical value.

The best you can do is to acclimate yourself to the relatively rockier world of academic-author relations. Bear in mind that along with the frustrations described above, you will also, according to the same surveyed journal editors,

---

1. Leah M. Christensen & Julie A. Oseid, *Navigating the Law Review Article Selection Process: An Empirical Study of Those with All the Power—Student Editors*, 59 S.C. L. Rev. 175, 206 (2007).

2. *Id.* at 207.

3. *Id.* at 206.

4. *Id.*

5. *Id.* at 207.

6. *Id.* at 206–07.

have "very pleasant interactions with professors who ma[k]e this process fun and exciting."[7] And you'll "frequently be[ ] impressed with the quality of the intellectual endeavors that the professors have undertaken and the professionalism with which they interact with students."[8]

You might come to find that authors' strategic maneuverings actually help you with the article-selection process. The requests to expedite might help you pinpoint promising articles—though this wouldn't be welcome news to authors who refuse to play the game and who worry that they may suffer for their civility.

2. Same-school academic authors

One scenario undeniably sharpens the edge on author relations: interacting with an author from your school's faculty. And this scenario surely redoubles the usual discomfort associated with communicating a rejection.

Your school's faculty shouldn't expect special treatment, but some might. Even if a faculty member shows no expectation of special treatment, you may still see fit to modify your practices a bit, recognizing that these authors are valued members of your school's academic family.

Consider appointing special editors to handle faculty submissions, meaning editors who haven't taken a course (or otherwise interacted) with the author. This lends a greater sense of objectivity to the evaluation process and the editorial work that occurs after acceptance.

Some journals choose to communicate with their school's faculty authors in person, which may lend an uplifting, celebratory air if you're delivering good news. But delivering a rejection to one of your own professors would surely test any student's fortitude.

Whether your rejections are written or in person, let your faculty advisor know first and ask their advice on how to best deliver the disappointing news. Your faculty advisor may offer to deliver the news or appreciate a chance to speak to their colleague before your official notification. If the rejection is left to you, be sure to tactfully offer concrete reasons for your decision. Those reasons might help the author improve the article and will dispel any suspicion that the journal's motives were personal.

---

7. *Id.* at 207.

8. *Id.*

Exercise restraint and decorum by not sharing your professor's rejection with friends or faculty, unless in the context of a genuine request for advice or support.

3. Symposium authors

Symposium authors come in many varieties, and their identity and preferences might depend on whether your symposium consists of a live event, a special theme issue, or both.

Your invitation to prospective symposium participants should clearly outline your expectations. State whether the invitation is contingent on their submitting an article and, if so, when the first draft is due. Requesting a first draft before a live event helps both you and your author; it ensures that your author is primed for the event, and it helps your moderator prepare probing, fruitful questions. Authors also benefit from the chance to revise and refine their draft after the event, perhaps infusing some new point or idea that emerged during a panel discussion.

Some symposium authors are academics with a passion for publishing. Others may have expertise well-suited to a panel discussion but no strong desire to publish. The upshot is that although your symposium authors will surely include eager scholars, you may also find yourself needing to prod a bit, coach a bit, help a bit, or concede a bit. This doesn't change the rules of communication. But it does mean that your author relations may be more varied with symposium authors.

For less experienced symposium authors, take extra care to define your expectations for their article—and give them samples to mimic. Be clear about your word-count or page expectations. Give your authors a clear vision of what your goal is and what their goals should be.

For symposium panelists who are eager, prolific authors, your communication might include strategic questions about how the authors intend to refer to their previous works. Experts naturally revisit issues and themes. But some careful messaging to these authors might help you protect against submissions that amount to a recycling of the author's previously published works.

4. Judicial authors

Judicial authors may pose additional communication challenges for two reasons. First, with judicial authors, journal editors must often communicate through a go-between, usually the judge's administrative assistant or law clerk.

Second, journal editors may be slightly intimidated by the prospect of interacting with—and suggesting edits to—judges. Remembering a few things should help you through the process.

When you write an email to the judge's assistant, always treat that person with respect and assume that the judge will read every word of it. Don't let your guard down. You are still communicating with the judge.

Also remember that your judicial author is an actual person. Despite their job title and robe, they have the same concerns as any other author. In fact, the judge's concerns about possible errors may be heightened, given the judge's public stature and the scrutiny that judge-written articles receive. Thus, be ready for—and tolerant of—a judicial author's requests for additional author reviews, especially at the galley stage.

5. Practitioner authors

Practitioner authors are probably your least typical. They come from all walks of practice and offer an almost unlimited variety of interests and experiences.

Some practitioners may have been journal editors during law school and may still keep their dog-eared, early-edition citation manual within reach. That author might meet your expectations with flying colors and leave you little to wrestle with during your edits.

Other practitioners may have caught the scholarship bug after 20 years in practice. These authors might have a unique and highly valuable perspective to offer. But some aspects of their work may fall short of your expectations.

It's dubious to attribute common characteristics to practitioner authors. But if you were to anticipate typical practitioner–author traits, they'd likely be traits that make author relations easier, not harder. As infrequent journal authors, practitioners may be more open to your edits and suggestions—and quicker to defer to you. The typical practitioner may also be less concerned about your publishing timeline than an academic author feeling the pinch to publish before a promotion deadline.

The notable exception is a practitioner eyeing an academic career. That practitioner may feel intense pressure to build a body of scholarship worthy of professorship applications. And they must produce that scholarship while also meeting the demands of daily law practice.

6. International authors

Communicating with international authors may pose special challenges, notably challenges concerning language differences. Even if your author is fluent in English, they may have relied on resources written in a language that's foreign to you. This might be an occasion when your journal's diverse membership is especially helpful. One or more members may be able to translate the non-English resources or may be able to communicate with the author in their native language. The happy byproduct might be an enhanced bond between your journal and the author.

You can also ask a librarian to help you find translations for non-English sources—and help determine how to cite those sources properly. Some schools have librarians who specialize in foreign and international law. Ask those librarians about available resources (including free resources) for creating translations. Or you may contact someone elsewhere in the university for help—for example, a particular language department. The *ALWD Guide to Legal Citation* lists a number of helpful guides for citing international sources, including the *Guide to Foreign and International Legal Citations* (published by NYU's *Journal of International Law and Politics*). You'll also find rules on citing international sources in *The Bluebook*'s online Table T2 ("Foreign Jurisdictions"). But a librarian's knowledge of international legal systems may prove invaluable when applying those rules.

C. Typical Author Concerns

Most author concerns are universal. Whether your author is a federal judge, a local trust specialist, a new academic, or a shining star in the academic firmament, they will worry about rejection and, after crossing that hurdle, will worry about embarrassing errors or someone changing their work without fully understanding it. The author's name is on the work, and errors will be attributed to them. Yes, the finer points of citation deserve your attention. But no journal faculty advisor has ever gotten an angry phone call over a *supra* that wasn't italicized. The text is paramount. Authors want it clean.

Yet no two authors are alike, even if they come from the same segment of the legal profession. For instance, at first blush, academic authors would all seem to have the same goals and concerns. Yet their feelings may vary greatly when submitting articles. Most academic authors try to place their articles in the highest-ranked journal possible. Yet a tenured law professor from an elite school can rest easy that their work will be welcomed and read with care.[9] The same isn't true for professors from lower-ranked schools. Those authors may fear that no matter how excellent their work, it won't be considered by highly ranked journals. They may also fear that if their work is published in a lower-ranked journal, it will not garner the same level of credibility from peers and from those evaluating their tenure dossiers.[10] To put it more frankly, professors from lower-tiered schools may feel an added pressure to overcome editorial bias against them.

Other author concerns are far more practical. Timing is a big one. If your author is from the academic world, they may be facing a promotion deadline that requires publication or at least a written publication offer by a date certain. After you've accepted an article, the author may, for the same reason, begin to worry if you experience delays during the editorial process.

Authors are always on the alert for editorial changes that compromise accuracy. So if your edits affect the text's core substance, meaning the author's description or analysis of the law, expect heightened scrutiny.

Finally, authors can be sensitive about their authorial voice, meaning their fingerprint diction, cadence, and tone. If your author is, for example, a plain-language advocate, you'll face friction if you suggest lawyerisms such as "pursuant to." And a judicial author renowned for a direct, conversational style may balk at an editor's attempt to impose a wordier, stiffer style.

D. Communicating with Your Author

1. Offers to publish

Your most vital communication with an author is your offer to publish, which should state any special conditions or expectations. You might attach your journal's standard publishing agreement, though many journals prefer to wait until after an author accepts.

A typical offer to publish imposes a deadline to encourage acceptance and discourage author delay. A reasonable deadline might be two weeks, although the deadline could be longer or shorter depending on myriad factors, such

9. *See id.* at 188–89 (describing survey indicating that journal editors consider where an academic author teaches and the employer school's ranking and reputation).

10. *See id.*

as the author's status, the journal's publication schedule, and whether you have other articles you would be excited to publish if the author declines. As mentioned earlier, some authors will use your offer to publish—and your deadline—to seek expedited reviews from higher-ranked journals. But other authors will simply wait and see whether they receive other offers during your acceptance window. If not, they'll accept. Some will get antsy and accept well before your deadline expires.

A twist on the standard acceptance deadline is the so-called exploding offer, which adds an element of competition. When a journal makes an exploding offer, it informs the author that it has offered the same publication slot to multiple authors; once one author accepts, the other offers are automatically revoked. This technique turns the tables on authors and may put off those who resent, after all their careful work, seeing the process devolve into an unseemly sprint for a publication slot. The counterargument is that exploding offers give journals a legitimate safeguard against authors who view traditional acceptance windows as opportunities to jockey for better offers. As exploding offers become more common, each journal will need to settle on a policy that suits its needs, situation, and reputational aspirations.

As for an offer's form, consider creating a PDF of a signed hardcopy and attaching that to your acceptance email. Academic authors may want to include it in an application for renewal, promotion, or tenure. The letterhead promotes your journal and your school. And if you're from a prestigious journal, your author might want this acceptance letter as a keepsake. In any event, creating a letter in PDF form is a small gesture with a big impact.

Whether you accept with a formal letter or an informal email, be sure to invite the author to email you with questions or concerns. Although this step is fairly standard, it reassures authors that you value them and understand that the article reflects their hard work and maybe their professional future.

2. Rejections

According to Scholastica, "many journals" don't bother notifying authors of rejections.[11] Some frustrated authors have referred to this omission as a

---

11. Elli Olson, *5 Reasons Your Law Review Should Be Sending Rejections*, SCHOLASTICA (Mar. 29, 2016), https://blog.scholasticahq.com/post/5-reasons-your-law-review-should-be-sending-rejections [https://perma.cc/JE5E-NG8B].

stealth rejection.[12] If your journal doesn't formally reject submissions, consider changing your practice.

During high-submission periods, it can be burdensome to send individual rejections to every author. Yet a flat rejection through the Scholastica website takes about eight seconds.[13] An email takes a bit longer, but not much, especially if your journal has a template. Either way, an explicit rejection gives authors a clear resolution and allows them to pursue other publishers. It also gives authors the courtesy they deserve.

In a perfect world, you might add a word or two about why you've declined the article. This may be impractical if your journal receives a high volume of submissions. (Some receive thousands of submissions per year.[14]) But giving authors a reason for your decision will reassure them that you've actually considered their work. The reason might be that the work is ill-suited to your journal's focus, that you've recently published on the same or a similar topic, that the jurisdictional focus is too narrow, or that you've already filled your next issue. Whatever the reason, a succinct explanation is a laudable courtesy and also shines some light into what cynics call the article-selection "black box."[15]

Avoid, however, form rejection letters heaping generic words of praise. Online academic forums and blogs are dotted with notes by authors who prefer a simple, straightforward rejection. Those authors believe that a journal's rote praise for rejected works is unnecessary or disingenuous, especially when the correspondence is an obvious form letter. Also avoid negative comments about the author or author's writing style that could lead to a defamation claim.

3. The need for regular communication

After you accept an article and the author signs on the dotted line, be sure to keep in touch with the author. Like lawyers who become so immersed in their day-to-day work on a case that they lose track of the client, journal editors can become so immersed in processing and editing an article that they lose track of its author. But your author is always there. Remember that point, even

12. *See id.*

13. *Id.*

14. Christensen & Oseid, *supra* note 1, at 203–04.

15. Jason P. Nance & Dylan J. Steinberg, *The Law Review Article Selection Process: Results from a National Study*, 71 ALB. L. REV. 565, 568 (2008).

as the work gets heavy. Give your authors occasional progress reports, even if just a few lines in an email.

Responsiveness is crucial. Many things that you do as an editor take a great deal of time and effort, whether it's reading and evaluating submissions or checking citations and author sources. But replying to an email is not one of those time-consuming tasks. It takes little time or effort.

Even if an author's email raises something that may take some time or reflection, a quick "I'll check on this and get back to you as soon as I can" will do wonders to make your author feel less detached from you and the editorial process.

And though you may sometimes feel overwhelmed by the sheer volume of submissions, you only have a few accepted authors. There's no reason to shirk on your communication with them.

4. Expect a positive experience

Before addressing the possible challenges associated with author communications, it's worth noting that one of the great joys of editorial work is communicating and collaborating with authors. Your author interactions will usually blossom into positive experiences that produce a shared sense of accomplishment. You'll sense the author's appreciation for your hard, careful work. And once the editing is done and the volume is published, the author will remain a professional contact—and a potentially valuable one.

Academic authors have devoted their lives to helping students grow and succeed. So even if your author teaches at another school, you should expect the same nurturing attitude that you get from your own school's faculty members. Judges and practicing lawyers especially enjoy interacting with law students. Interacting with you reminds them of their own law-school days and the optimism of youth. To a busy practicing lawyer, your energy is an antidote to the toil of day-to-day law practice.

So expect a positive experience, but be realistic. Occasional exceptions may arise (as discussed later).

5. Author preferences

In your effort to communicate effectively with authors, many little things (that don't take much time) can make a big difference. Your first priority should be to learn how your author prefers to communicate. They may prefer a certain email address, or they may want periodic phone or online meetings. They may be a judge who prefers that you email their administrative assistant. Try to confirm and record these preferences soon after the author accepts your offer to publish.

6. The internet factor

Online submission platforms have added a notable wrinkle to author communication. As of this writing, Scholastica is the most visible service, and it offers a number of electronic avenues for quick, clear interaction with submitting authors. If your journal uses Scholastica, much of your author interaction may flow through the website's "Discussions" feature. Double-check your Scholastica settings to ensure that you receive email notifications of authors' Discussion posts. Some authors may prefer to communicate exclusively through the Discussions feature—and may even reply to your emails that way. Email notifications reduce the risk of missing a message.

Be aware that your authors may have gotten advice on how to communicate with you from internet-based third parties. For instance, Scholastica has an author-tips page that advises authors on "law review communication best practices."[16]

If your journal puts a high value on its reputation for author-friendliness, be sure not to let online communication options create even more distance between you and your accepted or prospective authors. It would be easy to reduce author interaction (especially at the submission stage) to a series of rote mouse-clicks. Ask whether that's how your journal prefers to do business. For journals that receive very high volumes of submissions, the answer might be a frank "*yes*." But if your journal is interested in building relationships with legal professionals and leaving a good taste in authors' mouths, consider augmenting those mouse-clicks when possible, even if just slightly.

7. Author attentiveness

An essential part of author relations is keeping up with your busy authors and ensuring that they fulfill their end of the publishing bargain, whether it's

---

16. *Top Law Review Submission Tips for Authors: 2021 Edition*, SCHOLASTICA (Jan. 27, 2021), https://blog.scholasticahq.com/post/law-review-article-submission-tips-for-authors [https://perma.cc/VJ7E-3ESH] (recommending, for example, that authors keep their emails brief and use clear subject lines).

responding to your request for rewrites or a final galley review. Your authors may include professors transitioning to new academic posts, busy practitioners immersed in major cases, or new law graduates who are simultaneously studying for the bar exam, going to job interviews, and moving to a new city. As excited as these authors are to be published in your journal, they may, at times, treat your requests as lower-priority items.

Fundamentals matter: be sure to keep your author contact information current. And compassionate pressure helps. When reaching out to authors with requests, try to impress on them the need for reasonable timeliness and attentiveness. You're publishing more than their article in the designated issue.

8. Mistakes

We all make them. Perhaps a late edit knocked some footnotes off-kilter. Or maybe you went to print with a conspicuous spelling error or a patch of discrepant font. If your journal has made a mistake, a simple, direct apology can go a long way, preferably with a plan for remedying the error.

E. Defending Your Edits

Part of an editor's job is responding to authors' questions about edits. Though it's common to back off some edits in deference to your author's wishes or voice, on other occasions, you'll want to stand firm. When you do want to stand firm, a number of techniques can help you to defend your edits.

1. Cite a specific rule in your preferred style manual

Most journals look to *The Redbook*, the *Chicago Style Manual*, or another manual to guide their decisions on style, usage, and mechanics. That manual is your best resource for reassuring an author who questions an edit. Just like a lawyer who's ready with authority for a skeptical judge, editors should be ready with supporting authority when discussing a disputed edit.

For instance, citing the *Redbook*'s Rule 1.60(b) to explain why you've inserted hyphens in the phrase *breach-of-warranty claim* is far more effective than merely insisting that your crack editorial staff knows the phrasal-adjective hyphen rule. Citing a neutral authority objectively supports your edit. Citing the manual also removes you from the debate. If misgivings remain, the author's beef is now with the nation's leading usage expert and lexicographer, not you.

Most authors relent once they see and check your citation to authority. Often, the author learns something new and appreciates the experience. In fact, the late Richard Wydick, author of the venerable *Plain English for Lawyers*, acknowledged just such a usage awakening during his give-and-take with an astute student editor.[17]

2. Rely on house style

Most publishers have preferences on style, usage, and typography. For instance, *The New York Times* has a style manual that outlines its house preferences, and those preferences sometimes differ on certain points from the Associated Press's style manual.[18]

Your journal may also have its own house style on certain points of usage, such as insisting on the Oxford comma. House style ensures your journal's consistency. When faced with author questions, invoking house style insulates you from the dispute and puts the onus back on the author. After all, an author who opposes a house-style edit would be asking for special treatment or for you to break your journal's internal rules. Most authors won't feel comfortable doing that.

3. Stay tactful

Stay tactful when communicating with an author. Don't let any tension surrounding a disputed edit shake your civility. Remember that editors are meant to help authors.

Even when you're digging your heels in on an edit, the conversation should remain calm and positive. Help your author understand why you want the edit to stick. Focus on how the edit improves the author's work product, maintains your journal's style consistency, or protects the author from potential criticism. Try to foster a spirit of collaboration. But if the author is unyielding, ask yourself whether the author's version is offensive, unethical, inaccurate, or

---

17. Richard C. Wydick, *True Confessions of a Diddle-Diddle Dumb-Head*, 11 Scribes J. Legal Writing 57, 58–63 (2007) (recalling when a student editor taught him to use "that" for restrictive clauses and "which" for nonrestrictive clauses).

18. Allena Tapia, *AP Style Cheat Sheet*, Balance Small Bus. (Sept. 4, 2019), https://www.thebalancesmb.com/associated-press-cheat-sheet-1360728 [https://perma.cc/RGT4-BWW4].

embarrassing to your journal. If not, then it's probably time to relent. In the end, it's the author's article.

For much more about the editorial process, consult Chapter 14, "The Editorial Process: Substantive and Technical Editing."

F. Coping with Tinkerers

There's one in almost every issue: that author whose definition of "finished" is a bit, well, elastic.

The negative side of late author changes is that it upsets your carefully charted schedule. If an author asks to make late changes or submits unsolicited additions or edits, you might caution the author that each phase of the editorial process is carefully timed to ensure careful, quality checks—checks meant to protect both the author and your journal from miscues or inaccuracies. Every late-stage change forces your journal to retrace aspects of that process. And if those editorial checks and balances are retraced in haste to meet an impending deadline, you face increased risks that an error might find its way into the final product.

Still, there are positive sides to late author changes. Your author has lived with the article since its inception and may be acutely aware of weaker spots. Authors sometimes supplement research and discover some authority that plugs a hole. Or an author might revisit a difficult patch of text and discover a better way to articulate a point. Any of these late discoveries might enhance the article.

The best approach is to keep an open mind while reminding the author of your commitments and deadlines. And remember that a tinkerer is an author who cares. Some of the best writers are notorious tinkerers, and their editorial instincts can help you.

G. Problem Authors

True problem authors are rare. You'll likely get through your journal commitment without experiencing anything more dramatic than the odd squawk about delays or commas. But alas, problem authors do exist.

Some authors plagiarize. And often you can't discover this problem before accepting the article. Plagiarists usually fit one of two categories. Some are blithely ignorant. They don't realize, despite completing law school and practicing for years, that a mere citation, without quotation marks, is insufficient after lifting a passage verbatim. These errors will unsettle you, but they can be innocent and corrected quickly.

Other authors are calculating and unethical. Perhaps they've found some felicitous language in an uncommon source that they don't expect you to find and want to borrow it to impress readers. They omit not only quotation marks but also the citation.

This scenario warrants consulting with your faculty advisor. Your faculty advisor can review the article with you, get a sense for the level of deceit, and discuss your options. Those options would include invoking your right (under the publication agreement) to withdraw acceptance. Your faculty advisor can also serve as a buffer between you and your indignant or defensive author.

A twist on this is so-called self-plagiarism: when an author has borrowed heavily (and perhaps verbatim) from their own previous works. In a perfect world, your preemption checks would expose this issue before acceptance. If not, your choices are to rescind acceptance or work with the author to freshen retread passages. If you're leaning toward dropping the article, check your publishing agreement for language reflecting the author's warranty that the article hasn't been published elsewhere, in whole or in part.[19]

Less dramatic than the plagiarist—but no less problematic—are authors who might be called careless. Think of an author who submits an article and expects you to refine it. When this carelessness is pervasive and obvious, you can simply reject the article. But sometimes an author's lack of diligence emerges only after acceptance and editorial scrutiny. Seemingly well-supported ideas don't match their cited sources, quoted passages can't be found, and so on. Unraveling these mysteries and cleaning them up can cause resentment among journal members, who feel as if they're *doing* the author's work rather than *checking* the author's work. This scenario may well test your patience and politesse during author interactions.

If addressing such an article's shortcomings becomes too onerous, consult your faculty advisor. Sometimes the extra effort to rescue an author's sloppy work is worth it. After all, you saw enough in the article to accept it. But if rescuing the article could compromise your ability to meet your publication

---

19. For more information about publishing agreements, review Chapter 18 of this *Manual*.

goals, your editorial board or faculty advisor may need to approach the author and ask for prompt corrections on pain of forfeiting acceptance.

Again, look to your publishing agreement if you decide to rescind acceptance. You'll surely find language about unforeseen deficiencies in the author's work (including the research) and your journal's right to back out. Whenever you rescind acceptance, be sure to do so in writing. Quote and cite relevant language from the publishing agreement. And be sure to describe the article's shortcomings in a professional manner, expressing your concerns without appearing to belittle or chastise the author.

H. Asking for Rewrites or Supplements

If you accept an article despite a few wobbly spots, it's best to ask for rewrites or supplements right away, preferably in your acceptance letter, so that your memory is fresh, and the author has more time to work.

It's fair to condition acceptance on the author's willingness to rewrite or supplement portions of the article. But give a firm deadline for the rewrite. If the article isn't time-sensitive and presents a worthy, compelling thesis, you might decline the article but invite the author to resubmit it—noting that this invitation isn't a promise to publish the revised version.

The need for rewrites or supplemental research often emerges during the editorial process. When possible, ask the author to do the heavy lifting rather than committing staff time and resources. If the rewrite is sizeable, an author is unlikely to be satisfied with your attempts to rework passages. Plus, for all the flaws you've discovered, the author is still the expert, having considered the subject deeply for quite some time. Thus, the author's rewrite is more likely to be apt and accurate.

Be clear about your deadline for revisions so that your publication schedule remains intact.

I. Final Author Signoff—Sharing the Galley

Always share the final galley proof with the author. And inform authors about this practice from the outset. Sharing the final galley is the single most reassuring gesture that you can make for an author.

Some journals don't volunteer a galley review to their authors for fear that it invites last-minute tinkering and could slow the publication process. Resist that fear and stifle your reluctance. If it's not your regular practice to let authors review the galley, allow it if an author asks. Remember that their name is on the article, not yours. Sharing the galley gives you an added layer of protection. Most authors will print out the galley and review it with a keen eye. Their review could spot and correct an error that escaped your editorial team's notice.

J. Authors' Marketing Concerns

As an issue nears publication, expect author inquiries about article promotion. If your journal doesn't have clear, updated policies in place, adopt them to reassure authors that their intended use of their article, before and after publication, is permissible. The wave of recent sentiment has been toward open access—as evidenced by the 2008 Durham Statement on Open Access to Legal Scholarship—with no requirement that authors assign their copyrights to journals.[20] And scholars have questioned the propriety of copyright assignments in this digital age.[21]

Whether your journal continues to require a copyright assignment, accepts a nonexclusive license, or allows authors unfettered use of their articles, be clear and upfront with your authors. If you intend to control or restrict your author's use, communicate this in your acceptance letter even if it also appears in your publishing agreement's fine print.[22]

The internet has changed authors' attitudes about a law journal's role. Some in academia now liken a law journal to an archival repository—an article's "final resting place" after its life (and previous incarnations) on the internet.[23] Many of your authors will post their articles on SSRN, without discussion or a request, before you publish. In fact, they may post their article before submitting it to journals to receive helpful peer feedback or to start earning coveted

---

20. Brian L. Frye, Chistopher Ryan & Franklin Runge, *An Empirical Study of Law Journal Copyright Practices*, 16 J. Marshall Rev. Intell. Prop. L. 207, 212–14 (2017).

21. *Id.* at 214.

22. For additional information about copyrights and publication agreements, see Chapter 17 of this *Manual*.

23. Barry Friedman, *Fixing Law Reviews*, 67 Duke L.J. 1297, 1332 (2018).

downloads. Peer commentary may help your author (and you) shore up an article's shaky spots. And SSRN postings may lead to blog posts about the article (including your journal name, if you've accepted the piece).

If you make articles available online and rely on downloads to measure your publication's reach and popularity, you might encourage authors to rely on your website's download statistics rather than posting on SSRN or another platform. Yet academic authors will likely remain eager to post on SSRN to bolster their overall download statistics, so you may meet some resistance if you suggest total reliance on your journal's website downloads.

For more about how your journal can influence an article's scholarly impact post-production, review Chapter 16.

K. Negative (or Hostile) Reactions to an Author's Work

Part of your journal's job is to publish articles with a fresh or unique take. Some articles may challenge conventions or rebuke our judicial system or society. Some may test your ability to balance your journal's editorial spirit with your school's sense of decorum.

Your editors will readily identify submissions that are overtly political, ideological, or provocative. Some authors court controversy or aim to stir ideological rivals. Some target certain segments of society. This tactic usually jumps off the page. If your journal is tempted by such a submission, consult your faculty advisor, and consider whether to alert the Dean (who may, in turn, want to consult with the school's General Counsel, Provost, or President). Your faculty advisor can offer perspective, including an institutional perspective. Allow time for this consultation process to conclude before accepting the article, even at the risk of losing it to another journal.

If your journal accepts a patently controversial article, you won't be surprised by backlash from your school community, your readers, or the larger community. Nor will your author. Presumably, you, the author, and your faculty advisor will already have a strategy in place for addressing complaints.

If the critical outcry builds while an accepted article appears online but before you've gone to print, you may start to second-guess your decision to publish. If so, your author will surely point out that you expected controversy from the outset. This is all the more reason to exercise great care before accepting such a piece. When you deliberate, remember that controversy is easy to withstand when it's in the abstract; once it's real, your stomach will feel the difference.

In other instances, however, you and your author might be blindsided by criticism, and this unanticipated criticism may shake your confidence. These moments also require effective communication.

If you learn about prepublication criticism, discuss it with your author. Is the criticism substantive, suggesting a flaw in your author's understanding of the law? Is the criticism subjective, or does it concern an objectively verifiable flaw? Did your author rely on bad law? Did the law underlying your author's analysis change? Whatever the nature or source, if the criticism is valid and arrives before you go to print, consider it a blessing, albeit one that may sting your author's ego. You can react to it and adjust the article.

Other unexpected prepublication criticism may be more problematic and tempt—or cause—you to rescind acceptance. For example, some in the legal or wider community may complain that the article is insensitive, implicitly biased, or otherwise offensive in ways that weren't apparent to your editors.

Sometimes, that concern may arise from a word choice or term ("illegal aliens," for example) that you and the author can change. But other times, those negative reactions might expose an intrinsic or pervasive perspective that didn't jump off the pages during your review. If this situation arises, your board should meet and discuss whether to move forward with your offer to publish. Again, consult your faculty advisor and consider whether to alert the Dean. You'll all need to consider the institutional implications of publishing an article that some believe to be implicitly biased or that has otherwise become controversial. Editors might consider this scenario when reviewing the journal's publication agreement.

If harsh, unanticipated criticism arises after you've published an article, then you'll want to communicate with the author about whether or how to react. Sometimes criticism simply comes with the territory, and there's nothing to do but accept it and move on (perhaps anticipating a future response article). Journals sometimes invite response articles, affirmatively embracing the debate. This step might underscore that the original author's views were worthy of publication but did not necessarily reflect your journal's views. But you'll want to be careful to avoid the appearance of throwing your original author to the wolves. When fielding media inquiries, it's advisable to consult the author before commenting. This gives you and the author a chance to formulate a thoughtful reply.

KEY TAKEAWAYS

- Your author is a friend of your journal and a potential ambassador for your journal and school. Every aspect of your editorial work and communication should reflect this reality, including how you communicate rejections.
- The article is important to the author and will always carry the author's name.
- Good communication, like a doctor's good bedside manner and a lawyer's diligent case updates, will prevent headaches before they arise. Be responsive to author inquiries.
- Cite a style manual or usage authority when an author questions an edit.
- Ask your faculty advisor for help with problem authors or articles.
- When your author succeeds, your journal succeeds. Think of your relationship as a true collaboration. And remember that authors are valuable professional contacts.

14

The Editing Process

Substantive and Technical Editing

Michael J. Higdon

LEARNING OBJECTIVES

After reviewing this Chapter, editors will be able to

- distinguish the various rounds of typical edits;
- employ an editing process that maximizes efficiencies; and
- differentiate the role of the writer from that of the editor and incorporate editing strategies that recognize the distinction.

A. Introduction

Just as it is the mission of law journals to publish legal scholarship, it is the job of journal editors to prepare the works contained therein for publication. Indeed, that is a very important job—one not to be taken likely. After all, these journals will become permanent resources for future scholars, legislators, judges, practitioners, and students. Publishing works that contain errors or are not fully researched and sourced will reflect poorly on the author, those who edited that issue, the journal, and the journal's affiliated law school.

With those concerns in mind, editors will spend much of their time editing the various pieces selected for publication. Typically, each piece will go through multiple rounds of edits, with different editors and staff members playing different roles in the process. Given how time-intensive it can be to move an article from initial acceptance to final publication, journals must institute efficient processes for completing these editing rounds. Additionally, through the editing process, editors will interact with those authors whose work will appear in the journal. For that reason, a journal's editing process contributes greatly to building that relationship and, in the process, improving the efficacy of the editing process and encouraging future submissions.

In this Chapter, we explore the typical edits that editors regularly complete, how those edits might be structured to streamline the process, and what role the "editor" plays in making the work better while, at the same time, supporting the author and respecting the author's voice.

B. The Various Rounds of Edits and Journal Efficiency

Given the pressures journals face in publishing excellent work, articles selected for publication must be reviewed multiple times before they can be published. Between those edits, the journal will need to afford authors an opportunity to provide feedback on suggested edits and, in some cases, respond to requests by the journal for additional information. Further complicating matters is that academic articles have many different components, and each usually will require individual rounds of edits focused exclusively on certain areas. Thus, without a plan for how to structure these various edits, editors may not be using their limited time most effectively.

1. The layers of a journal article

In the movie "Shrek," the eponymous ogre describes his species as being "like onions" in that both "have layers."[1] Well, so too do journal articles. Before turning to efficient editing processes, editors must understand the various components of an article and appreciate that each component will require attention during the editing process. Indeed, very few articles will be publication-ready at the time of acceptance. But even if such an article did exist, that fact would not be evident from a single read. Instead, the editors would still need to review the article carefully, checking and double-checking the various components.

The first layer, as one might imagine, will be the substance. Does the piece make an original contribution, and does that contribution hold some value for the legal community? After all, at the end of the day, the goal of most law

1. SHREK (DreamWorks Animation 2001).

reviews is to publish articles that advance the dialogue on various legal topics. Now, no doubt the article editors were already impressed by the piece before offering to publish it. However, between acceptance and publication, the editing process will force the editors to develop a deeper understanding of the subject at hand. For example, as the process unfolds, counter-arguments might appear in the minds of the editors that they might not have thought of when they first read the piece. Thus, the question of substance is one about which editors should be continually mindful of as the article winds its way through the editing process.

More importantly, editors should ask several smaller but no less important questions related to the overall substance of the article. First, does the article supports its thesis? Whatever the article is advocating—be it a new remedy, a different lens through which to view an existing problem, or even simply a new problem no one has yet identified—does the body of the paper support the author's point? Additionally, has the author identified and engaged with obvious counter-arguments? Authors are typically attempting to persuade (to one extent or another), but to do so, they must be objective about the current state of the law, anticipating and exploring all counter-arguments relevant to the overall inquiry. Of course, to meaningfully address these questions, the editor might need to first expand their own understanding of the topic at hand, as it is difficult to truly engage with something that one does not adequately understand. To do that, an editor might consider talking with faculty members who teach in that area of the law or conducting independent research using a treatise, hornbook, or even the foundational sources that the author of the piece relied upon.[2]

The second layer will be the organization, which examines whether the article is optimally structured to be well-received by and useful to those who might rely on it in the future. For instance, if the author is advocating a new way of thinking about the law as it relates to nonmarital cohabitation, does the author first explain the existing law before articulating the author's case for change? As is true of all layers, organization and substance can (and often do) overlap. Above, we noted the need to address counter-arguments, but in an edit focused on structure, an editor would want to ensure that any counter-argument appears at the appropriate time. If the author fails to identify and engage with an obvious objective until the very end of the article, readers

2. For a reading list about different philosophical movements editors might encounter when evaluating and editing articles, consult Chapter 5 of this *Manual*.

might find themselves distracted by that objection during earlier parts of the article, unaware that the author will eventually engage on that topic. In that instance, the editor should suggest the author move that discussion to an earlier point in the paper (or at least reference it with a *see infra* citation earlier in the article).

The third layer will be citations—a category that could easily be the subject of an entire chapter.[3] Journal articles, like all scholarly publications, require support for the various assertions upon which they rely and build. It is common for law review articles to be submitted for publication with hundreds of footnotes already in place. The law review editor's job is to ensure that those citations (1) support the portions of the article for which they are offered; (2) where appropriate, are up-to-date and are still good law; (3) conform to the system of citation the journal requires, which will typically be either *The Bluebook* or the *ALWD Guide to Legal Citations*; and (4) most importantly, are sufficient to avoid plagiarism. The editor must likewise ensure that the footnotes correctly cross-reference one another. For instance, if footnote 181 says, "*See* Higdon, *supra* note 95, at 102," then footnote 95 should contain the full citation for that source. Last but not least, the editor must determine whether additional citations are needed. Collectively, this round of editing is often referred to as cite-checking or "cite and source."

The final layer will involve grammar, punctuation, and usage. Nobody is perfect, and no matter how preeminent the author, they likely missed at least a few mistakes. Thus, editors must conduct a careful review to ensure that commas are where they need to be, every opening quotation mark has a closing quotation mark, "statue" has not been inserted for "statute," and the author did not use "fewer" when it should have been "less," to name just a few of the errors that many authors make from time to time.

2. Efficient edits

In light of the layers, a dilemma arises. Specifically, how does a journal structure the editing process so all components are addressed, but editors are making the best use of their time? Consider, for instance, a journal that elects to edit first at the level of grammar and punctuation. The editors may subsequently find those efforts to have been a waste of time if the eventual edits for substance and organization require large sections of the paper to be removed

3. *See, e.g.*, Darby Dickerson, *Citation Frustrations—and Solutions*, 30 STETSON L. REV. 477 (2000).

or rewritten. Had the journal edited for structure and organization first and, only upon resolving those issues edited for grammar and punctuation, the editors could have made more efficient use of their time.

For that reason, first-round edits typically focus on large-scale issues like substance and organization. Only after those areas are resolved will editors move to smaller-scale issues like citations, grammar, and punctuation. That is not to say that editors should ignore small-scale issues during the initial edits, but merely that they should not be the focus. It is not uncommon, however, for cite-checking to begin immediately, given the time it typically takes to verify the large number of footnotes found in the average law review article. In fact, once an offer has been accepted, many journals will immediately task staff members to start assembling the author's sources. Thus, often the first cite-check takes place simultaneously with the first substantive edit, even though cite-checking focuses on details that could be eliminated or rewritten.

This advice does not suggest that, if the editing process is structured properly, a journal will need to review certain aspects of an article only once. Instead, given the stakes involved in ensuring that any published article is reliable and reflects well on the publishing journal, articles typically go through several rounds of edits with multiple opportunities for the author to weigh in on the suggested edits. Indeed, many journals have adopted an editing process that often looks something like the following:

Step 1 The journal accepts the article for publication.

Step 2 Editors begin a substantive review of the piece.

Step 3 At the same time, staff members begin checking the citations provided and identifying places where additional citations are required.

Step 4 The primary editor for the piece collates the edits from that round into a single document that can be returned to the author.

Step 5 The journal returns the edits to the author to review and responds to all requests for more information and edits made thus far.

Step 6 Following receipt of the author's responses, the editors review any new material and begin to focus more on technical edits, such as organization, grammar, punctuation, usage, and citation format.

Step 7 The journal again returns the article to the author to review the new edits.

Step 8 Once the author returns the piece, a senior articles editor or the Editor in Chief performs a final review, paying particular attention to the technical aspects (e.g., grammar, consistency of headings, cross-references).

Step 9 The journal returns the article to the author for one final review.

Not every journal, of course, will follow this identical schedule. Some may have fewer rounds of edits, while others may have more. Regardless, for any schedule to be truly efficient, the author will have to stop making substantive changes at some point. After all, each time the author submits additional material, all new material must proceed through the full editing process. For that reason, most journals typically select some point (often around Step 4) when the author can no longer make substantive changes.

As a final note, it is imperative that all edits sent to an author be collated into one single document for each round of edits. Not only would it be quite cumbersome to force the author to respond to various documents with different edits, but such a process would present more obstacles for the journal to track the edits. For this same reason, journals should ensure that all drafts sent to an author clearly identify the edits that are being suggested (i.e., using something akin to "track changes" and noting the edit stage and date in a header). The journal should request that the author return edits in the same manner. Failure to do so can lead to some edits being overlooked (and perhaps forgotten) and duplicated efforts for the journal and the author.

C. Being an Effective Editor

Author Dene October once said that "[a] good editor is someone who cares a little less about the author's needs than the reader's."[4] This statement does not imply that the editor and author are at odds. In fact, one of the editor's jobs is to help the author best realize the author's underlying goals. At the same time,

---

4. Scott A. MacMillan, Entrepreneur to Author: 5 STEPS to Writing and Publishing a Nonfiction Book That Builds Authority and Grows Your Business 156 (2020).

the editor is primarily responsible for ensuring that the work meets the level of excellence required by the journal and the expectations and professional standards of the legal academy.[5] Thus, in many ways, editors perform a crucial gatekeeping function, making sure that published work will interest readers and provide a reliable resource for other scholars writing in that area.

The different edits discussed above touched upon some specific concerns and how the rounds of editing can best address each. Below are some more specific guidelines editors should keep in mind as they discharge their responsibilities.

1. Respecting authorship

An editor has a duty to make sure that the published work aligns with the journal's publication standards. These standards typically include things like ensuring that representations regarding legal and other authorities are correct and supportable and avoiding plagiarism by making sure the author has given credit where credit is due. In addition, many journals have adopted internal style manuals to (a) foster some sense of cohesion among the various articles published in a given volume and (b) promote consistency in volumes published over the years, given that journals typically select a new editorial board every year.

At the same time, perhaps the most important thing editors must keep in mind is that, at the end of the day, the work remains that of the author. After all, once published, it is the author whose name will appear on the piece and thus the person to whom readers will attribute most positive or negative reactions they have when reading it. Plus, most authors feel a great deal of pride in the things they write and, although grateful for feedback that will improve the work, still want the published piece to reflect both their intent and voice. With those considerations in mind, editors must refrain from attempting to turn the author's piece into the piece the editor would have written.

How, then, does the editor balance this duty to the journal while still respecting authorship? For much of the editing process, those two responsibilities will not conflict. Being ever mindful of the author's intent, the editor should feel free to offer suggestions that enhance the piece. And the various

---

5. *See, e.g.*, Philip C. Kissam, *The Evaluation of Legal Scholarship*, 63 WASH. L. REV. 221 (1988); Deborah L. Rhode, *The Professional Ethics of Professors*, 56 J. LEGAL EDUC. 70, 72 (2006).

rounds of edits are ideally aimed at doing just that. Asking questions like "How can the thesis be better supported?" "Is this organization the most efficient way to engage the reader?" and "Are these citations sufficient?" help maximize the potential for readers to be more receptive to and more persuaded by the author's arguments. Similarly, edits related to smaller-scale issues like readability and flow can go a long way to helping an author realize the goal of publishing an accessible and easily readable piece.

When the journal's requirements conflict with the author's aims, the calculus becomes more complicated. As an initial matter, editors must first distinguish between the journal's technical *requirements* and the editor's individual *preferences*. As noted above, many journals have adopted technical requirements—through a style manual or some less formal document—for the pieces they publish, and obviously editors need to become familiar with those requirements. In addition, editors are encouraged to identify and comment on other things not explicitly listed as a requirement. However, editors must recognize that they, too, have writing preferences and not become unduly wedded to edits flowing from those preferences as, again, it is ultimately the author's piece. Consequently, while editors can share their preferences, the journal should respect an author's decision to reject them.

To the extent a conflict arises between an author's desires and the journal's technical requirements, many problems can be avoided simply by communicating with the author upfront (typically through the publication agreement or the initial offer of publication) about what requirements the journal will insist upon. To the extent a dispute arises about something not covered in those materials, the editors will need to decide whether the author's preferences can be accommodated in some way that will not adversely impact the journal's reputation. For instance, a stylistic preference might be excused if an author is adamant that they cannot do otherwise without fundamentally harming the piece. On the other hand, a dispute about whether a certain passage has been plagiarized will not be a risk most journals would be willing to take. Again, though, such disputes are mercifully uncommon and will often be resolved through a mutually agreeable compromise.

2. Restraining oneself

Editors achieved their positions, at least in part, by being talented writers, and the perspective they bring to the table can be invaluable to those authors with whom they work. As noted earlier, editors are free to offer whatever comments they think may assist an author in realizing the full potential of the piece, regardless of whether that comment stems from some requirement imposed by the journal or simply the editor's sense that the item in question can be improved. That being said, inundating authors with too many comments can be overwhelming, which in turn can damage the journal's relationship with the author, who may start to suspect that the journal does not respect the original work. Additionally, excessive edits can delay the journal's publication schedule, as it will take more time for the author to process and respond to them.

For those reasons, editors would be wise to recognize that, despite the expertise the editor brings to the task, the editing process is not intended as an opportunity to demonstrate the full extent of those talents. Some editors may wish to impress the author with whom they are working and mistakenly think that offering voluminous edits is the way to do just that. While some authors might respond positively, many would not. Instead, an effective editor chooses their battles, showing restraint in the items upon which the editor comments. One technique is to comment on one example of a particular issue of concern that the editor sees throughout the article, noting that the author made this choice multiple times and suggesting an alternative that might work better.

Additionally, editors should remember that the article will go through multiple rounds of edits, and perhaps not every item needs to be commented on immediately. As noted earlier when talking about efficient editing, it would be a waste of time to carefully edit text that is likely going to be rewritten in light of larger, more substantive edits typically offered in the earlier rounds. Instead, editors might analogize their role to those working triage in medical facilities. Those individuals evaluate patients upon intake to determine the most pressing health issues facing the patient and treat those issues first. For instance, consider someone admitted to the emergency room with an open chest wound. The doctors and nurses would spend their entire time focusing on that injury before turning to a minor problem, like a knee scrape.

3. Phrasing edits

Assume an editor, mindful of the need for the restraint referenced above, has gone through the document and identified areas to bring to the author's attention. The next question is how the editor might best formulate those comments to maximize their potential for getting a favorable response from the author and not harming the journal's relationship with the author in the process.

A helpful technique is to phrase edits in terms of the editor's reaction and a brief explanation. For example, an editor might say, "I was confused by this statement because, as I understood it, you earlier said that case X stands for a different proposition." The reason for this approach is that one's reaction is never incorrect. Thus, an author cannot respond to such a statement by saying, "No, you aren't confused." Instead, the author has to accept that feedback as true and then hopefully try and figure out how to clarify so that future readers are not likewise confused. If the editor had simply commented, "You are misrepresenting this case," then the author is likely going to respond with a defense, which fails to advance the concern of bringing clarity to the current words on the page.

As this last example demonstrates, tone is also important when phrasing edits. Most authors recognize the value of having others edit their work but nonetheless hate receiving edits. Most authors are understandably proud of the things they have written; thus, even feedback that is constructive can be difficult to take. Somewhat related is that most people are quite sensitive when it comes to their creative expressions, which writing—even in a scholarly academic context—definitely is. Just as most people would be sensitive to criticism regarding how they dress, so too are their feelings regarding their writing. For those reasons, a constructive but kind tone can go a long way toward recognizing those sensitivities and promoting a strong relationship with writers. Statements like "you are misrepresenting this case"—or other negative edits that begin with the word "you"—do just the opposite.

Another helpful strategy for achieving an appropriate tone is to phrase edits in terms of a question, somewhat analogously to the Socratic method law professors often utilize in class. For instance, returning to an earlier example, an editor could say, "Might the reader be confused by this statement given that, as I understood it, you earlier said that case X stands for a different proposition?" Other examples include, "I question whether this sentence is needed given . . ." and, "I notice you use 'indeed' as a transition quite a bit; do you think the reader might be distracted by that repetition?" Phrasing edits in such a way recognizes and affirms the author's ultimate authority over the content. This technique also more directly communicates the idea that the editor is looking out for the author's interest in making the work as strong and accessible as possible.

4. Managing writers' expectations

Finally, editors need to manage the author's expectations regarding the editing process. One method is to provide authors upfront with journal policies regarding technical requirements. In addition, it is important that the journal inform authors of the overall publication schedule, noting how many rounds of edits the article is likely to go through, what each round will entail, and which editor will be the author's contact during the process. The journal should also inform authors as early as possible when they can expect to receive edits from the journal and the due dates for responding to those edits. Providing this information allows authors to plan their schedules so there will be less chance the author will require an extension and potentially upset the journal's publication schedule.

D. Conclusion

Journal authors love to share negative experiences they have had with the editing process, and, in listening, one can discern a few common complaints:

- overwhelming edits where the editor had comments on almost everything the author wrote;
- changes that relate to stylistic choices and reflect that the editors seemed to think that their style choices should trump those of the author;
- deadlines that did not provide the author with sufficient time to review and respond to the editors' comments;
- edits that would require the author to provide footnotes for such things as the author's original thoughts and topic sentences that merely introduce an idea for which subsequent sentences provide relevant citations;
- comments provided simultaneously by more than one editor that contradict one another; and
- failure to communicate to the author all the changes made by the editor, either because the author was not given a chance to review those changes prior to publication or the editors failed to signal those changes when returning the draft to the author.

The purpose of providing this list is two-fold. First, it demonstrates that the process of having one's work published in a law review is incredibly important to authors, and they are quite sensitive to editing processes that are less-than-ideal. Second, this list underscores the need to implement those approaches discussed earlier in this Chapter. Namely, those include editing policies that are both responsive to the time constraints of law review editors and those that respect the role of the author, ever mindful of the authors' needs and expectations.

KEY TAKEAWAYS

- Journals need to develop a system for performing edits in an efficient manner; that system typically will require edits of larger-scale issues before edits involving smaller, more technical issues.
- Authors and editors play different roles, and editors need to balance upholding the journal's interest in setting certain technical requirements with the author's interest in retaining a full sense of authorship over the published article.
- Effective editing is a distinct skill set and, if not approached properly, can damage a journal's relationship with an author and create more work in the long run for the (likely already overworked) law review editor.

15

Journal Production and Dissemination

Brent Domann

LEARNING OBJECTIVES

After reviewing this Chapter, editors will be able to

- evaluate and select publishing media;
- evaluate and select vendors for services and supplies; and
- produce their journal in a consistent and high-quality manner.

A. Introduction

While much attention is given to staffing, editing, and author relations, editors should remember that a journal exists to put out a *product*. This Chapter provides guidance on how to go from edited content to physical copy and examines the wide range of options for journals to tailor production to their needs. This Chapter contemplates a journal moving from primarily digital format or traditionally published format to a print-on-demand model, which is becoming more common among journals facing budget reductions or wishing to reduce their environmental impact.

Traditionally outsourced to third parties, publication and printing can now take place largely in-house. Shifting to in-house production gives journals increased control over specific aspects of the finished product, reduces the environmental footprint of bulk printing, and—with a little "do it yourself" attitude—results in significant cost savings.

Incoming editors may find the publication details covered in this Chapter well-established in their journals and opt not to change them. Nevertheless, understanding the publication and printing process is crucial to managing day-to-day operations effectively and responding to unexpected circumstances outside of journal control. In other words, printers go out of business, administrators demand significant budget cuts, and "stuff" happens—so journal leadership must be prepared.

B. Choosing a Publishing Medium and Printer

1. Print vs. digital

Digital publication is nearly ubiquitous among law journals. Content is edited digitally and delivered to printing companies in digital format. Legal researchers use computer databases like Westlaw, Lexis, and HeinOnline (along with indexes like Google) to search the full text of documents. The citators that efficiently cross-reference content do so with automated, digital technology. Accordingly, the question becomes, "Does the journal want to produce a physical product?" This question is likely settled for incoming leadership, but it is a question that should be revisited regularly.

If a journal wishes to produce physical copies, a further question is whether that print status should become *primary*; print versus digital is not an all-or-nothing proposition, and the greatest benefits may come from a hybrid approach. A primarily print journal can easily distribute digitally and should do so to increase its reach. A primarily digital journal may benefit from printing even on a tiny scale for authors who appreciate and often request personal copies. Additionally, print production bears on the identity of a journal and could affect its rankings (some rankings systems and digests historically prioritized print, though many such as the Current Index to Legal Periodicals no longer do).[1] Ultimately, the decision to be primarily print or primarily digital

1. Due to established rankings methodologies and publication dissemination tools, primarily print journals maintain a visibility advantage over digital-only ones. *See, e.g.*, *Ranking Methodology*, W&L LAW JOURNAL RANKINGS (last visited Jan. 22, 2022), https://managementtools4.wlu.edu/Law Journals/Default3.aspx [https://perma.cc/EG8R-J5NC] (detailing the use of citation metrics in ranking journals); *Current Index to Legal Periodicals*, HEINONLINE (last visited Jan. 22, 2022), https://home.heinonline.org/content/current-index-to-legal-periodicals/ [https://perma.cc/L3H6-CPT6] (which no longer prioritizes print over digital); *see also* Sarah Reis, *Deconstructing the Durham Statement: The Persistence of Print Prestige During the Age of Open Access* (Working Paper No. 2785307, 2016), https://dx.doi.org/10.2139/ssrn.2785307 [https://perma.cc/48KP-FXYY].

is strategic, so a journal should focus on its goals and the incentives within whatever ranking or other system it would like to use as a benchmark.

Editors can apply the same factors discussed below for selecting vendors to choose an appropriate print-on-demand service.

Since journals are created digitally and find their finished form in Word or PDF format, digital distribution is simple and inexpensive. A journal website comes at minimal cost or may even merit support and web space as a student organization. Additionally, database vendors have email submission accounts or upload pages for journal content that accept PDFs, and some will even scrape data from journal websites if they are maintained and up to date.

Physical production and subscription distribution are much more involved and should be pursued only if doing so will directly aid in achieving journal goals. Assuming a journal chooses to pursue primarily print production, this Chapter will cover some basic options and responsibilities.

2. Traditional print publishing or print-on-demand?

The next big question for print publication is whether to use a traditional publisher or a print-on-demand service. Using a traditional publisher can be convenient. When using a traditional publisher, a journal delivers a Word or PDF file and then has only to wait for a shipment—and invoice—to arrive. Traditional publishers also offer services beyond printing, including cover design and layout, formatting and proofing services, printing and storage of archival copies, drop-shipping to subscribers or subscription vendors, and offprint production.

There are drawbacks, however. The first is cost. Traditional publishers can be expensive and may impose ordering minima that leave a journal with boxes of unneeded copies. Second, and perhaps more important, is the loss of control. Publisher contracts or policies can limit a journal's ability to make changes, fix errors, and scale production. And, as with any other industry, publishers can go out of business or be sold with little or no notice.

To choose a traditional publisher, journals should research available services, production minima, and other terms and policies. In comparing services, the journal should keep in mind its goals and limitations (such as budget restrictions); any services that a publisher cannot provide must be sourced elsewhere, and it is good to know how much each service costs independently. Production minima impact the budget by setting cost floors and increasing related overhead by requiring storage or disposal of unused copies. If minima are acceptable, it is best to find a publisher with quotas that most closely match expected circulation.

Review every contract or set of terms or policies very carefully. Left unread, these can turn into surprises impacting everything from costs to delivery times. Further, ensure the journal has appropriate authority to enter into the contract at hand and that journal leadership is authorized to enter into contracts on behalf of the journal or institution.[2]

3. Print-on-demand services

Another option is a print-on-demand service. By nature, these services avoid many drawbacks of traditional printing: costs are variable and, to some degree, controllable (the thinner the book, the less it costs), production minima are significantly reduced if not eliminated, and turnaround times are often shorter.

But drawbacks exist. First, when compared to traditional publishers, on-demand printers offer a significantly reduced range of services; and, even if available, they come at additional cost. Second, print-on-demand services may have policies or restrictions incompatible with journal needs, such as prohibiting consecutive pagination across issues or imposing metadata restrictions.[3] And third, due to more limited services, a journal or law school must often handle technical issues. For example, traditional publishers provide editorial services that ensure consistent layout, font size, margins, and overall "look" across issues and volumes; without access to these services or the tools used to provide them, a journal must spend the extra effort necessary to ensure consistent quality.

a. Choosing a print-on-demand service

Editors should select a print-on-demand service based on journal goals and requirements. Start by reading reviews and researching the background

---

2. For more information on contracting authority, see Chapter 3 in this *Manual*.

3. *See Members' Top 10 File Specification Challenges*, CREATESPACE.COM, https://createspacepublish.wordpress.com/2014/11/12/members-top-10-file-specification-challenges/ [https://perma.cc/37BZ-TCKQ] (stating that CreateSpace "cannot accommodate... page numbers that begin where a previous volume ended"); *see also id.* (stating that "the author name and title name are checked to ensure they are consistent in the title information, the cover file, and the interior file," which in the author's experience has resulted in errors when an interior title page (as is typical in law journals) lacks issue or author information).

and ownership of each prospective vendor. As print-on-demand is a growing and changing industry, a journal should err on the side of an established company or one owned by a large parent company to preserve continuity.

Next, a journal should sign up for a few accounts to test user interfaces and explore printing options. It is possible to read about available options on vendor websites or in user agreements, but it is much easier to make choices based on experience.

This second step of testing and exploring options is crucial. This step is when burdensome policies or restrictions would most likely show themselves, quickly helping to identify services whose use could wreak havoc on law journal publishing. The need for testing is especially important for journals that are long-established and moving online rather than starting there from scratch, as continuity might be limiting to flexibility.

Finally, a journal should explore payment and delivery options. It is helpful to take a back issue and recreate it on a few different prospective printing websites to test features and the ordering and delivery processes.

Fortunately, long-term contracts are atypical with print-on-demand vendors, so journals can change services if issues arise.

b. Typical limitations

Limitations in print-on-demand services that a journal may encounter include restrictions on physical size, book characteristics like paper type, thickness, color, and finishing options. This section covers some of these limitations and how they relate to traditional law journal publishing.

A restriction on physical size is the first frequent limitation. Law journals have traditionally been published in books that are 6.75 x 10 inches or similar. Many web-based print-on-demand services (such as Lulu.com, BookBaby, and Kindle Direct Publishing) limit size options to streamline delivery, and often the closest size available is that of a trade paperback, or 6 x 9 inches. For journals moving to print-on-demand, the difference is enough for subscribers to notice, and fewer words will fit per page compared to traditional sizing, making issues thicker on average. However, scaling down pages does not render text too small to read and so back issues can be reprinted with little trouble. And while a change in dimensions may seem drastic, providing advance notice to subscribers can minimize complaints. Further, if dimensions are a significant issue, some traditional law journal printers (such as Christensen Printing and Sheridan) can maintain traditional dimensions and may also offer print-on-demand options.

Law journals have also been traditionally "perfect bound" with off-white paper. Most print-on-demand services offer perfect bound as an option but may have limited options for paper thickness and color. A journal transitioning from traditional publishing may find itself having to accept thinner or thicker white paper, but this change will be immaterial to most readers.

c. *Formatting for print-on-demand*

Some traditional printers provide templates or word-processing macros that automatically format edited content. Templates and macros save significant staff time and effort and serve as quality controls for the printer to maintain consistency. If transitioning from traditional publishing to print-on-demand, these macros can be useful. However, they may be password-protected from editing and cannot be altered to fit a new page size. As a result, a journal may need to create its own formatting tools when using a print-on-demand service. If doing so, several resources are available to help with choosing things like typeface, font size, etc.[4]

C. Managing Subscriptions

Managing subscriptions requires attention to detail but is a task that a well-organized journal can successfully in-source. To do so, journal staff should build and maintain positive relationships with faculty advisors, the parent institution's or law school's business office, and the law library.

Faculty advisors and administrative staff maintain institutional memory that can be invaluable as journal staff turns over. Further, most understand the publishing process and have often served on journals.

The business office can help editors understand payments and receipts and may not be as surprised as an editor when something like an invoice or check arrives unexpectedly. They also sometimes forward or receive journal mail; having a strong relationship can facilitate communications.

---

4. *See, e.g.*, Matthew Butterick, Practical Typography (2d ed. 2021), https://practicaltypography.com [https://perma.cc/DR6C-FZJ8]; Matthew Butterick, Typography for Lawyers (2d ed. 2015), https://typographyforlawyers.com [https://perma.cc/BZ56-HRUH]; Ambrogino Giusti, *The Typography of Law Reviews: A Typographic Survey of Legal Periodicals* (2016), https://digitalcommons.law.uw.edu/law-lib_borgeson/28.

Finally, it is an excellent idea to make and keep acquaintances in the law library because they can provide essential information and advice. Librarians can explain the purchasing side of journal subscriptions and deal with prominent vendors like Hein, EBSCO, Lexis, and Westlaw. Understanding how these operations work for subscribers can be crucial when an editor receives an unanticipated communication or a demand for some action.

Beyond building these relationships, a journal will need to maintain a subscriber list, calculate production costs to set prices, decide whether subscription fees should cover offprints for authors, and more.

1. Maintaining a subscriber list

A journal must keep an updated list of subscribers or entities that pay regularly for print copies. Editors should consult and cross-reference several sources of subscriber information to ensure the list is complete. If any subscriber is missed when mailing copies, a journal may receive a "claim" form. If one shows up in the mail, the journal can rectify the situation by mailing the claimant a replacement copy.

Hein is a vendor with a long history of providing access to law journals and other legal publications. Hein acts as an aggregator; subscribers select the journals they want from a list and then pay in one transaction every year. Hein then forwards subscriber lists to each journal along with a single payment for that year's collected subscription fees. Many law libraries have reduced print subscriptions significantly but still maintain access to scans through HeinOnline. In this newer digital-access model, Hein can still provide subscriber lists and forward payment, whether for subscriptions or royalties.

EBSCO also collects the content of journals and makes that content available as part of various subscription packages. Like Hein, EBSCO can provide a subscriber list and collect and forward subscription payments and royalties. Journals may encounter other vendors like Hein and EBSCO, and most will work in similar ways.

A journal may have direct subscribers, many of whom are alumni. With direct subscribers, editors or an assigned law school staff member must make a strong effort to keep track of them, collect annual fees, update addresses, and ensure they are not missed when copies are sent out. Vendors like Hein have claims processes and systems for requesting unmailed copies that direct subscribers lack.

2. Calculating production costs

Calculating production costs is straightforward and helps to set subscription prices. These costs include printing, packaging, postage, and supplies. One important point to keep in mind is that institutional policies may bear on the ability or willingness to recoup costs or even generate income. For example, an independent law school registered as a nonprofit organization will want to be careful about selling journal copies above actual cost to avoid triggering tax implications. When making pricing determinations, editors must always involve faculty advisors and law school representatives so all factors and impacts can be addressed.

Editors should regularly review production costs to ensure subscription fees are sufficient to cover them. The optimal time to do so is between volumes (typically annually), and subscription vendors like Hein and EBSCO serve as reminders when they request updated quotes for their own marketing materials. Editors should consider the factors below, along with any communications from production vendors regarding upcoming price changes.

a. Printing costs

The journal's contract with a traditional printer should outline production costs. If using a print-on-demand service, past issues provide good estimates. Calculating such an estimate involves surveying page counts over several years to generate a cost-per-issue average. Shipping costs are also crucial considerations; while editors should consider the costs of shipping to subscribers and authors as a separate item (discussed below), costs for shipping copies to the journal for redistribution are more appropriately lumped in with printing costs.

b. Packaging costs

Packaging costs are the easiest to estimate. The price and usage of custom-ordered or standardized boxes are less variable than those of printing or postage. Further, low per-item costs mean that variations have less of an effect on the annual cost.

c. Postage costs

Postage is variable. Often, larger universities centralize mail administration, so postage can be challenging to predict. For that reason, editors may want to separate postage costs from subscription cost calculations and place them under another budget line. Alternatively, a journal could use a set amount of annual postage to calculate subscription cost and pull overage from another line.

d. Including offprints in subscription costs

One more consideration for subscription costs is whether a journal should use them to offset costs for offprints. Production costs can feasibly include these "author copies." However, they can make subscriptions very expensive compared to similar publications, in which case it might be best to exclude them from production cost calculations.

e. Additional considerations

Journal staff should expect unanticipated overhead. Although usually small, handling claims for undelivered issues, needing to switch suppliers, or accommodating author agreement variations (e.g., extra offprints) can become unwieldy. But journals also receive some unanticipated revenues. For example, some vendors remit royalty payments to the journal based on usage. These payments may not flow to the journal for budgeting or tax reasons but are worth discussing when calculating production costs.

D. Delivering Physical Copies

If a traditional publisher or print-on-demand service will not drop-ship physical copies to customers or other vendors, the journal will have to re-box and re-ship copies, increasing cost and workload. If the journal is re-shipping, its main jobs are to ensure that clean, protective packaging is used and that postage is handled appropriately given institutional norms.

You should research whether the journal or school has a bulk mailing or nonprofit rate. There are considerations of tax status and institutional contracts that may save the journal money. Therefore, it is important for a journal to explore its responsibilities and options before simply paying for postage. A call or email to the business office can often provide the information necessary to mail in bulk. If no special rate exists, the U.S. Postal Service offers a "book rate," which is less expensive but takes longer for delivery.[5]

---

5. *See What Is Media Mail® (Book Rate)?*, USPS (last visited Jan. 22, 2022), https://faq.usps.com/ s/article/What-is-Media-Mail-Book-Rate.

1. Subscription vs. author copies (offprints)

Even if a journal is primarily published in digital format or maintains no print subscriber base, it may be worth providing full issues and offprints to authors as a perk.

Offprints are copies of individual articles from an issue. Journals often provide ten or so copies of these to each author for free, and authors use them to distribute to colleagues, employer repositories, and others. Traditional publishers often provide this service as part of a package, but it is not difficult to do in-house—simply export an individual article as its own PDF,[6] edit the cover design to include only that article's title and author information, and ensure quality controls are met.

While seemingly a small gift, attracting well-cited authors can sometimes be a challenge, and every little bit can help. Producing these copies is the same as producing a print-only publication; the only difference is how many a journal will order for redistribution.

2. Sourcing mailing materials

Mailing materials can be purchased as needed from local supply stores and online, but journals should consider custom-made shipping boxes. Available options include varying thicknesses of cardboard and customized dimensions. Boxes are inexpensive and can be used for various tasks, and a quick search online can turn up several reputable vendors. Custom boxes can add an air of professionalism to journal subscriptions, and, for extra flair, some can even be printed with logos.

E. Digital Delivery

1. Digital production standards

Journals are free to set their own standards for font size, layout, etc., but production standards for files are a significant consideration. Print-on-demand services tend to be rigorous about file types that can be submitted and often

---

6. Some print-on-demand services have minimum page counts; adding blank pages to the end of an article can solve this problem. *See, e.g.*, LULU BOOK CREATION GUIDE 13, https://assets.lulu.com/media/guides/en/lulu-book-creation-guide.pdf [https://perma.cc/BSL7-V24D] (noting a 32-page minimum for paperbacks and a 24-page minimum for hardcover books).

rely on industry standards. Most will take a PDF processed for commercial publishing (PDF/X-1a is commonly requested because it includes embedded fonts and color standardization for images); this process provides both high-image resolution and underlying text that allows indexes like Google to full-text index documents. While the resolution serves printing needs, the text improves search engine optimization and so the printing file can also be used in institutional repositories or on journal websites.

2. Working with database vendors

Once a final file is saved, it can be submitted to databases for inclusion. Large legal databases like Lexis and Westlaw have data gathering systems in place. Westlaw has a submission account system where a journal can log in and upload a PDF of its publication to be included in Westlaw's journals database. Lexis's system has specific email addresses to which journals submit PDFs for inclusion. In both cases, database vendors will then subject publication files to OCR if necessary, generate links for references, and convert the files to text or HTML for use in the databases themselves.

HeinOnline is also a major source for journal publications, and journals can submit PDFs to Hein for inclusion. Editors at Hein split files into individual articles and add metadata consistent with recordkeeping standards. EBSCO is an example of a large, not-just-legal-database aggregator that may be interested in publication files.

It is important to remember that in addition to increased availability of the journal (i.e., increased exposure to potentially citing readers), Hein and EBSCO also help maintain subscription lists as described above.

F. Miscellaneous Considerations

1. Handling royalty payments

Vendors who remit royalty payments may send an annual check to cover the calculated amount owed. This check often goes directly to the institution's business office but sometimes may land in the journal's mailbox. If a journal editor receives a check from Hein, EBSCO, Lexis, or Westlaw for thousands of dollars, the first step is to contact the business office to see if it is the usual recipient. If so, there is likely an arrangement in place for the check to bypass the journal budget. It is fair to confirm this fact, but policy-wise, it may not be worth the trouble to pursue this money unless a shift to print-on-demand provides the opportunity for budget discussions.

2. Copyright considerations

Copyright considerations exist throughout the publication process, and much more detail is provided in Chapter 17 of this *Manual*. However, it is essential to remember that the journal will be bound by both copyright law and author agreements when dealing with publication and distribution. If the journal decides to attempt new avenues of publication or engage with new vendors, a thorough review of author and copyright agreements is necessary to ensure compliance.

3. Preserving publications

Journal websites serve as an excellent platform for hosting content, but more permanent storage is a good idea. A journal should ensure that its publications are stored in an institutional repository if available. These repositories, which are discussed in Chapter 16 of this *Manual*, are built on platforms and with policies designed for long-term preservation and access and are often managed by someone in the institution with a skill set for such work.

Chapter 16 of this *Manual* also discusses preserving sources, which is a separate concern from preserving publications. Both are important and improve journal utility.

KEY TAKEAWAYS

- When considering publication format, the most important goals are that the journal content is formatted properly to facilitate publication and that content, regardless of primary medium, is submitted to databases like Westlaw, Lexis, and HeinOnline; journal policies and procedures should not introduce barriers to these goals.
- Before changing the publishing medium or process, journals must consider journal goals, brand, rankings criteria, etc.
- Editors should consult their business office, faculty advisor, and librarians before entering or changing any vendor agreement.

16

Post-Publication Consequences

How a Law Review Can Influence an Article's Scholarly Impact

Christine Anne George

LEARNING OBJECTIVES

After reviewing this Chapter, editors will be able to

- differentiate between traditional citation metrics and alt-metrics for measuring scholarly impact;
- give examples of the challenges authors face with the current system for calculating scholarly impact;
- use persistent identifiers as part of the publication process;
- propose actions to help authors maximize their scholarly impact; and
- describe the citation gap that exists between men and women scholars.

A. Introduction

Given the tremendous effort that goes into an article pre-publication, it may be easy to think that the work ends once the article is published. But publication is actually the start of the article's journey. Placement—referring to journal-level ranking—is one metric used to measure scholarly impact. But once the article is available, the question becomes whether it will generate any scholarly impact.

"Scholarly impact" varies from one academic discipline to another. In legal academia, "scholarly impact" is the measure of an article's influence in the field, or when applied to an individual, the degree to which their scholarship has influenced a particular field. If that sounds nearly impossible to quantify, you are correct. There is no perfect metric or ideal system for calculating scholarly impact; any metric or system is inherently flawed and unfair. But because scholarly impact plays into faculty hiring and tenure decisions, it must be quantified. The challenge then becomes understanding the rules and learning how to maximize impact.

Editors make decisions during the publication process that can have a ripple effect on an article's scholarly impact. Specifically, decisions involving citations, copyright permissions, and promotion can assist or impede an author's quest to maximize scholarly impact. This Chapter provides an overview of various considerations for calculating scholarly impact and the steps a journal can take to show authors that your publication will support them and their articles. The Chapter also addresses the gender-based citation gap that exists in legal scholarship.

B. Citation Metrics

"Citation metrics" are the first piece of determining scholarly impact. While different fields have developed different metrics—including the H-Index that works better for the sciences—many platforms, such as Scopus, Web of Science, or Publish or Perish, that institutions use to calculate impact do not work well for law because most academic journals in law are student-edited, not peer-reviewed. For law, scholarly impact comes down to two types of metrics—traditional and alt-metrics.

1. Traditional metrics

"Citation counts" are a traditional citation metric. As the name suggests, "citation counts" involve counting the number of times that a work is cited within other works. Citation counts can be gathered manually or through a sampling system or computer-generated program. This Chapter discusses only articles because most means of counting citations rely solely on articles, not on other types of publications, like books. Citation counts are a way to show the impact of a particular article, working off the assumption that the more it is cited, the more important it is. Citation metrics can be used during the faculty hiring or tenure process, which means accuracy matters.

The accuracy of citation counts depends on the citation format. To improve an author's scholarly impact, the author's name must appear in the citation. While this point may seem incredibly simplistic, for works with more than two authors, the *ALWD Guide to Legal Citation*[1] and *The Bluebook*[2] allow users to insert "et al." after the first author's name. Thus, some authors' names are divorced from their articles, which means that only the lead author will get credit for that citation. Both manuals, though, permit all authors' names to be listed "when particularly relevant."[3] When it comes to scholarly impact, all author names are extremely relevant.

Every author deserves to receive credit for a citation to their article. If a name is not listed, it cannot be counted. Law reviews that use "et al." for individual authors are negatively impacting citation counts for some authors. Regardless of the ALWD Guide or Bluebook convention, consider creating an internal rule that requires footnotes in your publication to list every author of a work. Implementing this policy will show that your law review understands how citation metrics are a part of the scholarly impact calculation and that you strive to ensure all authors are acknowledged.

Once all names are included in the citation, the next hurdle is how those names appear. Consistency is extremely important when it comes to calculating impact. Adding or dropping an initial or including a middle name can impact counting, as can an author changing names. Section C of this Chapter addresses this name challenge and recommends using persistent identifiers as the solution.

Finally, if citation counts come from published articles, then at least one publication cycle must occur before any citation counts can be accumulated. This delay may mean that authors who have been publishing for longer are more likely to have higher citation counts for their older pieces that have had the opportunity to be cited in other articles.

---

1. CAROLYN WILLIAMS & ALWD, ALWD GUIDE TO LEGAL CITATION R. 20.1(b)(2), at 216 (7th ed. 2021) [hereinafter ALWD GUIDE].

2. THE BLUEBOOK: A UNIFORM SYSTEM OF CITATION R. 15.1(b), at 148–49 (Columbia L. Rev. Ass'n et al. eds., 21st ed. 2020) [hereinafter Bluebook].

3. *Id.*; *see* ALWD GUIDE, *supra* note 1, R. 20.1(b)(2), at 216.

2. Alt-metrics

"Alt-metrics," or "alternative metrics," are metrics other than citation counts that are used to show impact. Alt-metrics can show impact more quickly than traditional citation metrics because most of what is calculated is done in real-time—such as downloading an article or tweeting about it—instead of waiting until the article has been formally published.

One of the most common alt-metrics is "download counts." A download count is the number of times an article has been downloaded from a particular site.

Download counts are associated with the Social Science Research Network (SSRN) and the Bepress platform, Digital Commons. While an institution may subscribe to SSRN, law faculty can independently create profiles and upload their articles. Many institutions use the Digital Commons platform as their institutional repository (IR). An IR is an open-access platform that allows an institution to provide free, public digital access to scholarship produced by faculty, staff, and students and special collections.

Using download counts as a metric to indicate impact has been criticized. The first concern is what a download actually measures. Just because an article is downloaded does not mean it will be cited, let alone read.

Another concern is that authors who have had their articles available on these platforms for a longer period are more likely to have more downloads. For example, an article that has been available on SSRN for ten years is more likely to have more downloads than an article that has been available on SSRN for one year, regardless of when it was first published. This criticism raises the inequities of impact between senior versus junior scholars. It also highlights the disparities between those who are more digitally minded in terms of their scholarship—or whose institutions are more digitally minded—and those who have not sought to expand access to their work by uploading their pieces to SSRN or Digital Commons.

A final criticism is that the articles available on SSRN and Digital Commons are those that have the proper permission to be shared. Law review publication agreements may limit an author's ability to share their article. The agreement may allow only a pre-edited version of the article to be posted or refuse permission to post at all.

To help authors make their articles more accessible—and thus hopefully increase the scholarly impact—law review publication agreements should give authors blanket permission to post the final version of their article on SSRN and their IR (like Digital Commons). Law reviews should also announce their position about posting to SSRN and IRs on their websites to attract potential authors. Including this information on the law review's website can also help librarians and administrators who often manage SSRN and IRs for their schools. Seeking copyright permissions is a time-consuming task, and the more time it takes to obtain permissions, the longer it takes to post the article. If you rely on a service, such as the Copyright Clearance Center,[4] make sure that option exists for SSRN and IRs.

Law reviews that post published articles online to improve accessibility should consider how they are sharing those pieces. If a law review simply links to its own website, the author will not receive credit for any downloads from that site. But if the law review posts the article on the school's IR, the author should be able to track and receive credit for those downloads.

On a related point, when the law review posts to the school's IR, ensure that all of the author's information, including their current email address, is entered into the article's metadata so that the author will be able to receive download reports. You may want to consult the person who administers your school's IR (usually a librarian) to verify that you are taking all steps required to get the download counts to your authors.

Having an article on a platform like SSRN or Digital Commons is the first step to sharing the article via social media. While there is no hard and fast way to calculate impact via social media, sharing the link to the article may help lead to downloads, especially if one or more well-read blogs then features the article.

The service PlumX[5] is integrated with both SSRN and Digital Commons and can show the number of times an article—tracked by the platform-specific link—was shared on Twitter. On Twitter, it may also be possible for the author to see who is engaging with the article, but if the author is not tagged, that information may be difficult to track and preserve since social media can be ephemeral.

If a law review plans to use social media to promote articles once they are published, ask the authors if they—or their institution—have Twitter handles

---

4. For additional information about copyright, including the Copyright Clearance Center, see Chapter 17 of this *Manual*.

5. *About PlumX Metrics*, PLUM ANALYTICS (last accessed Jan. 29, 2022), https://plumanalytics.com/learn/about-metrics/ [https://perma.cc/34AC-Y2E5].

that should be used. Also ask who else should be tagged in a post to amplify it and spread awareness.

Law reviews also should consider how they share the article on social media. For example, if the article is published in the institution's IR, link to the abstract page, rather than the PDF, so that anyone who wants to read the article will have to download it, thus increasing the download count. If you link to the PDF and twenty people then click on the link, it will count as only one download for the author.

C. Persistent Identifiers

At the most basic level, calculating scholarly impact links an author with their article. That article is then cited, downloaded, or digitally discussed, which metrics are then used to show impact. So, it is extremely important that articles are correctly matched with the author who wrote them. One way to ensure that information is correctly matched is to use "persistent identifiers." Persistent identifiers are a long-term link to something. The two most relevant to this discussion are ORCID, which is used to identify the author and their associated scholarship, and DOIs, which are used to identify digital objects, like the article.[6]

1. ORCID

ORCID is an organization that allows authors to register for an Open Researcher and Contributor Identifier (ORCID iD).[7] ORCID iDs are unique for each author and allow an author to populate a profile with their scholarship. Similar to SSRN, authors can sign up for an ORCID iD, but institutions also can subscribe. While ORICD is not discipline-specific, it has become more popular in law only recently. ORCID has an integration with HeinOnline Author Profiles, which may make adopting ORCID iDs essential for law faculty.

---

6. *See generally* Aaron Retteen & Malikah Hall, *Persistent Identifiers and the Next Generation of Legal Scholarship*, SSRN (last accessed Jan. 29, 2022), https://papers.ssrn.com/sol3/papers.cfm?abstract_id=3168863 [https://perma.cc/S99U-GY62].

7. *What Is ORCID?*, ORCID (last accessed Jan. 29, 2022), https://support.orcid.org/hc/en-us/articles/360006973993-What-is-ORCID-.

One of the greatest challenges with citation counts involves the author's name. To be accurately counted, a person must be referred to consistently. But authors often change names or the way they present their names. An author may begin publishing with just their first name and last name. Then they may publish with their first name, middle name, and last name. And perhaps an article appears with the author's first name, middle initial, and last name. If the author publishes in another discipline, the citation method may include just their first initial and last name. And those are just some variations for an author who maintains the same name. For any number of reasons, a person's name could change, which makes tracking even more difficult. Including the author's ORCID iD with their credit line or in their biography and the acknowledgment note before the substantive footnotes creates a much-needed link between author and article.

Since 2016, more than 100 publishers have signed an open letter requiring ORCID iDs for submissions.[8] Requiring an ORCID iD to submit an article for consideration is the best way to ensure that authors adopt ORCID iDs. The more publications that require ORCID iDs during the submission process, the quicker ORCID iDs will be universally adopted.

Other disciplines require masters and Ph.D. students to register for an ORCID iD before they submit their thesis or dissertation. The idea is for authors to build the habit of this best practice early so that it is second nature as they embark on their academic careers. Law reviews can employ the same practice with their members who write articles. By registering for an ORCID iD while a student, any members who opt to continue publishing or decide to move into academia will be off to a good start in terms of tracking their scholarly impact.

2. DOIs

A DOI is an identifier used to track digital objects, like an article. The DOI is assigned by a registration agency (the International DOI Foundation) and provides a persistent link to the article on the internet.[9] The DOI that is registered for a particular article, which appears like a URL, will remain

8. *ORCID in Publications*, ORCID (last visited Jan. 29, 2022), https://info.orcid.org/requiring-orcid-in-publications/ [https://perma.cc/DF5W-W3VT].

9. *DOI Handbook*, DOI, at intro (last updated Oct. 17, 2015), https://www.doi.org/doi_handbook/1_Introduction.html#1.6 [https://perma.cc/GJH4-V2EF].

consistent, even if the location of the article—such as the website where it is hosted—changes. While there is a cost associated with registering the DOI and maintaining the information—the benefits of having the persistent identifier to help calculate scholarly impact are compelling.

Assigning DOIs as a part of the publication process is a forward-thinking act that benefits all authors. Law reviews that include DOIs as a part of the publication process, rather than relying upon individual authors or their institutions to assign DOIs retroactively, are helping to standardize DOIs. As assigning DOIs becomes the standard, the means for calculating scholarly impact—whether by traditional or alt-metrics—will be smoother.

Law reviews should take two steps to use DOIs. First, the law review should assign each article accepted for publication a DOI. The article's DOI can be placed in a similar location with the author's ORCID iD, either below the credit line or above the biography and acknowledgment note before the substantive footnotes. Second, as part of the cite-checking process for all articles it publishes, the law review should incorporate DOIs, when available, into citations. Although Bluebook does not yet provide guidance about DOIs, it can follow ALWD Guide's lead by including it at the end of a citation.[10] Putting the DOI at the end of the citation follows Bluebook's rules concerning archived internet sources—such as the Internet Archive or Perma.cc—where the archived website is added to the end of the full citation in brackets.[11]

A DOI is an asset to both traditional metrics and alt-metrics and, like ORCID iD, is widely used in many academic disciplines. The DOI can be included in citations to assist with the traditional citation counting in the same way that an ORCID iD is used for names. With alt-metric-focused platforms, such as PlumX and AltMetric, which are used to track social media engagement with articles, having a single URL that does not change is ideal. Otherwise, the author may have to track the various URLs associated with the article, such as SSRN and various IRs, to discover when someone tweeted about their article.

10. ALWD GUIDE, *supra* note 1, R. 30.3(c), at 337.

11. *See* BLUEBOOK, *supra* note 2, R. 18.2.1(d), at 177.

D. HeinOnline Rankings and the Citation Gap

In June 2019, *U.S. News and World Report* announced that it would be using HeinOnline's Author Profiles to gather citation information and create a scholarly impact ranking.[12] In June 2021, *U.S. News* abandoned the proposed ranking.[13] During those two years, in anticipation of the new ranking, HeinOnline's Author Profiles gained much attention.

The *U.S. News* announcement also generated discussion about whose articles were being published in law reviews and cited in other law review articles. As explained below, articles written by women are cited less frequently than those authored by men. Discussions about this citation gap became even more important in the wake of a global pandemic that has affected scholarly productivity.[14] While *U.S. News* ultimately abandoned its proposed ranking, new methods of calculating scholarly impact will continue to emerge because no one has yet crafted a satisfactory and equitable method.

1. HeinOnline's author profiles

The HeinOnline Author Profiles feature is meant to gather all of an author's articles that exist within HeinOnline's collections and show how many times each article has been cited.[15] The Author Profiles also collect other metrics, such as how many times an article has been cited in cases, the number of times the author self-cites, and the number of times the article has been accessed on HeinOnline.

One initial criticism was that the Author Profiles did not recognize name variations. Thus, if an author changed names or used variations of their name,

---

12. Robert Morse, *U.S. News Considers Evaluating Law School Scholarly Impact*, U.S. News & World Rep. (Feb. 13, 2019), https://www.usnews.com/education/blogs/college-rankings-blog/articles/2019-02-13/us-news-considers-evaluating-law-school-scholarly-impact.

13. Joshua Fischman & Michael A. Livermore, *Rankings Shift Could Force Big Changes at U.S. Law Schools*, Bloomberg L. (Aug. 19, 2021), https://news.bloomberglaw.com/ip-law/rankings-shift-could-force-big-changes-at-u-s-law-schools [https://perma.cc/Z2LC-8BAG].

14. *E.g.*, Collen Flaherty, *Women Are Falling Behind*, Inside Higher Ed (Oct. 20, 2020), https://www.insidehighered.com/news/2020/10/20/large-scale-study-backs-other-research-showing-relative-declines-womens-research [https://perma.cc/4NL2-GL85].

15. *Author Profile Pages*, HeinOnline (last visited Jan. 29, 2022), https://heinonline.org/HeinDocs/AuthorPortal.pdf [https://perma.cc/L69S-YCZG].

HeinOnline would create an Author Profile for each variation. Fortunately, law librarians took the lead in identifying the name variations for their faculty so that the multiple profiles could be combined. One way HeinOnline has addressed this name-variation issue was to introduce an integration with ORCID in August 2020.[16]

Methods for calculating scholarly impact are constantly evolving. HeinOnline Author Profiles did not become relevant to the conversation until a few years ago. Consequently, law reviews must stay informed about potential changes. Law librarians keep up with the latest breaking news concerning anything that may affect their faculty's scholarly impact or potential rankings. Designating an editor to check in with the librarians regularly will allow the law review to understand how the situation may be evolving and discover different ways the review can support its authors.

2. The citation gap

In May 2020, when HeinOnline released a ranking of the top 250 scholars based on five HeinOnline "ScholarCheck" metrics, fewer than 40 of those scholars were women.[17] A 2021 study also notes that, when amassing rankings of the top-cited legal scholars, far fewer women than men make the list.[18] The stark difference in numbers begs the question of why women are cited less frequently and calls for more awareness of who is being cited in articles.[19] If the metrics that show scholarly impact are tied into citation counts, and scholarly impact is used when considering faculty hiring, promotions, and tenure, this citation gap has been causing—and will continue to cause—real harm. Several law school faculty members drew attention to this issue by writing a public

---

16. *Phase II Complete: ORCID Records Appear in HeinOnline*, HeinOnline Blog (Aug. 26, 2020), https://home.heinonline.org/blog/2020/08/phase-ii-complete-orcid-records-appear-in-heinonline/ [https://perma.cc/39YU-DHUF].

17. *ScholarRank's Top 250 Authors in HeinOnline*, HeinOnline (last visited Jan. 29, 2022), https://home.heinonline.org/top_authors/ [https://perma.cc/5CEL-RSF7].

18. Fred R. Shapiro, *The Most-Cited Legal Scholars Revisited*, 88 U. Chi. L. Rev. 1595, 1609 (2021).

19. For more information about diversity, equity, and inclusion issues, including barriers to publication for POC and women faculty, see Chapter 4 of this *Manual*.

letter to journal editors and faculty promotion and tenure committees.[20] More scholarship and discussion about this issue are likely on the horizon.

Law reviews can lead the push to close this citation gap. Specifically, they can publish more articles by women, non-binary, and POC faculty. They also can review the citations in articles they are considering or have agreed to publish and note the percentage of citations to women, non-binary, or authors from other underrepresented groups, though this presents an entirely new challenge of relying on legal scholars to publicly self-identify into these groups. One academic journal outside of law has begun analyzing the percentage of women who are cited in articles under consideration; if the analysis reveals a gender gap, the journal asks the author to explain why the gap exists.[21]

When it comes to citation gaps, there is no way to correct the past. The only possibility is improvement moving forward. Knowing how important citation counts can be, ensuring diversity in citations is one action that your publication can take to close the gaps.

Editors should remember that events may limit the productivity of a group of authors in a submission cycle. For example, the COVID-19 pandemic has disproportionately impacted the scholarly productivity of women scholars. Being aware of those outside events and figuring out ways to support impacted authors are important steps in preventing citation gaps from widening or new citation gaps from opening.

E. Conclusion

Publication is just the start of an article's journey when it comes to scholarly impact. While authors do need publications, they also need the citations in others' publications. By acknowledging the post-publication life of an article and the metrics that need to be gathered, your law review may be able to assist its authors post-publication. Whether by incorporating persistent

---

20. Cyra Akila Choudhury, Meera E. Deo, Angelique Eaglewoman, Jennifer S. Hendricks, Saru Matambanadzo, Shruti Rana & Maybell Romero, *A Letter to Law Review Editors and Promotion and Tenure Committees at Law Schools* (last visited Jan. 29, 2022), https://docs.google.com/forms/d/e/1FAIpQLSdqwGgGSOR-P6WaHqonHb1Gfp20BVjZL9v264fzuTSg9_ZHzw/viewform.

21. Rachael Pells, *Understanding the Extent of Gender Gap in Citations*, Inside Higher Ed (Aug. 16, 2018), https://www.insidehighered.com/news/2018/08/16/new-research-shows-extent-gender-gap-citations [https://perma.cc/V8SS-5MTT].

identifiers—such as requiring authors to use an ORCID iD during the submission process or assigning a DOI to the article at the time of publication—your law review will show a dedication to linking authors to their articles and making citation counting easier. Giving copyright permission for authors to post articles on SSRN or an IR will allow them to have download counts as an alt-metric. Tagging an author or their institution on social media will help draw attention to the article and hopefully lead to downloads and, ultimately, citations.

Scholarly impact does not occur in a vacuum. External actors like *U.S. News* might create a new ranking system that dictates how scholarly impact should be calculated. When changes occur, law reviews should consider how they can support and maximize their authors' scholarly impact.

Outside forces like a pandemic also may impact who is able to produce articles. Acknowledging that cycles may occur when certain groups are not able to produce the scholarship they would have under "normal circumstances" is only the first step. To avoid exacerbating or creating a legal citation gap, law reviews need to seek articles from women, non-binary, and POC authors.

Choosing to publish an article does not mean that decisions made during the publication process affect only the author of that article. Those decisions will also affect every author who is cited within that article, and many who are not. While no perfect way to calculate scholarly impact currently exists, in light of our current flawed metrics, it is important for law reviews to make a concerted effort to support their authors and push them to consider the equities of their citation practices.

KEY TAKEAWAYS

- Law reviews should incorporate persistent identifiers into the publication process.
- Editors should evaluate law review policies to ensure all authors are visible in citations by removing "et al." from citations and listing every author.
- Law reviews should require that all submissions include an ORCID iD.
- Law reviews should use DOIs for and in articles they publish.
- Law reviews should adapt their current practices to respond to issues that affect scholarly impact and develop a plan to stay current on issues, like citation gaps, involving scholarly impact.

17

Managing Copyright Issues for Law Reviews

Benjamin J. Keele

LEARNING OBJECTIVES

After reviewing this Chapter, editors will be able to

- evaluate whether material is protected by copyright and whether exceptions apply to a particular use of the material;
- assess potential copyright issues in articles under consideration for and edited for publication; and
- develop appropriate copyright policies governing authors' rights, use of copyrighted material, and management of copyrights owned by law reviews.

A. Introduction

When editors assume leadership of a law review, they likely have little idea that they are using and managing copyright-protected works. These responsibilities require familiarity with an area of law they may not have studied in law school.

Suppose an author asks to include an image from a news story in their article. Or suppose an author wants to have their article translated into another language and republished in another journal. Or suppose an editor receives a request from a casebook publisher to reprint portions of an article published in the law review fifteen years ago.

Copyright infringement (real or perceived) presents a risk of conflict with the copyright owners and, in circumstances that would be unusual for a law review, monetary damages. More often, a claim of copyright infringement could result in an article being withdrawn or edited to remove the infringing material, or perhaps some permission fee would be charged without resorting to court. While these situations would be unpleasant, following the guidance in this Chapter will make these risks quite low. Another important way to reduce risk is to consult the school's general counsel, especially if a copyright complaint is received or an author proposes to use material extensively that has high commercial value.

This Chapter will summarize the fundamentals of U.S. copyright law and discuss copyright questions that may arise for law review editors. Part B discusses the motivations driving law review writing and production and how that relates to the interests protected by copyright. Part C reviews the fundamentals of copyright rights and exceptions. Part D considers the law review as a user of copyrighted material and focuses on when and how to obtain permission from the copyright holder. Part E focuses on the law review as a publisher and negotiating copyright issues with authors. Part F regards the law review as a manager and discusses appropriate policies for stewarding copyrights for the long term.

B. Economic Value of Law Review Articles

For all the thought, time, and energy that goes into producing law review articles, there is not much of a market for buying and selling individual articles. Relative to other scholarly fields, law reviews have very inexpensive subscription rates, and law reviews are increasingly moving toward an open-access model in which articles are freely available.[1] Law review articles certainly have value, but the resources for producing and distributing articles are not provided through directly selling content to buyers.

Law review authors generally write articles without compensation from the law review. Instead, academic authors write as part of their employment responsibilities and are thus paid through their salaries or other compensation from their employer. Attorneys and judges write as part of their professional duties or public service. Members write for academic credit or the credential of having their work selected for publication. Authors, then, are not writing

1. Jessica Litman, *The Economics of Open Access Law Publishing*, 10 Lewis & Clark L. Rev. 779, 783 (2006). For additional information about open-access models, see Chapter 16 in this *Manual.*

for money but for professional or academic recognition, which may later lead to monetary benefits.

Likewise, law review editors mostly work for academic credit or professional recognition for their services. Law schools subsidize law review operations, to various degrees, with staff assistance, office space, and technology support. Law schools support law reviews to offer educational opportunities for members and support schools' scholarly reputations. Law review editors and authors work for reputational goods rather than direct financial compensation.

This model is quite different from the one that U.S. copyright law is designed to protect. Copyright has been designed to help creators control the reproduction and distribution of their creative works. This arrangement usually means creators want to be able to demand royalties or other compensation for using their works. For many creators, copyright provides a legal mechanism that supports the economic model by which creators make their livelihoods, but this motivation is not true for most law review authors.

It is crucial to recognize this mismatch between how copyright is usually used by content industries and how law reviews can use copyright to further their educational and scholarly missions. In many cases, law reviews will strategically move away from copyright's default rules and invoke exceptions built into copyright law.

C. Copyright Law Fundamentals

Part C reviews basic copyright concepts. First, it explains what works can be copyrighted and who owns the copyrights. Second, it considers what rights are conferred by copyright. Third, it discusses exceptions to copyright that are particularly useful to law reviews.

1. Eligibility and ownership

Copyright provides certain rights for creators of original, creative works. The originality and creativity requirements are low bars (a phone book merely listing names alphabetically was found not to be creative[2]), so virtually anything a law review publishes would meet these requirements. Copyright protects

---

2. Feist Publ'ns, Inc. v. Rural Tel. Serv. Co., 499 U.S. 340 (1991).

text, images, sculptures, music, motion pictures, and others works.[3] Copyright is vested upon creation and goes to the creator. In practice, copyright in works employees produce as part of their jobs is granted to their employers under the work-for-hire doctrine, and creators may also sign contracts transferring copyright in exchange for payment.[4] However, most academic institutions have policies allowing professors to retain copyright in their scholarly works.[5]

What is not eligible for copyright is just as important as what is eligible. First, ideas and concepts are not subject to copyright.[6] For example, this Chapter on law reviews and copyright can be copyrighted. But the ideas contained in it cannot be, so someone else can write another chapter on the same topic, using a different combination of words, and that second chapter would also be a copyrightable work. Law reviews, as part of legal academia, have norms on citing sources and giving credit for some ideas. When authors credit earlier works, they mostly do that to comply with these scholarly norms, not to avoid infringing copyright.

Second, copyright expires 95 years after first publication or, for works by authors published after 1995, 70 years after the author's death.[7] Thus, as of 2022, any work published in or before 1926 is no longer protected by copyright. Works that are not copyrighted are commonly described as being in the public domain. For works published between 1926 and 1977, some formalities (including a copyright notice or registering the copyright with the U.S. Copyright Office) were required; thus, works that failed to comply are now in the public domain.

Third, virtually all primary legal sources (statutes, regulations, judicial opinions, treaties, etc.) and works of the federal government are immediately in the public domain.[8] Primary legal sources and federal government data are particularly useful for law review authors.

---

3. 17 U.S.C.A. § 102 (West 2021).

4. 17 U.S.C.A. § 201 (West 2021).

5. Eric Priest, *Copyright and the Harvard Open Access Mandate*, 10 NW. J. TECH. & INTELL. PROP. 377, 409 (2012).

6. 17 U.S.C.A. § 102(b).

7. Peter H. Hirtle, *Copyright at Cornell Libraries: Copyright Term and the Public Domain in the United States*, CORNELL U. LIBR., https://guides.library.cornell.edu/copyright/publicdomain [https://perma.cc/NP44-G6PB] (last updated Jan. 4, 2022, 9:26 AM).

8. *E.g.*, Georgia v. Public.Resource.Org, Inc., 140 S. Ct. 1498 (2020); Eric E. Johnson, *The Misadventure of Copyrighting State Law*, 107 KY. L.J. 593 (2019); Katie Fortney, *Ending Copyright Claims in State Primary Legal Materials: Toward an Open Source Legal System*, 102

If a work is in the public domain, that means anyone can copy or use it for any purpose. If a law review wants to republish a judicial opinion or an article from 1915, it can do so without permission from anyone. At the same time, the law review cannot claim copyright over the public domain material it has republished.

2. The bundle of sticks

Copyright confers six rights: reproduction, distribution, public display, public performance, derivative works, and digital transmission. These rights can be separated—an owner could sell the reproduction and distribution rights but keep the rest, for example—so the rights are often referred to as a "bundle of sticks."[9] Each right lets the owner control how others can use the copyrighted work. If a work is copyrighted and none of the exceptions discussed below apply, then the owner can require users to seek permission and perhaps demand compensation.

The rights most relevant for law reviews are reproduction and distribution. The reproduction right covers making copies of a work in any format, and the distribution right covers sharing or selling those copies to the public. When a law review posts an article on its website, it is making and distributing copies to its readers.

The public performance right is usually for publicly playing music, theater, or choreography, while the public display right applies to artwork, images, sculpture, and video recordings. Law reviews would use these rights if they played a video at a symposium or published an image in an article. Law reviews organizing online events or producing multimedia publications might also implicate public performances and displays.

The derivative works right covers making new works that are based on an earlier one. While it is unlikely a law review article would ever be adapted into a movie or television series, they might be translated into another language, recorded into an audio format, or adapted to a presentation. Any of these uses could involve the derivative works right. The digital transmission right applies only to musical recordings and is least likely to come up in law reviews' work.

Law Libr. J. 59 (2010); Irina Y. Dmitrieva, *State Ownership of Copyrights in Primary Law Materials*, 23 Hastings Comm. & Ent. L.J. 81 (2000).

9. 17 U.S.C.A. § 201(d).

Understanding which rights one would need to achieve a goal is useful when making copyright agreements or making permission requests. The more tailored the permission request is to a specific purpose, the more likely the law review and owner will be able to agree. In many instances, though, law reviews will not need permission because an exception in copyright law covers its use.

3. Library exception and the fair use doctrine

Copyright law provides for several exceptions, thus allowing certain socially advantageous use of copyrighted works without permission. The two exceptions that are particularly useful for law reviews are the library exception and the fair use doctrine.

Law reviews often use library collections for verifying citations and gathering research for symposia or other projects. The library exception provides that copies for research purposes made by libraries are not infringing.[10] If a law review's library does not have a particular source, the library can request a copy from another library that does have it, and this copy is covered by the library exception. In digital research platforms, access and copies are authorized by subscription agreements the library has negotiated and purchased.

While the library exception covers making copies, the fair use doctrine can apply to any right protected by copyright. Fair use is broad and meant to enable socially beneficial uses of copyrighted works. Uses that are educational, not for profit, and for comment and criticism are strong candidates for fair use. Fortunately, these are common uses law reviews make of copyrighted material when publishing articles.

Courts consider four key factors when deciding whether a use is covered by the fair use doctrine: the purpose of the use, the nature of the copyrighted work, the amount and substantiality of the work used, and the effect on the potential market for the work.[11] The flexibility of the doctrine permits innovative uses that were not anticipated when the statute was enacted (such as Google and HathiTrust Digital Library's creation of search indexes from scanned books[12]), but it also makes it challenging to develop bright-line rules.

---

10. 17 U.S.C.A. § 108 (West 2021).

11. 17 U.S.C.A. § 107 (West 2021).

12. Authors Guild v. Google, Inc., 804 F.3d 202 (2d Cir. 2015); Authors Guild, Inc. v. HathiTrust, 755 F.3d 87 (2d Cir. 2014).

A brief example will illustrate applying fair use. Suppose a law review accepts an article by an author that analyzes claims made in advertisements for pharmaceuticals. These advertisements appeared in magazines, newspapers, TV broadcasts, and websites. The article will be significantly more effective if it contains reproductions of images from these advertisements. While it may be possible for the author to request permission from every drug company that produced the advertisements, this would demand a great deal of time and energy, and the companies may very well deny permission or require substantial fees. If the article reproduces an appropriate amount of the advertisements for purposes of supporting the article's arguments, then there would be a strong case that the use is protected by fair use. Later, this Chapter discusses how editors should familiarize themselves with fair use and develop policies for including copyrighted material in articles.

In sum, copyright protects most creative works. However, copyright also eventually expires, primary legal materials are not copyrighted, and there are exceptions of which law reviews can avail themselves to support their educational and scholarly activities.

D. Law Reviews as Users

1. Deciding when permission is needed

Challenging copyright questions can arise in articles the law review has decided to publish. Authors certainly quote and excerpt from other copyrighted works, and some may want to reproduce significant portions of these works. Editors must decide whether and when to ask an author to obtain written permission from the copyright owners.

Before making that request, editors should consider whether the work is copyright-protected or if an exception applies. Earlier, the Chapter discussed how primary legal materials, federal government works, and works whose copyrights have expired are all in the public domain. Editors should also check if a Creative Commons license (a widely recognized way to grant prospective permission and further discussed in Part E(2)) or other permission has already been given. Notices of such licenses or permissions are usually found at the beginning or end of the work, or where a copyright notice would usually be placed. Once those options are investigated and found to be unavailable, invoking the fair use doctrine is appropriate.

The International Communication Association has published recommendations on fair use for communication scholars, and its advice is relevant for legal scholars.[13] The guide reduces the fair use analysis to two fundamental questions: First, is the copyrighted material being used for a different purpose than originally intended? Second, was the amount and kind of material used appropriate, given the nature of the use and the copyrighted work?[14] If both questions can be answered in the affirmative, there is a strong case for fair use.

The guide also discusses using copyrighted works for commentary and analysis and quoting copyrighted material for illustrative purposes.[15] These categories encompass most uses law reviews make of copyrighted materials. When the uses are tailored to articles' educational and scholarly purposes, law reviews and authors can be confident they are covered by fair use. Law reviews should have a documented policy on deciding when permission is needed. When making decisions on fair use, a checklist can be helpful and demonstrate the law review's good faith efforts to avoid infringement.[16]

2. Obtaining permissions

When the law review or author decides they need permission from the copyright owner, the law review may decide to assist the author, though obtaining copyright permissions typically is the author's responsibility.

The first step is locating the copyright owner. The two most likely candidates are the work's creator or the publisher. Look for a publisher's contacts for permissions or licensing inquiries. Some publishers have delegated licensing administration to collective management organizations or copyright collecting societies. Different organizations exist for each content industry; for example, many textual works are administered by the Copyright Clearance Center, while many musical works are handled by ASCAP or BMI.

If an author is deceased, their estate might administer their rights. For works published since 1978, the U.S. Copyright Office has a public catalog in which

---

13. Int'l Comm. Ass'n, Code of Best Practices in Fair Use for Scholarly Research in Communication (2010), https://cmsimpact.org/code/code-best-practices-fair-use-scholarly-research-communication [https://perma.cc/LW39-N44M].

14. *Id.*

15. *Id.*

16. Am. Libr. Ass'n, Fair Use Checklist, http://www.ala.org/advocacy/sites/ala.org.advocacy/files/content/copyright/FairUseChecklist.pdf [https://perma.cc/6T4G-527H] (last visited Jan. 8, 2022).

one can search for copyright registrations and recorded transfers. If a work is commercially valuable, it will probably be registered. If you cannot obtain permission from the author, publisher, or a collecting society, the work may be an orphan work—a work whose owner is undetermined or unavailable—and you will have to choose between relying on fair use or not using the work.

If you find someone who can grant permission, be specific about how the work will be used and where it will be published. Obtaining permission may take time and money, so it is wise to make decisions about copyright permissions relatively early in the editing process.

E. Law Reviews as Publishers

Once a law review has accepted an article for publication, the rights of the author and law review in the published article should be established. The author is the default copyright owner, so establishing the rights is typically done with a signed agreement with the author. These agreements often are called a "copyright agreement," "author contract," or "publication agreement." Some law reviews also use this agreement to articulate other matters, such as editing timelines. When writing or revising a publication agreement, the law review should consider three critical decisions: whether the copyright in the article will go to the journal or the author, what rights the author will retain, and whether to automatically grant permission for certain uses.

1. Copyright transfer or license

The first decision is whether to ask the author to transfer copyright in the article to the law review. As recently as the 1990s, transfer was a common practice, but in the last decade, the practice has become less common.[17] An advantage of transferring the copyright to the journal is that the law review is a central organization from which people can make permission requests. In addition to distributing articles through their websites and print issues, law reviews also send articles to research platforms like Lexis, Westlaw, and HeinOnline. When law reviews were the primary conduit for distributing articles, copyright transfers may have made some sense.

---

17. *See generally* Benjamin J. Keele, *Copyright Provisions in Law Journal Publication Agreements*, 102 Law Libr. J. 269 (2010).

However, over the past twenty years, authors (and their employing institutions) have taken a more active role in distributing scholarship. Authors post drafts and edited articles on SSRN, their personal websites, and their schools' institutional repositories. This decentralization of scholarly communications is largely beneficial and reduces the need for law reviews to hold copyright in articles. Managing permissions requests is an administrative task for which some law reviews are not well-equipped. Copyright lasts for 70 years after the author's death; most law reviews will not maintain complete records of copyright agreements for that long.

For most law reviews, a license strikes a better balance between the law review's and author's interests. A license means the author keeps the copyright, but the law review has permission to make specified uses. The agreement can be drafted to give the law review broad rights to make appropriate uses, such as distributing the article and authorizing others (like research platforms) to do so. Since the author retains copyright, they will also be able to share the article as they see fit.

Licenses can be exclusive or non-exclusive. An exclusive license means only the law review can exercise those rights for a period of time. If a law review wishes to preserve subscriptions or attract readers to the review's online presence while the article is new, then an exclusive license lasting six to twelve months may be worthwhile. Exclusivity periods longer than twelve months are uncommon and probably counter-productive. A non-exclusive license, in which both the author and law review equally can distribute the article and grant permission to others, will, in most cases, benefit all involved. Attention and recognition are the rewards of valuable articles, and the flexibility of a non-exclusive license will help maximize the distribution of articles to readers.

Whether the law review or author is sharing an article, the other party should be properly recognized, so copyright agreements should include a mutual promise to attribute authorship and venue of first publication on all copies in a format appropriate for the field. Some agreements ask that the parties notify each other of any republications or permissions; this is courteous but almost impossible to enforce and should not be an obligation.

A law review should also post the template copyright agreement on the law review's website and provide it to the author with the publication offer.[18] If the agreement provides for a copyright transfer or exclusivity period,

---

18. Duke L.J., Licensing Agreement for Single Author Works (2013), https://dlj.law.duke.edu/wp-content/uploads/sites/2/2013/09/authorjournalagreement_single.pdf [https://perma.cc/PX76-VG3U].

some authors may negotiate for shorter exclusivity or specific rights to use or distribute their articles, such as making copies for academic presentations or including excerpts in later work. Since law reviews are publications of the parent institution, when writing or revising a copyright agreement, editors should consult the institution's general counsel or office responsible for contracts. Editors should also be clear about their authority to amend agreements with authors.

2. Creative Commons and educational use licenses

For law reviews wishing to encourage frictionless copying and sharing of their articles, a Creative Commons license is a good option. When readers later want to use an article, perhaps as a reading assignment for a course or presentation or reprinting an excerpt in a book, unless they want to rely on an exception to copyright, they will need to contact the law review or author for permission. While this process may not present a major inconvenience for the first few years after an article has been published, the transaction costs can increase significantly over the years. Fifty years after an article has been published, it may be quite difficult to determine who owns the copyright and how to contact them for permission.

Creative Commons licenses are a widely recognized way to grant permission prospectively to potential users and avoid many issues by telling readers what they can do with articles without obtaining further permission. Copyright holders can place several conditions on the license; users can copy, adapt, and distribute the work if the conditions are followed. Several possible combinations of conditions exist, but two examples of the most restrictive and most permissive varieties will suffice.

The Creative Commons BY license has one condition.[19] The attribution (BY) condition requires all copies to provide appropriate credit to the author. Since the only condition is attribution, users can copy, republish, adapt, and transform the work. This license has been widely adopted by many scholarly journals that make their articles openly available and is expected by funding organizations, such as the Gates Foundation and Wellcome Trust.

---

19. Creative Commons, Attribution 4.0 International, https://creativecommons.org/licenses/by/4.0/ [https://perma.cc/WQF2-BDJ4] (last visited Jan. 8, 2022).

If a law review or author is not comfortable granting expansive permission, then the Creative Commons BY-NC-ND license may be more appealing.[20] First, the attribution (BY) condition applies as discussed above. Second, the use must be noncommercial (NC), which means the primary purpose of the use must not be for commercial advantage or compensation. Third, no derivative (ND) uses are authorized. Potential users are not permitted to adapt or transform the article. Putting these conditions together, the Creative Commons BY-NC-ND license permits noncommercial copying and sharing, but not much beyond that. Fair use and other copyright exceptions still apply, of course, and users can require permission that goes beyond the license, but that decision would be for the author or law review.

Before Creative Commons drafted its licenses, many law reviews granted prospective permission for educational and classroom copying, provided the user gave attribution and did not charge anyone more than the cost of the copies.[21] These educational licenses are appropriate given law reviews' educational missions. Law reviews should consider replacing their educational licenses with at least the Creative Common BY-NC-ND license because many worthwhile uses—such as posting articles on online learning management systems or sharing in professional training sessions—exist outside the traditional classroom.

F. Law Reviews as Managers

As mentioned before, copyright lasts a long time. A law review editor may be retired from law practice before the articles they edited enter the public domain. Law reviews may become long-term stewards of the copyrighted works they publish, especially if they ask authors for copyright transfer or exclusive licenses in their copyright agreements. With this long-term perspective, we should expect that people will invent new uses and formats for legal scholarship. For example, law review editors in the 1970s probably did not envision ebooks or full-text searchable research platforms. Thus, editors should prepare for the future by maintaining flexibility for authors and future editors.

---

20. Creative Commons, Attribution-NonCommercial-NoDerivatives 4.0 International (last visited Jan. 8, 2022), https://creativecommons.org/licenses/by-nc-nd/4.0/ [https://perma.cc/W3AS-BLS6].

21. Duke L.J., Copyright Permissions Policy (last visited Apr. 2, 2021), https://dlj.law.duke.edu/permissions/ [https://perma.cc/XD8C-USNT].

The simplest way to prepare is to use a Creative Commons license or a non-exclusive license. This option grants both the author and law review the power to distribute and transform the article. The copyright agreement should specify who can grant permission to third-party uses. The law review should anticipate receiving these requests and either retain the ability to grant permissions or maintain updated contact information for authors so the requests can be promptly forwarded.

If the law review owns copyrights in articles published with copyright transfers, it should develop policies describing when permissions will be granted and what licensing fees will be charged. The parent institution may have an office responsible for managing all intellectual property interests, so this question would warrant consulting the general counsel. If no one is interested in handling permissions, the law review could apply a Creative Commons license to all copyrighted works it holds, or it could offer to transfer the copyrights back to the authors. Transfers require a written instrument and can present some logistical challenges.

G. Conclusion

Making responsible decisions about using and managing copyrighted material may not be in the job description for law review editors, but it is a necessary part of publishing scholarship. Editors can minimize the chances of difficulties by familiarizing themselves with the basics of copyright law, keeping good records, and consulting with the general counsel when needed.

KEY TAKEAWAYS

- Copyright law accords research and scholarship considerable freedom to use copyrighted works.
- Law reviews should develop policies to use copyrighted material responsibly and allocate and manage copyright in published articles.
- Copyright terms are very long, and law reviews should develop policies and maintain records with future editors and researchers in mind.

18

Policies for Law Reviews on Archiving Internet Sources

Clanitra Stewart Nejdl

LEARNING OBJECTIVES

After reviewing this Chapter, editors will be able to

- recognize and articulate the reasons for link rot and reference rot in published legal scholarship;
- identify and discuss key tools available to preserve internet sources cited in legal scholarship; and
- develop and execute policies to ensure the preservation of internet sources cited in legal scholarship.

"All text is ephemeral. Some texts are more ephemeral than others."[1]

A. Introduction

The impermanence of internet sources cited in scholarly works has been the subject of studies across multiple disciplines.[2] A 2020 study by Fayaz Ahmad

---

1. Faith Oguz & Wallace Koehler, *URL Decay at Year 20: A Research Note*, 67 J. Ass'n for Info. Sci. & Tech. 477 (2016).

2. *See, e.g.*, Robert P. Dellavalle, Eric J. Hester, Lauren F. Heilig, Amanda L. Drake, Jeff W. Kuntzman, Marla Graber & Lisa M. Schilling, *Going, Going, Gone: Lost Internet References*, 302 Sci. 787 (2003); Dion Hoe-Lian Goh & Peng Kin Ng, *Link Decay in Leading Information Science Journals*, 58 J. Ass'n for Info. Sci. & Tech. 15 (2007); Edmund Russell & Jennifer Kane, *The Missing Link: Assessing the Reliability of Internet Citations in History Journals*, 49 Tech. & Culture 420 (2008); Cassie Wagner, Meseret D. Gebremichael & Mary K. Taylor, *Disappearing Act: Decay of Uniform Resource Locators in Health Care Management Journals*,

Loan and Ufaira Yaseen Shah found that, out of 358 internet references cited in 221 scholarly articles published between 2007 and 2011 in the *Journal of Informetrics*, 32.12% (115) references were "missing or dead."[3] As with other disciplines, the continued ability to access internet sources cited in legal scholarship—whether those sources are cited solely in the footnotes or referred to in the main text—remains a serious concern. Changes in the content and availability of these cited sources threaten the long-term usefulness of the published legal work.

This Chapter examines two common reasons for the loss of internet sources cited in legal scholarship and the impact of that loss on law review articles that cite those sources. This Chapter then describes two popular archival tools used to prevent this loss of information. The Chapter concludes with guidance for journal editors on key considerations related to establishing policies on the archival process for internet sources cited in works they publish.

B. Link Rot and Reference Rot

"Link rot" has been defined as "a phenomenon wherein hyperlinks to a specific URL or website lead to a dead end."[4] It has also been explained as a "URL no longer serving up any content at all."[5] A related condition called "reference rot" refers to "when a link still works but the information referenced by the citation is no longer present, or has changed."[6]

Potential causes of link rot and reference rot are predictable, obstruct the author's purposes for citing the source, and burden readers. For example, an internet source may no longer be located at a cited URL because that URL or domain name has changed. Although the cited source might be found at a new location online by using an internet search engine, it is not guaranteed that a researcher would be willing to take additional steps to find the source at its

---

97 J. Med. Libr. Ass'n 122 (2009); Jason Hennessey & Steven Xijin Ge, *A Cross Disciplinary Study of Link Decay and the Effectiveness of Mitigation Techniques*, 14 BMC Bioinformatics S5 (2013) (Supp.).

3. Fayaz Ahmad Loan & Ufaira Yaseen Shah, *The Decay and Persistence of Web References*, 36 Digital Libr. Persps. 157, 157 (2020).

4. Jorge Juarez, *Fighting Link Rot and Preserving the Future of Legal Research*, Va. Law., Feb. 2020, at 45, 45.

5. Jonathan Zittrain, Kendra Albert & Lawrence Lessig, *Perma: Scoping and Addressing the Problem of Link and Reference Rot in Legal Citation*, 127 Harv. L. Rev. F. 176, 177 (2014).

6. *Id.*

new location. Even if the researcher is willing to take further steps to locate the source, it is hardly desirable to place that burden on the researcher. In some cases, the cited URL may no longer lead to any resource because the cited source has been removed, or it may lead to a completely different resource. In other cases, the cited source may have been changed to a degree that the content no longer supports the assertion being made by the citing author.

In the context of citing a webpage or other type of internet source, the effects of link and reference rot result in the information cited being unreliable, either because it no longer exists or has been altered. As a result, the citation has lost its effectiveness. If the author intended the citation to lead the reader to a new research resource, link and reference rot cause that effort to fail. Similarly, if the author intended to use the internet source cited to support a legal argument, that support is negated when the source disappears or changes over time.

Given these issues, the ideal solution for an author citing an internet source is to preserve the source exactly as it was when the author cited it. This preserved source would be unaltered and accessible in the long term through a reliable tool or process.

C. Citation Rules and Archiving Internet Sources

Fortunately, the two main citation manuals—the *ALWD Guide to Legal Citations* and *The Bluebook*—provide guidance on archiving internet sources cited in legal scholarship. Bluebook Rule 18.2.1(d) states, in part, "Archiving of internet sources is encouraged, but only when a reliable archival tool is available. For citations to internet sources, append the archive URL to the full citation in brackets."[7] The rule then provides example citations of resources cited with the inclusion of an archived URL. The two archival tools used in the example Bluebook citations are the Internet Archive and Perma.cc, both of which are reliable archiving tools.

1. The Internet Archive

The Internet Archive is a nonprofit organization that maintains an online repository of over 588 billion webpages and myriad other internet-based

---

7. *See also* Carolyn V. Williams & ALWD, ALWD Guide to Legal Citations R. 31.1(f), at 344–45 (7th ed. 2021) (stating that "if the webpage is archived on an internet archival tool, append the archived URL in brackets after the normal URL").

resources, including books, video and audio recordings, and images.[8] Started in 1996, the Internet Archive provides its archived resources to the public free of charge[9] and has over 13.4 million users.[10] The public can access the organization's archived information through the Internet Archive Wayback Machine, which has been available to the public since 2001.[11]

Internet Archive users can enter a URL into the Wayback Machine and see a webpage as it looked at an earlier date and information provided at a URL on various dates. The Wayback Machine works only for webpages that allow crawlers and are not password-protected, posted on a secure server, excluded from the archive by the owner's request, or excluded for another limited reason.

Authors and editors can use the Wayback Machine to archive webpages and other internet sources by entering the URL of the source into the site's capture feature. Through this process, internet sources cited in law review articles can be preserved for the future.

2. Perma.cc

Perma.cc is another option for the long-term preservation of internet sources cited in law review articles. Perma.cc is a tool created by the Library Innovation Lab at Harvard Law School that can be used to create a permanent and "reliable, unbreakable link to an unalterable record of any page."[12] These links, called "Perma Links," remain unchanged regardless of what happens to content at the original URL archived. The "Perma Linking" process creates both a capture and a screenshot of the archived webpage and returns a new URL to include in the citation for that source.

Perma.cc is unlimited and free for users from academic institutions that are Perma.cc registrars. Per the Perma.cc Terms of Service, linked sources must

---

8. *About the Internet Archive*, INTERNET ARCHIVE, https://archive.org/about [https://perma.cc/8ADP-3499] (last visited Jan. 8, 2022).

9. *Id.*

10. *User Statistics*, INTERNET ARCHIVE, https://archive.org/about/stats.php [https://perma.cc/7GR3-GCJD] (last visited Jan. 8, 2022).

11. *Wayback Machine General Information*, INTERNET ARCHIVE, https://help.archive.org/hc/en-us/articles/360004716091-Wayback-Machine-General-Information [https://perma.cc/6LY6-4AYV] (last visited Jan. 8, 2022); Sanjay K. Arora, Yin Li, Jan Youtie & Philip Shapira, *Using the Wayback Machine to Mine Websites in the Social Sciences: A Methodological Resource*, 67 J. ASS'N FOR INFO. SCI. & TECH. 1904, 1904 (2016).

12. *About Perma.cc*, PERMA.CC, https://perma.cc/about [https://perma.cc/35KS-N96H] (last visited Jan. 8, 2022).

be "freely available on the internet to the general public without paying, registering with the website, or the like."[13] Perma.cc does not make its archived pages available to internet search engines, nor does it preserve links embedded within a source.

Although the Bluebook does not explicitly mandate archiving internet sources cited in law reviews and law journals at this time, the detriments to legal scholarship caused by link rot and reference rot—in combination with the citation manuals' inclusion of citation formats for archived internet sources cited in legal scholarship—should spur each journal board to consider carefully how to proceed when cite-checking or drafting articles containing references to internet sources. Through consultation with faculty advisors and law librarians, editors can develop and implement practical policies for using tools like the Internet Archive and Perma.cc as part of the publication process to preserve internet sources cited in accepted articles.

D. Establishing Archival Policies for Law Reviews

The journal board would be wise to establish policies for the archival process if such policies do not already exist. In creating these policies, the board should at least consider the following questions:

- Which archival tool should be used?
- Whether the author or the journal will be responsible for archiving the cited internet sources in an article.
- If the author bears the responsibility for archiving the internet sources, whether that responsibility is clearly explained in the publication agreement with authors and the journal's submission guidelines.
- Whether the board bears the responsibility for archiving the internet sources, which board members should be assigned to complete the archival process and what training will be needed to enable them to do so.
- What steps should the board take to document the archival process for future boards so that continuity can be maintained?

---

13. *Perma Terms of Service*, PERMA.CC, https://perma.cc/terms-of-service [https://perma.cc/R3TQ-27Q3] (last visited Jan. 8, 2022).

1. Selecting an archival tool

If a board does not already use an archival tool, the board should consult with the school's law librarians before selecting a tool. The law librarians will be able to provide details on options for archival tools and methods, the support that might be provided through the law library or law school for such tools, and any practical concerns that might affect the selection decision. The law librarians should also be to provide insight to help determine which tool is most appropriate for the board's specific circumstances. While the Internet Archive is free to use for individual registered accounts, Perma.cc is free for a law journal only if it is authorized by its institution's law library.[14] Therefore, a board that selects Perma.cc as an archival tool would need to consult with the law library to obtain an authorized journal account.

2. Responsibility for the archival process

If a journal does not have an existing policy stating who is responsible for the archival process, then the editors will need to draft a suitable policy. If the policy dictates that the author is responsible for the archival process, then this requirement should be included in the submission guidelines and publication agreement. Some authors, particularly those who are associated with academic institutions, already may be familiar with tools like the Internet Archive and Perma.cc. However, authors who are judges and legal practitioners may be less familiar with the archival process and related tools and may need additional guidance.

Authors who have problems with the archival process may require more assistance than journal members can reasonably provide. To reduce the assistance needed from journal members, the members could refer an academic author to the law library at the author's institution for assistance with the process.

Another concern is that requiring authors to submit their own archival links will also require the journal to create a mechanism to record each author-provided link, if the journal wants to have an easily accessible record of the archival links for each article published. Thus, requiring authors to submit their own archival links results in a duplication of effort, especially when a resource like Perma.cc will retain the archival links within the journal's own organizational account if the journal members create the links.

---

14. *See About the Internet Archive*, *supra* note 8; *Perma.cc for Journals*, PERMA.CC, https://perma.cc/sign-up/journals [https://perma.cc/9J84-P3BA] (last visited Jan. 8, 2022).

Given these issues, the benefits of the journal handling the archival process will likely outweigh the potential difficulties of leaving the archival process in the hands of individual authors. Although first establishing the workflow for the process may be time-consuming, the archival process can soon become as routine as other journal-related tasks.

3. Preparing an archival policy

The archival policy should impress upon journal members the importance of the archival process and contain enough information to provide consistency in the link archival process over time. It should also specify the archival tool to be used by the journal, indicate that the journal will create the archival links, and include details about which specific journal members or editors will be responsible for completing the process.

Some boards limit archiving responsibilities to specific editors. For example, UNM Law Library suggests a process in which the lead editor for the piece creates the archival links for the appropriate internet resources and adds those links to the article's footnotes.[15] Other boards may decide to assign the archival process to one specific editors for all pieces or to allow a larger number of members to create links. If a variety of journal members complete the archival process, one or more senior editors should be responsible for reviewing the archived links to ensure the process has been completed correctly.

The journal should prepare its archival policy in consultation with the journal's faculty advisors to ensure that all relevant issues are considered. The editors should also consult their law librarians to request training on the archival process for the relevant journal members. This is a critical step since there are some types of internet sources (e.g., content behind paywalls, content that requires registration or a subscription to access, etc.) that are prohibited from being archived under some archival tools' Terms of Service[16] and journal members need to understand fully both the archival link process and the requirements of the archival tool used. The policy also should address general timelines for requesting and holding training on the archival process.

---

15. UNM Law Library, *Journals Administrative Handbook: Perma.cc—Navigating Perma.cc—Workflow*, https://libguides.law.unm.edu/c.php?g=413811&p=2819728#s-lib-ctab-8711322-2 [https://perma.cc/RC5N-4ZHF] (last visited Jan. 8, 2022).

16. *See, e.g.*, *Perma Terms of Service*, *supra* note 13.

4. Continuity for future boards

Once an archival policy is established, the editors should also create and maintain an internal document describing the reasons for the policy and different decision points within the policy that future editors and faculty advisors use when they consider policy revisions. To the extent possible, this document should address details about each part of the archival policy, including why the responsibilities for the archival process were divided as they were and why a specific archival tool was selected.

KEY TAKEAWAYS

- Link and reference rot are detrimental to the long-term preservation of internet sources cited in legal scholarship, such as law review articles.
- Using archival tools like the Internet Archive and Perma.cc can maintain the usefulness of citations to the sources in legal scholarship.
- The ALWD Guide and Bluebook expressly encourage the use of reliable archival tools to preserve webpages and other internet sources.
- Editors should, in consultation with faculty advisors and law librarians, develop an archival policy to preserve internet sources cited in articles accepted for publication.
- The archival policies and the rationale behind them should be detailed in law review documents such as submission guidelines, publication agreements, and cite-checking procedures to ensure that future authors and journal members fully understand and can continue the established preservation practices.

19

The Editorial Adventure

Five Universal Lessons

Brooke J. Bowman

LEARNING OBJECTIVES

After reviewing this Chapter, editors will be able to

- reconsider the chapters in this *Manual* from a new perspective, focusing on the five universal lessons presented in this Chapter;
- formulate effective plans to meet unexpected challenges; and
- identify additional lawyering skills they can develop through their editorial board service.

A. Introduction

Whether you read this *Manual* from front to back or just read select chapters, we hope you noticed that the *Manual* is chock-full of advice, tips, and strategies. We also hope some of you might have noticed that five universal lessons emerged. These lessons, which apply across journals and editor positions, are

- Pause, plan, then respond.
- Be aware of and use resources.
- Seek growth opportunities for yourself and your journal.
- Learn to listen actively.
- Be self-aware and self-reflect.

B. Lesson 1: Pause, Plan, Then Respond

Before starting my first job after college, I was told, "During the first year, you learn *how* to do the job. In the second year, you *do* the job. And in the third year, you look for the new job or the promotion." For journal editors, the schedule is compressed. Although you will be learning throughout your time as an editor, you must take advantage of the editorial transition period to absorb as much as you can.[1]

But because you will be learning while doing—and working with other editors who are doing the same—you need to expect challenges.[2] Some challenges may be minor hiccups: a journal member turns in their cite-checking assignment a day or two late, an author asks for a weekend extension on the page proof, or you and a co-editor disagree about which article should get that last slot in Issue 2. But other challenges may present major hurdles: you discover plagiarized material in a student-authored article published in the last issue; the budget is due to the law school, but no one told you in advance; or the symposium editor signed a contract with a hotel without following school policies.

Whether a hiccup or hurdle, you need a strategy for responding to challenges. And here's the lesson: pause, plan, then respond. Don't panic, and don't simply react without having developed a thoughtful response.[3] Planning adds some time to the process, but it yields significantly better decisions and results. It's also the professional way to proceed.

An initial step is to ground yourself. Handling a challenge can be stressful and bring out emotions. That's fine. Humans have emotions. Pause and take a few deep breaths and try not to take the situation or what people might say to or about you during the process personally.

Next, start developing the plan. Gather the relevant facts and learn the context by speaking with those involved or who may have relevant information, reading pertinent emails and other communications, and reviewing related material—possibly the article or assignment at issue.

---

1. For more information about the editorial transition process, see Chapter 8 of this *Manual*.

2. For more information about possible challenges editors can face, see Chapters 11, 12, and 13 of this *Manual*.

3. *E.g.*, Tony Belak, *How to Handle Difficult Behavior in the Workplace*, MEDIATE.COM (last visited Jan. 29, 2022), https://www.mediate.com/articles/belak4.cfm [https://perma.cc/DY34-JDR6].

Then evaluate which rules or policies apply. To complete this step, you may need to review the journal's constitution, bylaws, or previous "precedent"—documentation about previous situations that editors have faced and how they resolved them.[4] You may also need to review the law school's honor or conduct code or other policies.[5]

Next, apply the facts and circumstances to existing policies or precedent, if they exist, and analyze the situation (akin to what you would do on an essay examination or in a legal memorandum). If they don't exist, then turn to a logical school official—the journal's faculty advisor, the associate academic dean, or the assistant dean for student affairs. These individuals have probably faced situations similar to the one you are facing and can help you analyze the matter and develop an action plan.

You may discover you have many options to resolve the challenge. For each option, consider developing a pro/con list to help you choose the best path forward. Once you've decided, create the plan. Effective plans share several common features; specifically, they

- articulate the challenge to be resolved, including relevant facts;
- are based on the facts, not speculation or rumors;
- identify the root cause of the problem;
- are designed to resolve the challenge;
- comport with journal and law school policies and processes;
- are consistent with past practices, if any;
- include specific and measurable objectives that are achievable, relevant, and time-bound;
- anticipate and provide all necessary resources and training;
- are clear and unambiguous;
- are equitable and include an element of grace;
- address the consequences of failing to accept or abide by the plan;
- consider realistic contingencies that may exist or arise;

4. As editors, it is important to document decisions, so that future editors have knowledge of and can rely on those decisions. In addition, several chapters in this *Manual*, especially Chapter 3, address common types of journal documentation.

5. For additional information about school policies that typically impact journal members, see Chapter 2 of this *Manual.*

- can be applied in similar situations;
- include all necessary details, such as a timeline and steps that must be taken;
- are reviewed by the appropriate individuals (e.g., Editor in Chief, faculty advisor, associate dean for academic affairs, and potentially the school's General Counsel);
- are documented and shared with all appropriate parties—such as the faculty advisor, the associate dean for academic affairs, and possibly the assistant dean of student affairs; and
- are stored appropriately so the appropriate future editors can find the plan, but those without a need-to-know cannot access it.

When a student is involved, the plan typically should include an educational component designed to help the student develop professionally.

The process of preparing the plan may reveal gaps you need to fill or flaws in your initial logic. Don't be afraid to revise the plan. Time permitting, put what you think is the final plan aside for a few hours or a day. That break can bring new ideas and perspective. And as noted in the list above, seek input from other appropriate individuals, like your journal faculty advisor. But don't gossip or share information with students not involved in the situation.

As you move through the process, strive to examine the situation objectively by focusing on the situation, not the person involved.[6] Don't let emotions, friendships, or past feuds cloud your judgment or tempt you to overlook key information or create exceptions that don't exist.[7] If your best friend's conduct is at issue and you can't compartmentalize, then acknowledge that you have a conflict of interest and allow the faculty advisor or the next editor in the chain of command to assign another person to resolve the matter.

Bottom line: when an unexpected challenge arises, pause, plan, then respond.

C. Lesson 2: Be Aware of and Use Resources

Just as in the practice of law, the journal and law school have resources to help you in your editorial role. The resources can take many forms: governing documents, such as the journal constitution or bylaws; the law school honor or

6. *E.g.*, Belak, *supra* note 3.
7. For a discussion of ethical issues and favoritism, see Chapter 9 of this *Manual*.

conduct codes; and training materials like this *Manual* or guides created by the outgoing editor who preceded you. People are also resources: your predecessor, your current editorial colleagues, other journal alumni, the journal's faculty advisor,[8] law librarians,[9] associate or assistant deans, and law school staff members.

Realize that you usually don't have to recreate the wheel. Instead, learn what exists and find the materials and people that can help you fulfill your duties.

If you're not sure where to start, ask for help. Frankly, the only "silly question" is an unasked question. Ask questions when you are learning the responsibilities of your position or facing a difficult situation. But also ask questions when you start thinking about major initiatives, like revising the bylaws or the constitution, changing new member or editor selection processes, entering vendor agreements, or approaching donors and sponsors.

Bottom line: knowing and understanding your resources—and then using them—will save you time and stress and lead to better, more consistent decision-making.

D. Lesson 3: Seek Growth Opportunities for Yourself and Your Journal

The journal credential enhances your resume, but when you add "Editor," that credential further distinguishes you from your classmates. But adding "Editor" also adds expectations. When prospective employers see the "Editor" credential, they expect that you have developed advanced skills in legal research, writing, analysis, attribution, editing, proofreading, leadership, and teamwork.[10] But as an editor, you will have opportunities to develop an array of additional lawyering skills that will serve you and your clients well. Make an effort to learn about and hone these sought-after skills.

View your editor position as an opportunity to grow, not as a burden or a task to complete. Being an editor is much more than a resume booster; it is an opportunity to develop key professional skills, build lasting relationships, and contribute to the growth of the journal as an organization.

---

8. Many of the chapters in this *Manual* discuss faculty advisors; see the index for specific chapters.

9. For information about working with law librarians, see Chapter 6 of this *Manual*.

10. For a discussion on how being an editor can help you develop additional skills, see Chapter 1 of this *Manual*.

The Institute for the Advancement of the American Legal System (IAALS)[11]—after surveying more than 24,000 lawyers and conducting other research—has developed a list of 76 characteristics, competencies, and skills—the "foundations of practice"—new attorneys need as they enter practice.[12] The IAALS "Learning Outcomes Map" is reprinted below. Take some time to review the list of foundations. So many are ones you can develop through serving as an editor, and below are some that might jump out at you:

- Accept feedback;
- Adapt to demands;
- Attention to detail;
- Compassion;
- Conscientiousness;
- Cooperation;
- Curiosity;
- Diligence;
- Energy;
- Flexibility;
- Grit;
- Honor commitments;
- Initiative;
- Integrity;
- Meet goals;
- Multitask;
- Organized;
- Ownership;
- Punctuality;
- Resourcefulness;
- Responsiveness;

---

11. IAALS, *Trending Topic: Foundations for Practice*, IAALS (last visited Jan. 29, 2022), https://iaals.du.edu [https://perma.cc/E69E-Y896].

12. IAALS, *The Foundations Map*, IAALS (last visited Jan. 29, 2022), https://iaals.du.edu/projects/foundations-practice/foundations-map [https://perma.cc/J4SG-H4ZC] [hereinafter *The Foundations Map*].

- Seek advice;
- Self-awareness—*one of the five universal lessons addressed below*;
- Status updates;
- Tech savvy;
- Timekeeping;
- Work ethic; and
- Work under pressure.

You may not have realized some terms on this list are skills you can develop. Or you may have thought some items on this list are traits you're either born with or not. But each of the 76 foundations is a skill you can learn, polish, and hone. And working on a journal with other talented, dedicated individuals on a complex but common project—producing an academic journal—can accelerate your learning and growth, if you embrace the experience and accept the responsibility.

Source: IAALS, *The Foundations Map*, https://iaals.du.edu/projects/foundations-practice/foundations-map (last visited Jan. 29, 2022) [https://perma.cc/J4SG-H4ZC]. Reprinted with permission.

A corollary to seeking individual growth opportunities is considering how you and your editorial colleagues can improve the journal. You want to leave the journal better and stronger than when you joined.

While it may appear that all journal processes and procedures are set, and an editor's job is merely to follow them, opportunities for organizational growth often arise. Some opportunities arise out of challenges—finding a weakness when something goes wrong. But other times, opportunities arise because new editors bring fresh perspectives.

At its very core, seeking opportunities for organizational growth starts with ownership. You must learn not only your position, but you also need to learn about the journal's history, mission, and organization. You cannot be so focused on your department or responsibilities that you lose sight of the big picture—the business that the journal is running and the product it is producing. Learning about your position and the journal as a whole may spark creative ideas that will help the organization continue to grow. Maybe you can develop a streamlined cite-checking process using technology. Maybe you can increase alumni involvement through a mentoring program. To survive and thrive, organizations must change and evolve.

Bottom line: focus on building your foundations for practice but also consider how your editorial team can leave its mark in a positive way that will benefit future boards and the law school.

E. Lesson 4: Learn to Listen Actively[13]

Listening is a crucial skill for attorneys to have. IAALS identifies communication as one of the five overarching categories for the 76 foundations and characterizes a strong communicator as one who can "communicate by reading, writing, speaking, and *listening* in a professional manner."[14]

---

13. Fortunately, many helpful and free resources on learning active listening skills are available. *E.g.*, *The 10 Principles of Effective Listening*, SkillsYouNeed (last visited Jan. 29, 2022), https://www.skillsyouneed.com/ips/listening-principles.html [https://perma.cc/5J3Q-EXEP]; *Active Listening: Hear What People Are Really Saying*, MindTools (last visited Jan. 29, 2022), https://www.mindtools.com/CommSkll/ActiveListening.htm [https://perma.cc/375N-Y4RE]; *Effective Listening*, in LEARNING (last visited Jan. 29, 2022), https://www.linkedin.com/learning/effective-listening [https://perma.cc/ZB9W-5UB5]; Jennifer Romig, *A Model of Listening*, Listen Like a Lawyer (July 17, 2013), https://listenlikealawyer.com/2013/07/17/a-model-of-listening/ [https://perma.cc/RKW6-77UJ].

14. *The Foundations Map*, *supra* note 12 (emphasis added).

The goal should be learning to be an active listener—listening not merely to hear but also to respond effectively. Active listening forces you to be present and focus; it involves shutting down the thoughts roaming in your head and turning off the snap judgments and biases.[15] Active listening also involves understanding and paying attention to the non-verbals—facial expressions, tone, and body language—and thinking about what has not been said.[16]

Attentiveness and attention to details[17] are important to active listening.[18] Learning to be attentive and pay attention to details while listening can be a challenge, but the factors in Professor Judi Brownell's[19] HURIER model can help. "HURIER" is an acronym for the six factors that should occur when listening:

- Hearing;
- Understanding;
- Remembering;
- Interpreting;
- Evaluating, and
- Responding.[20]

Throughout your editorial service, you will need strong listening skills in many situations, from listening to a fellow editor present at a board meeting to listening to a student-writer discuss the thesis in their paper at a roundtable.[21] One tip to active listening is to prepare to listen.[22] This tip ties to the first lesson

---

15. *The 10 Principles of Effective Listening*, *supra* note 13.

16. *Id.*

17. *The Foundations Map*, *supra* note 12 (listing attentiveness and attention to details as 2 of the 76 foundations).

18. *The 10 Principles of Effective Listening*, *supra* note 13.

19. Judi Brownell is a professor emerita of management and organizational behavior at the Cornell School of Hotel Administration and wrote a book titled *Listening: Attitudes, Principles, and Skills*. Cornell Peter & Stephanie Nolan Sch. of Hotel Admin., *Judi Brownell*, Cornell U. (last visited Jan. 29, 2022), https://sha.cornell.edu/faculty-research/faculty/jlb18/ [https://perma.cc/P4R7-CKRK].

20. Romig, *supra* note 13.

21. For more information on working with student-authors and using roundtables, see Chapter 12 of this *Manual*.

22. *The 10 Principles of Effective Listening*, *supra* note 13.

in this Chapter—"plan, then respond." When preparing to listen, stop talking and focus on what the person is saying (and not saying).[23]

Bottom line: active listening takes conscious effort and practice but is critical for interacting with others effectively and ensuring common goals are met.

F. Lesson 5: Be Self-Aware and Self-Reflect

Improving your skills and developing your professional identity requires you to be self-aware and self-reflective.[24] Self-awareness is being aware of one's "strengths, weaknesses, boundaries, preferences, [and] sphere of control" in one's professional development.[25] We are all aware of our flaws—our "areas of opportunity," so to speak; we have learned those through years of educational feedback and interactions with those around us.

But there is more to developing professional skills than just being self-aware; self-reflection is also needed. Self-reflection involves evaluating your work to "identify successful actions, avoid prior mistakes, adjust current conduct based on past learning, and apply current lessons to future practice."[26] Unfortunately, "[m]ost of us do not have a personal trainer in the law to assess our strengths and weaknesses and design the drills to help us improve."[27] Thus, we each must develop the discipline to think about—to reflect upon—the feedback or criticisms we have received, how our skill development is progressing, and how we need to adjust our actions to improve.[28]

Consultant and business coach Kim Tasso has developed a simple reflective process:

- Description—what happened?
- Feelings—what were you thinking and feeling?

---

23. *Id.*

24. Essential Qualities of the Professional Lawyer xxiii (Paul A. Haskins ed., 2013).

25. Alli Gerkman & Logan Cornett, *Foundations for Practice: The Whole Lawyer and the Character Quotient* 20, 32 (July 2016), https://iaals.du.edu/sites/default/files/documents/publications/foundations_for_practice_whole_lawyer_character_quotient.pdf [https://perma.cc/Z4HS-PYK5].

26. Learning from Practice: A Text for Experiential Legal Foundation 203 (Leah Wortham et al. eds., 3d ed. 2016).

27. *Id.* at 19–20.

28. *Id.* at 20.

- Evaluation—what was good and bad about the experience?
- Analysis—what sense can you make of the situation?
- Conclusion—what else could have been done?
- Action plan—if it arose again, what would you do?[29]

As you are working through your editorial responsibilities, you will gain experiences—successful and not successful—to learn from. For example, assume you are the Editor in Chief, and you just ran your first editorial board meeting. After the meeting is over, use the Tasso process. Replay what happened. Reflect on what went well (e.g., you started and ended on time, you remembered to ask someone to take minutes, and all discussions were collegial) and what did not go well (e.g., you didn't distribute the agenda in advance, you made it through only half the agenda items and had placed the most important item at the end of the agenda, you forgot to take a vote on one issue, and only three other editors spoke during the meeting).

Think about the flow of the meeting and how you felt: maybe you felt proud and relieved that the discussions were collegial but frustrated that you didn't get to the most important agenda item. Then evaluate what you will change for the next meeting and what you will strive keep the same, which will require you to analyze how you can repeat the positive elements and improve the elements that fell flat or short.

Changes might include

- developing a shorter agenda with the most important matters at the top;
- distributing the agenda and minutes from the last meeting at least a week in advance;
- appointing a parliamentarian to help ensure you take votes on every action item; and
- encouraging other editors to share their input and ideas.

And remember to use your resources: debrief with your faculty advisor, chat with the other editors to learn their impressions of the meeting and why

29. Kim Tasso, Essential Soft Skills for Lawyers: What They Are and How to Develop Them 66 (2020). *See generally* Learning from Practice: A Text for Experiential Legal Foundation, *supra* note 24, at ch. 8 ("Reflection and Writing Journals"); Timothy Casey, *Reflective Practice in Legal Education: The Stages of Reflection*, 20 Clinical L. Rev. 317 (2014).

they did or did not participate in discussions, and read articles or take a short online course about how to run business meetings effectively.

For elements that went well, consider the why and how so you can replicate them. For example, starting and ending on time likely wasn't accidental. So, what strategies did you use? Maybe you shared with attendees in an email that you planned to start on time. Maybe you arrived early to make sure the room was unlocked and unoccupied. Maybe you set the meeting at a time and in a location that gave others sufficient time to arrive. Maybe someone reminded you that people needed to leave soon to attend class. But maybe you could have taken other steps, like setting timers on your phone for the starting and ending times.

Having completed the reflection process, you now have a solid action plan for the next editorial meeting.

Bottom line: be aware of your strengths and areas of opportunity and build in time to reflect on—and continually improve—your performance.

KEY TAKEAWAYS

- When the unexpected happens—positive or negative—never react, as reacting will take time and energy away from planning and responding. Pause, plan, and then respond.
- Whether documents or people, be aware of what resources are available and use them.
- Find a list of lawyering skills, such as the IAALS Foundations Map reprinted in this Chapter, and consider how you can learn and develop these skills as an editor.
- Leave your journal better and stronger than you found it.
- Look for opportunities to develop active listening skills.
- View every opportunity as an opportunity to learn. Be aware of your strengths and areas of opportunity and engage in reflective practices.

Index